THE ENTREPRENEUR'S GUIDE TO PREPARING A WINNING BUSINESS PLAN AND RAISING VENTURE CAPITAL

W. KEITH SCHILIT

Catalyst Ventures, Inc.

With a Foreword by Victor K. Kiam
CEO, Remington Products, Inc.
Author of *Going For It!*

PRENTICE HALL, Englewood Cliffs, New Jersey 07632

Library of Congress Cataloging-in-Publication Data

Schilit, W. Keith
  The entrepreneur's guide to preparing a winning business plan
and raising venture capital / W. Keith Schilit.
    p. cm.
  Includes index.
  ISBN 0-13-701301-9 (binder)
  ISBN 0-13-282302-0 (pbk.)
  1. New business enterprises—Finance—Planning. 2. Small
business—Finance—Planning. I. Title.
HG4027.6.S35 1990
658.1'592—dc19

        88-37103
        CIP

Editorial/production supervision
  and interior design: GERTRUDE SZYFERBLATT
Cover design: LUNDGREN GRAPHICS, LTD.
Manufacturing buyer: KELLY BEHR
Page make-up: JUNE SANNS

© 1990 by Prentice-Hall, Inc.
A Simon & Schuster Company
Englewood Cliffs, New Jersey 07632

The publisher offers discounts on this book when ordered
in bulk quantities. For more information, write:

    Special Sales/College Marketing
    Prentice-Hall, Inc.
    College Technical and Reference Division
    Englewood Cliffs, NJ 07632

Printed in the United States of America

15

ISBN 0-13-701301-9 {BINDER}
ISBN 0-13-282302-0 {PBK}

PRENTICE-HALL INTERNATIONAL (UK) LIMITED, *London*
PRENTICE-HALL OF AUSTRALIA PTY. LIMITED, *Sydney*
PRENTICE-HALL CANADA INC., *Toronto*
PRENTICE-HALL HISPANOAMERICANA, S.A., *Mexico*
PRENTICE-HALL OF INDIA PRIVATE LIMITED, *New Delhi*
PRENTICE-HALL OF JAPAN, INC., *Tokyo*
SIMON & SCHUSTER ASIA PTE. LTD., *Singapore*
EDITORA PRENTICE-HALL DO BRASIL, LTDA., *Rio de Janeiro*

To my loving wife Karen

CONTENTS

FOREWORD

I recently received a letter from a woman in Surrey, England. She was the proprietor of a tea and cake shop. Opened only three years ago, the shop had proven to be quite a triumph. Its success persuaded her that it was time to expand the operation. She wanted to open up a similar store in a nearby town.

I've also received correspondence from an Illinois farmer. He claims to have created a revolutionary hoe. His patent application had just been approved. Now this man wanted to know how he could transform his brainchild into an enterprise.

The CEO of a privately-held data base company—an organization that was experiencing some rocky times—called to ask how he could raise money to tide over his promising but troubled organization. These three, entrepreneurs all, came from diverse backgrounds but they were joined by a common thread. Each needed the capital to turn a vivid dream into glowing reality. It is the primary question faced by most entrepreneurs. I have a regular newspaper column that offers advice to entrepreneurs of all sizes. Seventy-five percent of the mail I receive contains questions pertaining to financing. There is investment capital out there, but how does one lay his or her hands on it? It's a lender's market. The competition for those dollars is enormous. How can you insure that your enterprise will stand out amongst all the others? Reading this book is an excellent first step.

There's nothing tricky about the title—*The Entrepreneur's Guide to Preparing a Winning Business Plan and Raising Venture Capital*. For my money, you can put the word *winning* in boldface. I've always said that business is a game and that you should play it to win. In these pages, Keith Schilit has mapped out a proven strategy that will increase your chances for victory. I applaud the way he's gone about this. I've always believed that the secret to a successful negotiation is to know what the other guy—the fellow sitting across the table from you—wants to achieve. How could you address his needs satisfying your own? This book approaches the preparation of a business plan in much the same fashion. It deals with the question from the perspective of the potential investor. This is the person you must impress and persuade and Keith does a first-rate job of letting you know how to achieve these goals.

It is certainly a complete package. Keith takes you step-by-step over a tricky terrain. He points out the smooth road and warns you of all the pitfalls. In sharing the investor's point-of-view he reveals not only what turns potential investors on, but what can very well turn them off. If heeded, such information is invaluable. I can't tell you how many times I've seen otherwise sound proposals self-destruct because they contained the very red flags the author alludes to in Section One.

Because Keith has covered so much ground—I can't think of anything he's left out—you're going to find that this book is more than just a primer for preparing a winning business plan. It is a first-rate guide for starting or expanding an enterprise. Just take a look at the section dealing with distribution. The queries and observations dealt with here are key elements to the initial planning of any enterprise. Even if you were not drawing up a plan to persuade investors, if you already possessed the necessary capital to finance your dream, these are questions you would have to raise before proceeding. Similar gems aren't just occasionally sprinkled throughout the book; they stand out on every page.

Early in my business career I made it a habit to put all my ideas down on paper before I brought them to my superiors. This would be an in-depth document and would outline all the steps that led me to my final plan of action. Why did I do this? Because the acid test of paper can prevent one from making a fool of himself. The natural hype that accompanies your latest brainstorm is considerably blunted when it's forced on display in impersonal black-and-white. No amount of enthusiasm can hide the holes that will show themselves on the printed page. In the same manner, a business plan will cast a hard, cold light on your enterprise. If your business is sound and you follow Keith's game plan, you'll welcome the inspection. This confidence will be well-founded. You'll know the document you've presented for scrutiny is hole-proof.

You'll also know that you've been working with advice received from someone who's been in the trenches. Keith Schilit is not one of those fellows from the "those who can't do, teach" schools. He's a successful entrepreneur who has started his own companies. You couldn't ask for a better mentor. If you tried hiring someone to teach you what you're about to learn in these upcoming chapters, it would cost you many times the purchase price of this book. These pages are lined with gold.

Victor K. Kiam
CEO
Remington Products, Inc.

PREFACE

How do you prepare a business plan to enable your company to secure financing? What do investors want to see in a business plan? How can you avoid the major pitfalls of most business plans?

The Entrepreneur's Guide to Preparing a Winning Business Plan and Raising Venture Capital provides practical answers to these questions. It presents an easy-to-follow step-by-step guide for developing a business plan to assist entrepreneurs or owners of small growth businesses in their quest for capital. Moreover, it explains how to prepare the plan *from the perspective of the investor*. That is, it tells you what information is considered valuable by the investor and why it is considered so valuable. There is even an appendix which provides one of the most comprehensive directories available of investors interested in funding emerging growth businesses.

Typically, entrepreneurs spend hundreds of hours and thousands of dollars to prepare a business plan. A very small percentage of those plans, however, will attract investors; a much smaller percentage will gain the favor of established venture capital companies. Thus, securing funding for a small business becomes a probability game. The purpose of this book is to put the odds more in the favor of the entrepreneur.

It is unfortunate that there are thousands of small businesses with successful or potentially successful products or services and with capable management teams whose growth is stymied solely due to a lack of capital. It is generally acknowledged that one of the most common reasons for the failure of small businesses is undercapitalization. This is supported by a recent survey in *Inc.* magazine, which reported that the biggest hurdle for successful new ventures was insufficient resources. B. Robert Jefferson, of the very successful Jefferson-Williams Energy Corp., noted that his company was "so undercapitalized [initially] that it was one continual crisis." How important is adequate funding for a business? As suggested by Alan Shugart, founder of both Shugart Associates and Seagate Technology, "cash is more important than your mother."

The Entrepreneur's Guide to Preparing a Winning Business Plan and Raising Venture Capital is designed especially for owners of such businesses in need of capital. In addition, it will provide bankers, investors, financial planners, CPAs, and others in the financial community with information useful for their clientele.

The search for funding begins with the preparation of the business plan, which is described here in an easy-to-follow workbook format.

W. Keith Schilit

ACKNOWLEDGMENTS

This book is the result of several years of practical and academic experience in the area of raising capital for emerging growth businesses. The preparation of such a book can certainly be an arduous task. For me, however, this entire effort has been one of the most enjoyable projects of my career. I attribute this largely to the inspirational guidance that I've received over the years. Several individuals have had a tremendous impact on my career and, therefore, have influenced the preparation of this book.

Anyone who has ever been able to cultivate a relationship with one or even possibly two role models is, indeed, fortunate. Having had at least a half dozen role models myself, I feel that I've been well cared for over the years.

Several years ago, while a graduate student at the University of Maryland, I was guided by three of the finest people anyone can imagine—Ed Locke, Frank Paine, and Lee Preston. Although they did not contribute directly to this book, they have been *the* intellectual guidance for me throughout my career; in their own unique manner, they each epitomize what a role model should be. More recently, three other individuals—Al Bartlett, Bob Cox, and Bob Leeds—demonstrated that role models arise throughout one's life. I am deeply indebted to all of them for their support and encouragement over the years.

I am also grateful to those individuals who have reviewed earlier drafts of this book. H. Steven Holtzman, partner in the Tampa based securities law firm of Shasteen and Holtzman, and Howard M. Schilit, CPA (as well as Ph.D.), of Rockville, Maryland, managed to explain the finer points of law and accounting to me. Rob Schilit, "wordsmith" extraordinaire, was able to find some redeeming qualities in my writing. I also appreciate the anonymous reviewers for their comments and Gertrude Szyferblatt and the outstanding editorial staff at Prentice Hall for helping me turn my ideas into a workable product.

I owe a special thanks to Victor K. Kiam, CEO of Remington Products, Inc. for preparing the foreword for this book. Somehow he was able to fit this task in while: travelling throughout the world to play in benefit tennis tournaments, negotiating to buy the New England Patriots, running one of the most admired and innovative corporations in this country, and serving as the ideal role model to thousands of young people ready to embark on an entrepreneurial career.

Finally, I thank my parents, my brothers, Rob and Howard, my sister, Audrey, and my wife, Karen, for their support and guidance. Each of them is an expert in either securing or spending capital.

ABOUT THE AUTHOR

Keith Schilit is an accomplished entrepreneur, consultant, author, and professor. He has founded or cofounded three businesses and has assisted in the startup of several others. Currently, he is president of Catalyst Ventures, Inc. (of Tampa, Florida), a consulting firm which assists small growth businesses.

Dr. Schilit has consulted to or conducted training programs for numerous businesses and other organizations including the U.S. Civil Service Commission (General Accounting Office), Niagara Mohawk Power, Corning Glass Works, Miller Brewing, National Tire Dealers and Retreaders Association, Syracuse Cable Systems, Robbins Manufacturing, Medcross, and the American Institute of Certified Public Accountants.

He has written approximately three dozen articles and cases on such topics as Starting and Financing New Business Ventures, Preparing Business Plans, Strategic Planning, Managing Professional Practices, and General Management, and has given numerous talks on these topics to corporations, societies, associations, and universities.

Dr. Schilit is presently a faculty member of the University of South Florida. He held previous faculty positions at the University of Maryland, where he earned his M.B.A. and Ph.D., and at Syracuse University. He has received several awards for his innovative approach to teaching.

He is a founding member of the Strategic Management Society, an international society of consultants, executives, and professors involved in the area of strategic planning. He also plays an active role in several national associations and is a member of the board of directors of several community groups.

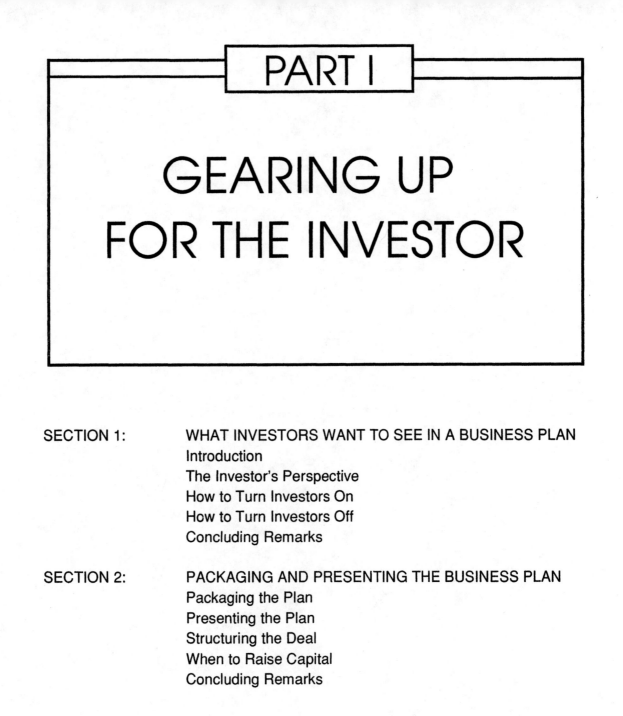

PART I

GEARING UP FOR THE INVESTOR

What Investors Want to See in a Business Plan

INTRODUCTION

When the CEO-founder of a computer software firm in Washington, DC recently visited his banker to request a $50,000 line of credit, he kept his business plan tucked neatly under his arm. When the president of a manufacturer of miniaturized electronic components in New York wanted to establish a set of five-year goals based on the company's current financial projections, he, too, resorted to a business plan. And when the management team of a citrus processing company on the west coast of Florida sought outside investors to finance their expansion, they made sure that their business plan was up to par. These entrepreneurs all recognized the value of the business plan for securing capital and for sustaining the growth of their companies.

Why Prepare a Business Plan?

The business plan serves as a blueprint for building a company. It is a vehicle for describing the goals of the business, why the goals are economically and technologically feasible, and how these goals can be reached over the coming years. Moreover, the business plan is a means to:

- Delineate individual responsibilities
- Project sales, expenses, and cash flows
- Explain to employees what is expected of them
- Improve company performance
- Assist managers in decision making
- Plan for new product development
- Raise capital for a business

Thus the business plan is not merely a report that is prepared and then left on the shelf to collect dust; rather, it is a working document that small business owners should use on a monthly—or even weekly—basis to ensure continuity of the business. (I prefer to use the word "plan" as a verb rather than merely as a noun.) As noted by Nolan Bushnell, founder of Atari and several other ventures: "Every time you prepare a business plan, you become a better entrepreneur."[1]

Despite the many reasons for preparing a business plan described above, the single most important reason for preparing such a plan for a vast majority of entrepreneurial companies is in securing capital. Investors agree that an effectively prepared business plan is a requisite for obtaining funding for any business — whether it is a new business seeking startup capital or an existing business seeking financing for expansion, new business activities, or a turn-around situation.

THE INVESTOR'S PERSPECTIVE

Due to the riskiness of the venture business—only a limited number of investments provide adequate returns—investors set rigorous standards in evaluating venture proposals. A large majority of proposals are rejected, due either to the nature of the product or service, the quality of the business, the capabilities of management, or the preparation of the business plan itself.

As a first step in preparing a business plan, it is crucial to understand how the plan is read and evaluated by the investor. How can you turn on the investor? How can you avoid turning off the investor? What is the basis of the investor's evaluation?

A Matter of A's, B's, and C's

Most entrepreneurs and other small business owners can prepare a *B* or a *B+* business plan without too much trouble. That would be fine if investors would fund *B* or *B+* plans. Investors, however, fund only *A* or *A+* plans. In essence, a *B* business plan is no better than a *C* or *D* plan because none of them is likely to get funded. Thus the real skill is in turning a *B* business plan into one that warrants an *A+*.

An *A+* business plan might be only a 10 to 20 percent improvement over a *B* or *B+* plan in the eyes of the entrepreneur; it might also take 80 percent more effort on the part of the entrepreneur to gain a 20 percent improvement. Yet that 20 percent improvement will seem like a 100 percent improvement in the eyes of the person that matters the most (i.e., the investor) and will therefore increase the likelihood of getting funded by close to 100 percent.

What separates a *B* plan from an *A+* plan? In general, the key difference is that an *A+* plan is written *from the perspective of the investor!* The *A+* plan gets the investor to believe in your product or service, your target market, your management team while it addresses the problems or the key concerns of the business. In addition, the *A+* plan demonstrates that something is unique about

---

[1]See J. A. Timmons, L. E. Smollen, and A. L. M. Dingee, Jr., *New Venture Creation,* 2nd ed. (Homewood, IL: Richard D. Irwin, 1985), p. 432.

this deal—something that distinguishes this investment opportunity from the scores of others that may be brought before a particular investor every week.

The simple rules that follow are designed to enable you to develop an *A*+ plan. You will know you have written an *A*+ plan when you have to turn away money.

HOW TO TURN INVESTORS ON

There are several specific guidelines to follow when developing a convincing business plan for investors—one that will warrant an *A*+ rating in their minds. These guidelines will not only help you in the preparation of your plan, but will serve as valuable advice to you in operating your business and in planning for long-term growth.

For a plan to receive a favorable review by an investor, it must demonstrate the following four features:

- A clear definition of the business
- Evidence of marketing capabilities
- Evidence of management capabilities
- An attractive financial arrangement

Let's examine each of these.

Definition of the Business

There are three basic questions regarding the business that, when answered, provide a working understanding of the "definition of the business"—also known as the "mission" or scope of operations of the business (i.e., what business are you in?):

a. What is the product or service?
b. What is the industry?
c. What is the target market?

These three questions underlie the basic strategy (or direction) of the firm.

No small business venture can be "all things to all people." In the earliest stages of a business it is critical that the company develop a logical, somewhat stable business definition or strategy and avoid any dramatic changes to it. Any alteration of one or more of these three features—the product or service, the industry, or the target market—results in a new—and riskier—strategy for the firm. Of course, as the business expands, the only way to accomplish significant growth will be to alter its current business definition, whether by expanding the product line, entering a new industry, or seeking a new market for a given product or service. Investors, however, will want to see some initial stability in the company's strategy or business definition.

Let's explore these three components of a company's business definition.

a. *What Is the Product or Service?* Investors are always looking for that "something extra" in a product or service that will provide the company with a decided advantage over its competitors. This may include a new product feature, a cost advantage, technical competence, or something else that will be a significant benefit to the customer.

A great way to win the favor of an investor is to have a unique product that is of a proprietary nature, either by copyright, trademark, patent, or by some other exclusive arrangement. Two classic examples of companies benefiting from their proprietary positions are Polaroid, with their instant printing process, and Xerox, with their xerography or photocopying process.

Keep It Simple: Although the product or service idea should be unique, it should also be kept simple. If you cannot describe the idea in a sentence or two, then it is too complex. Also, keep in mind that investors generally do not have technology backgrounds. So if you are dealing with a high-technology product, describe it in such a manner that nontechnical persons will understand it. Do not become more infatuated with the product than with the market for the product.

Finally, in the earliest stages of a venture, it is recommended that you avoid overdiversification of products or services. One or two product or service lines should be sufficient until the company has generated annual revenues of at least $1 million.

     b. *What Is the Industry?* The industry should be clearly defined and should have growth potential. Investors prefer to fund businesses in industries that have at least a 25 percent—and preferably, a much higher—growth rate. High growth is much more important than high tech, as evidenced by venture capitalists giving greater attention to specialty retailers than to technology companies in recent years.

Opening Up Industries: Many investors are particularly attracted to companies that have the ability to open up whole new industries, as was the case of McDonald's in fast food, Federal Express in overnight delivery, Head in ski equipment, Apple in personal computers, and Digital Equipment in minicomputers.

An excellent example of an entrepreneur opening up new markets is the case of Thomas Bata, who grew up in Czechoslovakia, where his father was the owner of a shoe company. After his father's death in 1932, Thomas assumed control of the company. When it became apparent that his country might fall to Hitler, Bata fled his country and opened up a factory in Canada. Today, the Bata Shoe Company sells ¼ billion pairs of shoes a year (one out of three pairs sold in the noncommunist world). A famous story told by Tom Bata summarizes his philosophy of opening up new markets:

> Two shoe salesmen were sent to a poverty-stricken country. One wired back, "Returning home immediately. No one wears shoes here." The other cabled, "Unlimited possibilities. Millions still without shoes."[2]

Riding the Growth Curve: Some investors prefer to fund businesses in the electronics industry. Others prefer biotechnology companies. Still others prefer to invest in companies involved in real estate development. As a rule, however, investors prefer innovative product-oriented companies in industries that are

---

[2]See E. Severeid, *Enterprise* (New York: McGraw-Hill, 1983), p. 13.

just beginning to approach their growth stage. The investors realize their greatest returns as they "ride the growth curve."

Investors shy away from revolutionary products in industries that have not yet been developed. Although such developments as the light bulb, the telephone, the television, the camera, and the automobile have had a dramatic effect on all of our lives, they would not have been prime investment opportunities for most venture capitalists today because their development time was extremely long and there was no evidence of consumer acceptance of these products until their development was completed.

c. *What Is the Target Market?* It is critical that you identify a specific target market for your product or service. The difficult issue here is that you want to demonstrate evidence of the market being substantial enough to provide adequate revenues for your business. Yet capital requirements will make it impossible for you to reach everyone, thereby necessitating that you clearly define or focus your target market. (See the following section on "Marketing Capabilities.")

Marketing Capabilities

There are four features that demonstrate the firm's marketing capabilities:

  a. Benefit to the user
  b. Evidence of marketability/past success
  c. Widespread appeal
  d. Selling ability

a. *Benefit to the User.* Perhaps the best indicator of a firm's marketing capabilities is the ability to demonstrate user benefit: that is, how the customer will profit, gain, or otherwise benefit from buying the company's product or service. Demonstrating user benefit will necessarily strengthen the entrepreneur's contention that the company can generate sales and will therefore be an attractive investment opportunity.

Benefits to the user vary considerably from product to product. However, there are a few guiding questions to demonstrate this characteristic:

  • Will the product save the customer money?
  • Will it save time?
  • Will it provide status?
  • Will it enhance the customer's life-style?
  • How long will it take to pay for itself?

Quantify User Benefit: You can strengthen your arguments of user benefit by quantifying the benefits. For example, a certain breakthrough patented genetic engineering process developed by a team of scientists was able to increase yields by more than 200 percent while it reduced costs to biotechnology companies (i.e., the users) by over 50 percent.

On a mass-appeal level, a residential energy-saving device which reduced energy consumption by 40 percent on average paid for itself within one year. This can be contrasted to an alternative residential energy-saving device with which I am familiar that sells for over $8000 and results in 10 to 20 percent savings in energy. Based on an average monthly energy bill of $250, the device will not pay for itself for nearly 20 years, thereby making its user benefit extremely questionable.

Thus you can quantify user benefit by describing the cost savings to the customer, which are generally measured in terms of:

- Lowered reject rate
- Lowered warranty costs
- Reduced labor costs
- Lowered storage costs
- Lowered inventory costs
- Reduced downtime
- Greater convenience
- Amount of time before the product pays for itself

Similarly, user benefits can be expressed in terms of increased earnings to the customer (e.g., through increased productivity) or in terms of various nonmonetary benefits (e.g., better health).

If you really want to catch an investor's eye, then you can explain what will happen to potential customers who do not buy your product. Insurance companies have used such an approach in their advertising campaigns for many years.

b. *Evidence of Marketability/Past Success.*   Even if the product has benefit to the user, a critical question is whether enough customers will buy it. A well-recognized market can certainly enhance the likelihood of your obtaining funding.

Investors generally want to see some indication that customers or clients have used the product or service—even if only on a trial basis (e.g., a prototype)—and are happy with it. Obviously, the best indicator of whether you will have customers in the future is if you have had customers in the past. Moreover, existing customers will be able to provide you with feedback to enable you to alter the product design or service features if necessary.

As a general rule, most investors prefer to fund companies with some operating history—this provides some assurance of success—although it is not necessary that the venture be operating profitably.

Stated another way, investors would prefer to have their money used for production and selling rather than for product development and market research, thereby reducing the risk and accelerating the time span for profits to be generated.

c. *Widespread Appeal.*   The growth potential of a business is often related to the widespread appeal of a product or service. As a rule, investors shy away from businesses whose basic product or service must be specially designed for each customer. In most such situations, costs are high due to specialized labor requirements, profits are low due to an inability to achieve advantages from economies of scale, and growth is slow.

For example, I am familiar with a biotechnology laboratory that was planning to develop a diagnostic test for laboratory technicians exposed to a specific strain of woodchuck virus. The interest in developing this diagnostic test resulted from their chief immunologist's research interests while in graduate school.

Unfortunately, however, only 10 or 12 laboratories in the country conduct research on woodchuck virus, thereby limiting the marketability of this product. On the other hand, diagnostic tests for AIDS or herpes, which have much wider market appeal, would be more attractive investment alternatives for investors.

d. *Selling Ability.* Even if the product or service has user benefit and has a demonstrated market available, it is still crucial that the company have the capabilities to sell and support it. For example, I recently encountered a young engineer-entrepreneur whose company developed a unique audio speaker system to reduce sound distortion. The company consisted of the engineer, who was responsible for designing the product, and three employees, who manufactured the product. Although he had a fairly sound business plan with carefully researched market projections, he was at a loss for words when a potential investor asked him, "Who's going to sell the product?"

Thus you must show how the product will move "from the shop floor to the customer's floor." This demonstrates a market-driven rather than a product-driven attitude, which is critical for the success of any venture. If I had to describe one essential characteristic of a successful entrepreneur, it would be the ability to sell. You could have the most impressive product imaginable and could be extremely well capitalized, yet without sales, the business cannot succeed. Numerous entrepreneurs have risen through the ranks in established companies in sales capacities prior to launching their own successful ventures. Victor Kiam was a leading salesperson at Playtex before purchasing Remington Products. Similarly, H. Ross Perot was a star salesperson at IBM—he would generally reach his annual sales quota for the year in January—prior to starting Electronic Data Systems (EDS). When EDS was recently purchased by General Motors, Perot's net worth was in excess of $2 billion.

Management Capabilities

Most investors feel that management is the key factor in securing funding for a venture. They invest in management rather than in products. One prominent venture capitalist goes as far as suggesting: "It's really the people who are important. The plan just gives the investor the opportunity to meet people and see what kind of people they are, to learn their visions, their philosophies, and see what kind of intelligence went into the plan."

There are three features that demonstrate the company's attention to the importance of management:

a. The management "team"
b. Experienced managers
c. The board of directors

Investors would much rather fund an experienced management team—especially if their experience is in the same industry as the venture needing the funding—than sole entrepreneurs. The management team should have a demonstrated track record and competences in each of the critical functional areas—marketing, finance, product design and production, control, and personnel. Furthermore, the board of directors should enhance the capabilities of the management team.

Let's explore these three features of capable management in greater detail.

a. *The Management "Team."* The effective use of management teams is becoming very evident in today's growth companies. Companies such as COMPAQ Computer, SAGE Systems, Linear Technology, AST Research, and Quantum Corp. have each avoided the "one-man show" and have assembled top management teams that are able to look beyond the narrow confines of specific functional areas to the broad concerns of the company as a whole.

The vice-president of finance or controller is an extremely important member of the management team, as he or she speaks the language of the investor. Furthermore, the vice-president or director of marketing is vital in that sales is, perhaps, the most important function of small growth-oriented businesses.

Investors will almost always prefer a first-rate management team with a second-rate product over a first-rate product with a second-rate management team. Perhaps the most attractive arrangement for an investor would be to fund a venture managed by a previously successful entrepreneurial team. If they have succeeded before, they will be likely to succeed again. For example, Tandem Computer was founded by several experienced managers, primarily from Hewlett-Packard. It is not surprising that the Mayfield Fund, one of the leading venture capital firms in the country, invested in this startup firm in 1975. Over the next 10 years, it returned nearly 40 times its original investment in the company.

How Investors Can Help: One of the biggest problems faced by less experienced entrepreneurs is that they have "gaps" in their management team. For such entrepreneurs, experienced investors can be valuable in assisting the startups in "filling in the gaps" by providing introductions to marketing or finance executives.

In some cases, investors will want to take on very active roles with the company that they are funding. For example, in addition to the venture capital firm Kleiner Perkins Caufield and Byers providing Genentech with the necessary capital to support its early levels of growth (their $200,000 investment in 1976 increased 800-fold in five years), they also provided Genentech with a chief executive officer, thereby enabling Genentech's scientist-executives to return to their research labs to develop new biotechnology products. That decision has been primarily responsible for Genentech's remarkable success over the past twelve years.

b. *Experienced Managers.* In recent years, we have seen numerous experienced managers with excellent track records with established companies become very successful in starting their own businesses. For example, Gene Amdahl left IBM to launch a computer company sporting his name, while Richard Greene left IBM to start Data Switch Corp.; Richard Blackmer founded Oxygen Enrichment Company after spending 25 years as an engineer with General Electric; and Dean Scheff started CPT Corp. after having worked for Univac and Honeywell.

Once Is Not Enough: Similarly, "repeat entrepreneurs" such as Nolan Bushnell (Atari and Pizza Time Theatre), Steven Jobs (Apple Computer and Next), William Poduska (Prime Computer and Apollo Computer), and Alan Shugart (Shugart Associates and Seagate Technology) have found that securing funding from investors becomes increasingly easy with experience. Investors invariably invest in the experience of the entrepreneur or the entrepreneurial team more so than in the growth potential of a given product or service idea.

c. *The Board of Directors.* Investors are also very sensitive to the qualifications and experience of members of the board of directors. In many cases, an experienced board will partially offset some of the "gaps" in the management team. At a minimum, such a board will enhance the capabilities and experience of any management team in the eyes of the investor.

The purpose of the board of directors is to aid, challenge, and replace (if necessary) the officers of the company. A passive unquestioning board (which is often the case if the board is composed primarily of either inside managers or friends and relatives) can have a disastrous impact on the business. Just as in the case of your top management team, selectivity is critical in choosing members of the board. You should consider having two or three "outsiders" (i.e., not members of the organization—for example, a banker, an attorney, a supplier, etc.) serve on the board to assist you in making decisions and in monitoring the environment. You will often be able to attract competent directors who would welcome the opportunity to work with a small growth venture and who will accept a minor token payment of cash and/or equity for their services.

Chester Kirk, founder, chairman, and CEO of Amtrol, Inc., a very successful privately owned manufacturing company in West Warwick, Rhode Island, has made extensive and effective use of outside directors over the past few years. Kirk has acknowledged that outsiders often possess expertise in areas where his own management team may be lacking. Outside directors with backgrounds in finance and international business were especially helpful in making recommendations related to selecting inventory accounting methods, choosing a computer system, developing an employee ownership plan, and in making general decisions on the long-term growth of Amtrol.

Principal investors will often make suggestions regarding potential members of the board of directors. In most cases, these investors will want to be represented on the board personally in order to remain involved in critical strategic decisions. This is highly advisable, as such investors can provide you with experience and important contacts—in essence, you want their advice as much as you want their money.

Financial Arrangement

Investors prefer to see a structured arrangement presented by the entrepreneurial team which describes the capital needs of the venture and which proposes a fair equity agreement for the two parties involved. Although investors expect to see such a structured financial arrangement, recognize that the terms are generally subject to intense negotiation.

The business plan should include a provision for a specific dollar amount of capital needed for the business. Proposals for any amount of capital may be appropriate. However, for venture capitalists, proposals that are accepted are generally in the range of $100,000 to $2 million. Due to the cost of investigating any venture (several thousand dollars per venture proposal), it is not cost-beneficial to evaluate smaller proposals.

In addition, the business plan should have the following financial features:

a. Acceptable return
b. Provision for an "exit"
c. Participation by other investors
d. Structured deal

a. *Acceptable Return.* Investors maintain a time horizon of five years (or a range of three to seven years) in which to realize their returns on their initial investment. During that period they expect their investment to increase in value by 5- to 15-fold net of inflation.

Risk and Return: What dictates the return on investment expected by a typical investor? Essentially, it is based on the riskiness of the investment. Thus the higher the riskiness of the investment, the greater the expected return for the investor.

Riskiness is generally based on two factors that were discussed earlier: (1) the nature of the product or service, and (2) most important, the quality of the management of the venture. Newly developed ideas are more risky than established products or services; investors generally wish to see products or services that are already being used and have been accepted by customers. (Having exclusive rights to a product or process via copyrights or trademarks, however, will make even a new product seem attractive in the eyes of the investor.) Similarly, individual entrepreneurs are seen as more risky than are established management teams.

Stanley Rich and David Gumpert have developed an evaluation system based on the two factors just noted.[3] The system identifies four levels to describe the status of the product or service and four levels to describe the status of management. In both cases, level 1 is the most risky type of venture and would therefore warrant the highest expected return by the investor, whereas level 4 is the least risky type of venture. The system is described below.

	Level 4 Fully developed product/service; established market; satisfied users	4/1	4/2	4/3	4/4
Most risky	*Level 3* Fully developed product/service; few users as of yet; market assumed	3/1	3/2	3/3	3/4
Status *of* *Product/* *Service*	*Level 2* Operable pilot or prototype; not yet developed for production; market assumed	2/1	2/2	2/3	2/4
	Level 1 Product/service idea; not yet operable; market assumed	1/1	1/2	1/3	1/4
		Level 1 Individual founder- entrepreneur	*Level 2* Two founders; other personnel not identified	*Level 3* Partial management team; members identified to join company when funding is received	*Level 4* Fully staffed, experienced- management team

←———————— Most risky ————————→

Status   of   Management

[3]See S. Rich and D. Gumpert, *Business Plans That Win $$$* (New York: Harper & Row, 1985).

Some investors would only invest in 4/4 (or possibly 4/3 and 3/4) ventures, whereas others would invest in riskier businesses. Regardless, as I mentioned earlier, the higher the risk, the higher the expected returns. Thus investors generally seek approximately four to five times their investment net of inflation in five years (or a 30 to 40 percent compounded annual return on investment) for a 4/4 company and would seek perhaps 15 times their investment net of inflation (or a minimum of a 60 percent compounded annual return) for a 2/2 company.

Typically, investors seek returns on their investment as follows:

State of Business	Expected Annual Return on (Percent) Investment	Expected Increase on Initial Investment		
Startup business (idea stage)	60+	10–15	×	investment
First-stage financing (new business)	40–60	6–12	×	investment
Second-stage financing (development stage)	30–50	4–8	×	investment
Third-stage financing (expansion stage)	25–40	3–6	×	investment
Turnaround situation	50+	8–15	×	investment

Please note that the figures above are merely general guidelines; each venture is evaluated on its own merit. Investors will often settle for a lower return on investment if (1) the company has sufficient capital, (2) there is a good cash flow (for example, as a result of monthly or other recurring revenue streams), or (3) the original owners of the business have invested a sizeable portion of their own funds in the business, thereby taking on a good deal of the risk themselves. For example, if the original owners invest 10 percent of the total capital, they can often expect to retain 40 to 50 percent of the ownership in the business; if they invest 30 percent of the capital, they can often retain two-thirds or more of the ownership in the business.

Certainly, the expected returns for the investor noted above are high. However, especially in recent years, during a period when blue-chip companies traded on the New York Stock Exchange—which are virtually risk free over the long term—have yielded compounded annual returns of 20 percent, 30 percent, or more, it is reasonable to assume that venture investors would be seeking double or triple those returns.

VCs Are VC: It is also important to understand the personality of the investor as it relates to risk and return. The initials VC stand for *venture capitalist.* Yet they stand for something else—*very conservative!* Venture capitalists are not just interested in making a lot of money. They are also interested in not losing the money that they have already invested in a company; they want to at least get their investment back. Thus it is crucial to demonstrate to them how they "can't lose" on their investment.

To go one step further, a battle often develops between the entrepreneur and the investor. The entrepreneur argues for the upside potential of the business, whereas the investor states a case for its downside risk. In most cases the investor has the leverage because (1) the investor is generally much more experienced in these battles than is the entrepreneur; and (2) the investor has something that the entrepreneur wants—*money!* Eventually an agreement is reached that will enable both parties to benefit. The important lesson is that the entrepreneur must understand the investor's needs and risk preferences prior to presenting a plan for raising capital.

An Example: Let's look at an example to see how a venture capitalist's investment affects the equity position of a company. Suppose that SUPER-PROD Corporation, a one-year-old company with excellent potential, is seeking venture capital. The company has developed a prototype but has not yet begun production due to its limited funds. Currently, the only persons working for the company are the two engineer-founders. Projected earnings for the company in five years are $3 million on $25 million in revenues. Let's assume that companies similar to SUPERPROD would be worth 10 times their earnings or $30 million in five years. Assume that SUPERPROD is now seeking $1 million to expand their production and marketing efforts. What percentage of ownership of the business would the venture capital company want to realize its expected return?

Let's first examine the riskiness of this venture. Using the evaluation system just described, we would classify this venture as a 2/2 investment, from which investors would be seeking a 60+ percent annual return or, perhaps, 12 times their investment in five years. Assuming no inflation, the $1 million initial investment should be worth $12 million or approximately 40 percent ($12 million divided by $30 million) of the ownership in the business. When we adjust for inflation, the ownership position of SUPERPROD by the venture capital company would approach 50 percent.

Recognize that the current owners of SUPERPROD will be expected to give up nearly one-half of their ownership in the company at this early stage. Yet there might be two or three more rounds of venture financing necessary during the next 5 to 10 years to enable the company to grow. Thus if the owners will be giving up so much equity at such an early stage, then it will be impossible for them to maintain a majority interest in the company as the business requires additional funding at a later time.

Do Investors Want to Control Your Business? From the preceding example, it might appear that investors want to become majority owners of a company. This is generally not the case. Investors in small growing privately owned companies are just like any other investors, yet they have a specific objective of earning a 40 to 60 percent annual return on their investment, net of inflation; this return is very much in line with the riskiness of such an investment. Unlike investors in blue-chip companies, who expect a 10 to 20 percent annual return in less risky companies over a 20- or 30-year period, however, venture investors generally want to realize their returns within five years. Furthermore, in a typical venture capitalist's portfolio, there may be only one major success and three or four minor successes, with the remainder either losing money or failing completely. Thus they expect higher-than-average returns to counterbalance the poor returns realized by many of their other high-risk investments. If they happen to secure a 51 percent ownership position in the company, it is merely a reflection of the potential returns necessary to invest in the venture rather than of the desire to "control" the company.

b. *Provision for an "Exit."* The only way for any investor to realize a gain on an investment is to sell (at least part of) his or her ownership position. For securities traded on a national stock exchange, there is always a market in which to sell shares of stock. However, for privately held companies, the market is considerably more limited. There are four basic ways in which the investor can "exit" from the deal or get his or her money out of the company:

1. A buyback by the founders of the company (which is not generally the preferred alternative of the entrepreneurial team). Why would the owners propose to pay 30 to 50 percent annual returns on money "borrowed" from investors when they could have borrowed at much lower rates from other sources earlier?
2. Finding a new investor.
3. An acquisition by a larger company.
4. "Going public" via an initial public offering (IPO)

Going public is seen as an attractive alternative because it suggests to investors that a ready market will then exist for them to get their original investment out of the business. It can also be a very profitable arrangement for investors as has recently been evidenced by such IPOs as Lotus Development, Apple Computer, COMPAQ Computer, Microsoft, and Genentech.

Before an investor invests in a business, he or she will want to know what provisions for exit will be available five years down the road. At that time the investor will want to liquidate a part of his or her holdings in the company in order to invest in other privately held growth business.

c. *Participation by Other Investors.* An excellent way to attract investors is to demonstrate that other investors—particularly, the existing top management team—have already invested in it, thereby reducing the risk and exposure of the investor. There is the story of Frederick Smith, who in his quest for $90 million to launch Federal Express used the tactic of asking *all* of his potential investors for that "last million" rather than for the "first 89 million."

d. *Structured Deal.* As mentioned earlier, investors prefer to see a structured deal. The answer to the following questions should be clearly stated in the business plan and, in fact, in the executive summary of the plan:

- Who is involved in the deal?
- How much money is needed?
- What is the minimum investment per investor?
- How is ownership translated into shares of common or preferred stock, convertible debentures, debt, and so on?
- What is the price per share of stock?
- What is the projected compounded annual return for the investor over the next three to seven years?

HOW TO TURN INVESTORS OFF

In addition to understanding what turns investors on, it is important to know what turns investors off. There are several key turnoffs, any one of which can set off a "red flag" that could undermine the reliability of the remainder of the plan, regardless of the quality of the product or service, the capabilities of the management team, or the terms of the financial arrangement. These include:

- A "prepackaged" package
- A product orientation
- Unrealistic financial projections
- Failure to deal with potential critical risks

Let's examine each of these.

Prepackaged Package

The sterile standardized business plan packages that many consultants will sell to small business owners will often set off a "red flag" to the investor. Such packages use a common skeleton of a business plan, regardless of the nature of the company or of the industry, and substitute a few words and names in the plan as appropriate. They are often lacking in their analysis of the industry and incorrect in their financial projections. Often, they suffer from "Lotusitis." Although Lotus and the other impressive spreadsheet programs can develop neat, mathematically correct rows and columns of numbers, their end product often fails to meet the needs of the investors, who are generally more concerned with the assumptions surrounding these numbers than with the numbers themselves.

Furthermore, as we discussed earlier, investors recognize that as important as the plan itself is, equally important is the process in which the entrepreneurial team must invest their time.

Product Orientation

One of the greatest pitfalls of entrepreneurs is to focus on the product rather than on the market for that product. Many inventors (or "tinkerers") fall prey to this pitfall. True, the product might be innovative and might have phenomenal features. The key issue, however, is: Will customers buy the product? For example, software entrepreneurs have developed numerous computer software packages priced at $200 to $400 which can do little more than already existing written directories priced at less than $20. Such software packages might be excellent products; yet investors, who generally have strong financial and/or marketing backgrounds and weak technology backgrounds, tend to shy away from entrepreneurs who are more enamored with the features of the product than with the market that must recognize the value of the product. After all, satisfied customers—not dazzling products—are the key to success in any business; all the successful businesses with which I have had contact are market driven rather than product driven. The red flag for investors is when the business plan devotes more space to describing the product than to describing who will buy the product and how it will be marketed.

Unrealistic Financial Projections

It is difficult to fool investors when it comes to the financial projections for the company. Specifically, entrepreneurs have a tendency of overestimating revenues or underestimating costs, which will result in a red flag being raised when the investor sees significant deviations from industry norms or questionable projections by companies in embryonic industries.

For example, projections of 50 percent growth rates and 60 percent gross profit margins by a company in an industry characterized by 10 percent growth and 25 percent gross margins would be questioned by an investor. Similarly, projections of 50 percent or 100 percent growth rates for a company that has developed a new, untested product would also be suspect.

It is important to avoid being overly optimistic in developing financial projections. Investors like to see a best case, a worst case, and a most likely case set of projections, thereby enhancing the believability of the entire plan.

Failure to Examine Risks

Undoubtedly, there will be numerous risks associated with the business. Recognizing that raising capital is the art of reducing risk—contrary to popular belief, investors are risk adverse—it is imperative that the business plan address the critical risks and problems that may be encountered. Investors will generally be aware of some of these risks, so failure to address them will probably undermine the credibility of the entire plan. In addition, investors would rather fund entrepreneurs who demonstrate that they are "cautiously optimistic" than those who are "recklessly optimistic."

Addressing the risks will often turn a *B* or *B+* plan into the *A−* range; turning those negatives into positives can raise it solidly into the *A* range.

CONCLUDING REMARKS

We have just presented some general guidelines for preparing a business plan to meet the needs of the investor. Investors tend to be turned on by plans that demonstrate the following four features:

1. A clear definition of the business
2. Evidence of marketing capabilities
3. Evidence of management capabilities
4. An attractive financial arrangement

Furthermore, investors are generally turned off by plans characterized by:

1. A prepackaged package
2. A product orientation

3. Unrealistic financial projections
4. Failure to deal with potential critical risks

We will now discuss how to package the business plan properly and how to present the plan to potential investors.

Packaging and Presenting the Business Plan

PACKAGING THE PLAN

How important is the way in which you package the business plan? As mentioned earlier, the quest for financing is a probability game, the goal of which is to avoid being eliminated. Having an attractive, well-prepared plan package will not offset the weak features of an otherwise ineffective plan. Yet having a poorly prepared plan package will undoubtedly result in the plan being discarded before it is ever read.

Covering the Basics

The first thing about the business plan that an investor will see is the cover. So let's start with the outside and work our way in. The most suitable type of cover for the business plan is a plastic spiral binding holding together two cover sheets. The plan should not be too amateurish in appearance; a stack of photocopied sheets stapled together would be inappropriate. It should also not be too lavish; a hardcover bound edition with typeset print may be indicative of extravagant spending on the part of the entrepreneur.

First Impressions. The general appearance of the entire plan—and more specifically, the cover itself—is extremely important, as it is the first impression that the investor has of the business. Unfair as it may seem, in the eyes of the investor, a sloppy cover will be indicative of a disorderly shop floor; incorrect titles will be indicative of shoddy cost control. This is quite similar to the analogy that Tom Peters of *In Search of Excellence* fame has made regarding coffee stains on the flip-down trays in airplanes being indicative of sloppy engine maintenance. Sure, it's unfair. It still is up to the entrepreneur, however, to make certain that the unfair assertion is not made by the investor.

Certain aspects of the cover can have a dramatic effect on investors' likelihood of reading the business plan and on their developing an initial—positive or negative—bias toward the plan when reading it. In a recent study conducted by noted author and lecturer Joseph Mancuso to determine the characteristics of business plans that investors would be most likely to read, it was found that investors would first examine the covers and pick up the plan based primarily on the name of the company. Next in importance was the geographic location of the business, followed by the length of the business plan (inversely related). The least important factor noted was the attractiveness of the cover. Therefore, developing a pretty cover should not be a primary objective of the entrepreneur, as the cover tends to be more of a factor in assisting the investor to eliminate plans than in improving the chances of the plan being read.

Format

The business plan should be neatly typed and devoid of errors in spelling, grammar, punctuation, and tabulation of numbers, any of which can give the reader the impression of a poorly developed plan. I always recommend that each member of the entrepreneurial team proofread the plan to make sure that the words and numbers are accurate. It is also advisable to have a professional writer or editor review the content of the plan and to have an accountant or financial advisor review its financial projections before it is presented.

Use a standard style of type to which investors are accustomed. It is also often appropriate to include graphs, charts, and pictures in the appendices, but only if they are of high quality.

Most investors prefer that the business plan be approximately 25 to 40 pages in length. It should be arranged appropriately with the following three main sections:

Part 1:   Executive summary
Part 2:   Body of the report—with logically arranged chapters or sections
Part 3:   Appendices—which support materials contained in the main body of the report

An outline is presented below.

OUTLINE FOR PREPARING THE BUSINESS PLAN

Part 1.   EXECUTIVE SUMMARY
Part 2.   BODY OF REPORT
    I.   Background and Purpose
        IA.   History
        IB.   Current Conditions
        IC.   The Concept
        ID.   Overall Objectives
        IE.   Specific Objectives
    II.   Market Analysis
        IIA.   Market Research
        IIB.   Overall Market
        IIC.   Specific Market Segment

IID.   Competitive Factors

IIE.   Other Market Influences

IIF.   Sales Forecasts

III.   Development and Production

IIIA.   Research and Development

IIIB.   Production Requirements

IIIC.   Production Process

IIID.   Quality Assurance/Quality Control

IIIE.   Contingency Plans

IV.   Marketing

IVA.   Marketing Orientation

IVB.   Marketing Strategy

IVC.   Contingency Plans

V.   Financial Data

VA.   Current Financial Position

VB.   Payables/Receivables

VC.   Cost Control

VD.   Break-Even Analysis

VE.   Financial Ratios

VF.   Financial Projections

VI.   Organization and Management

VIA.   Key Personnel

VIB.   Other Personnel

VIC.   Miscellaneous Issues

VID.   Contingency Plans

VII.   Ownership

VIIA.   Structure of Business

VIIB.   Financing/Equity Considerations

VIII.   Critical Risks and Problems

VIIIA.   Description of Risks

IX.   Summary and Conclusions

IXA.   Summary

IXB.   Scheduling

Part 3.   APPENDICES

A.   Photograph of Product

B.   Sales and Profitability Objectives

C.   Market Survey

D.   Production Flowchart

E.   Price List/Catalog

F.   Sample Advertisement

G.   Sample Press Release

H.   Historical Financial Statements

I.   Table of Startup Costs

J.   Current and Projected Profit and Loss Statement
K.   Statement of Cash Projections
L.   Current and Projected Balance Sheet
M.   Fixed-Asset Acquisition Schedule
N.   Break-Even Points
O.   Résumés of Key Personnel
P.   Individual and Organizational Tax Returns
Q.   Character References

The Executive Summary

The first and generally most important part of the business plan is the executive summary. Because venture capital firms and other investors receive so many business plans, they will generally spend only 5 to 10 minutes scanning a plan before deciding whether to read it in its entirety or not to read it at all. The executive summary is likely to be the only part of the plan that is read. Thus spend the time to prepare an A+ executive summary, as this might be your only chance to get the attention of the investor.

Another important reason for preparing an effective executive summary is that many investors prefer to read a preliminary proposal before requesting a formal business plan. The executive summary, if properly prepared, serves as a more than adequate preliminary proposal.

The Body of the Report

Although the business plan should be designed specifically for a given industry, there are a few major topics that must be covered to satisfy the concerns of the investor. As noted in the previous outline, there should generally be nine key sections of the main body of the business plan, as follows.

I. *Background and purpose:* provides a brief overview of the history of the company, its current state of progress, and its objectives over the coming years.

II. *Market analysis:* identifies the specific target market in which the product(s)/service(s) is(are) aimed and discusses the competitive forces that affect the company's long-term success. In short, investors want to know who will purchase the product (service), why they will purchase it, and how much of the product (service) they will purchase.

III. *Development and production:* describes the emphasis the company places on research and development (R&D), the production process, and quality control. Investors generally would rather see funds needed to support production scale-up (i.e., later-stage expenditures) than to support product development (i.e., early-stage expenditures).

IV. *Marketing:* describes how the company will sell its product(s)/service(s) to the target market described earlier. It should describe the specific marketing strategies that will be used and should justify the costs devoted to marketing.

V. *Financial data:* summarizes the past, present, and future financial position of the company. Actual financial statements should be presented concisely in the appendix. (Most investors avoid reading business plans with page after page of spreadsheet projections.) It is crucial that the financial projections should not deviate considerably from industry averages. For that reason, the appropriate financial ratios must be calculated and discussed.

VI. *Organization and management:* discusses the qualifications and responsibilities of the key management personnel involved in the venture. In most situations, the quality of management is the deciding factor in being funded.

VII. *Ownership:* discusses the financial arrangement proposed by the company. Investors want to see a structured deal in which there is an indication of:

- How much money is being sought
- The form of the proposed investment (i.e., debt, equity, convertible debt, etc.)
- How the funds will be used
- The percentage of ownership to be provided in exchange for the funding
- The projected compounded annual return for the investors
- The manner in which the investors will get their money out of the business

VIII. *Critical risks and problems:* describes the key risks facing the company, many of which will already be evident to the investor.

IX. *Summary and conclusions:* summarizes the key parts of the business plan and develops a schedule or timetable for future developments. The timetable gives the investor an indication of when the funds will be needed.

Appendices

Most investors prefer that the body of the business plan contain almost entirely text and that all financial data and other information that cannot fit neatly into the text be included in appendices. Photographs, advertisements and press releases, price lists, financial statements, résumés, character references, and so on, should be arranged in appendices at the end of the business plan.

Recognize that most venture capitalists and other investors have backgrounds in finance. Thus they will often quickly turn to the rows and columns presented in the financial statements when they receive a business plan. To them, the decision to fund a venture will be influenced greatly by the way the numbers are presented.

PRESENTING THE PLAN

Following completion of the business plan comes the challenge of finding an investor to fund the business.

Do Your Research

One of the reasons that business plans are rejected is that they are sent indiscriminately to investors who do not fund such ventures. For example, if a venture capital firm invests solely in land development businesses, it would be foolish to send a business plan for a high-tech venture to such a firm. Similarly, do not expect that a startup business will be funded by an investor who provides only second- or third-stage financing. I am amazed at how many entrepreneurs spend months preparing a business plan and then spend just a few minutes haphazardly sending out those plans to 20 or 30 venture capital companies, without regard to the investment priorities (i.e., type of business or industry, stage of financing, etc.) of those companies. Before sending out proposals, take the time to "prospect" for the investors who might be interested in funding a business like yours.

Obtaining Leads. Recognize that a majority of an investor's leads comes from the entrepreneurial companies in which he or she has invested. Therefore, one of the best linkages that you can establish is with an entrepreneur already in an investor's portfolio. Find out which entrepreneurial companies comprise the portfolio. Then get to know two or three of those entrepreneurs. They will often be able to provide you with assistance with your business plan and with introductions to investors who have already invested in them. Therefore, contact an entrepreneur rather than an investor directly.
As a backup, you can attempt to secure introductions to investors through:

- Other venture capitalists or investors
- Friends or associates of an investor
- Individual investors in a venture capital firm's portfolio
- Other business associates, such as lawyers, accountants, bankers, public relations specialists, or small business owners

The Informal Network. Certainly, the informal network is an ideal way to make contact with investors. One way to develop your informal network is to find some background information on an investor and to use that as a common ground for an introduction. For example, A. David Silver's *Who's Who in Venture Capital* (3rd Ed., Wiley, 1987) provides such information. Perhaps one of the venture capitalists went to law school or business school with someone you know or serves as a director of a company with which you are familiar. In any case, you want to avoid sending out an unsolicited proposal to an investor with whom you have had no direct or indirect contact.

Evaluating the Investor. Find out all that you can about an investor before contacting the person. You should get references from CEOs of firms funded by him or her. In addition, if possible, attempt to obtain information about the following:

- Past investments of the investor—especially those investments in your industry
- Characteristics of successful versus unsuccessful investments made by the investor
- How far the investor will go to support an investment (i.e., how deep are the investor's pockets?)
- The investor's commitment to firms during economic downturns

- The investor's access to other investors
- The type of investment (i.e., active versus passive) that the investor generally makes

Although the statistics suggest that there are only one or two chances in a hundred of getting funded by venture capitalists, recognize that by preparing an effective, convincing plan and by submitting it to the appropriate investors, you can enhance your chances tremendously. However, the plan must be prepared as well as possible, packaged appropriately, and delivered to the right people. That will be your only chance to get your "foot in the door."

Submitting the Business Plan

Once you have prepared your business plan and executive summary and have secured a few good leads, it is time to contact potential investors to see if they may be interested in funding your venture.

Contacting the Investor. Generally, it is recommended that you phone the investor directly after you have completed the plan. (Please note that venture capitalists and other investors tend to be very difficult to reach throughout the day. It has been my experience that they are most likely to be around the office either first thing in the morning or very late in the day.) Your initial conversation with the investor will be your opportunity to present a "two-minute summary" of your plan that describes your business and the type of deal that you are attempting to get financed.

It is essential that you prepare yourself for this conversation and that you cover the following points in a succinct, organized manner:

- A brief description of your business (i.e., product/service; target market)
- The unique features of your business or product/service
- The management team
- The type of funding desired (i.e., common stock; preferred stock)
- The general terms of the deal

If you can then arrange to meet with the investor to expand on your two-minute summary, that would be fine. However, at this point, most venture capitalists and other sophisticated investors will want you to send them either the entire plan or the executive summary before they choose to meet with you.

When sending out the plan or the summary, you should include a cover letter. Try to be as specific as possible in the letter (and refer to matters discussed in your earlier telephone conversation) so that the letter is not perceived as a mass mailing.

Then mark your calendar for the fifteenth day following your mailing of the plan to the investor. That will be the day to follow up with the investor to make certain that he or she has received the necessary information and to see if the person has questions that you can answer.

The Oral Presentation to the Investors

After a careful screening of the written business plan, investors will generally require you to make an oral presentation to them. The oral presentation should summarize the key features of the written plan. In addition, the members of your management team should be prepared to answer questions asked by the investors. You can certainly strengthen the oral presentation with the use of presentational aids such as handouts, overheads, flipcharts, and so on.

The investors will be interested in determining if your management team has the capability to make critical decisions and to function as a "team." They will be particularly interested in determining the expertise that your key executives have in finance, marketing, and perhaps production. All members of your management team should be prepared to provide input during the presentation to demonstrate the capabilities of a management team rather than of a single entrepreneur. In addition, investors will generally insist that all the key managers be owners of the company in order to foster the necessary teamwork to stimulate growth.

Evaluating the Venture Proposal

The evaluation process takes place in a series of stages:

- A large majority—perhaps over 80 percent—of the preliminary proposals (i.e., executive summaries) are rejected shortly after the investors receive them.
- After this initial screening of the preliminary proposal, the formal written business plan is evaluated by the investor. A large percentage of those plans are rejected.
- Further rejections are made on the basis of the oral presentation.
- A final evaluation is generally made two to four months following the oral presentation, after the investors have conducted background checks on the management team and have discussed the business with experts in the field as well as with suppliers, customers, and competitors of the business. Venture capitalists refer to this process as "due diligence."

Although the likelihood of obtaining venture funding is therefore rather slim, you can immeasurably enhance your chances of being funded by following the guidelines outlined throughout this book.

What Happens If You Are Turned Down?

Even if an investor chooses not to invest in your venture, you can use the experience very productively. For example, you might have been turned down because of the stage of the venture. In such a situation, the investor might be available for later-stage financing; he might even know of—and possibly provide an introduction to—another investor who would be interested at this time. Thus be certain to ask the investor:

- How should I proceed at this time?
- Who might invest in such a venture?

- Do you have a specific contact name?
- If we do receive funding for this stage, can we count on you for later financing?

Successful entrepreneurs use such negative experiences as opportunities.

Provisions of the Venture Agreement

If your proposal has been accepted by an investor, you would then meet to negotiate the final financing agreement as well as the ownership, control, and financial objectives of the venture (see below). Recognize that an investment in your company is not a "free loan"; you will have to make several sacrifices in order to obtain it.

Ownership can range from 10 percent (for established profitable companies) to 90 percent (for beginning or financially troubled firms). Most investors, however, do not want to own more than 50 percent of a business, to ensure that the new business be managed as an entrepreneurial concern by its current managers.

Operating control would generally remain in the hands of you and your management team. However, the investors will generally ask for representation (occasionally, major representation) on your board of directors in order to have some input in important strategic decisions that may alter the direction of your company.

Investors generally realize their profits by either providing for a stock buyback or by arranging for a corporate acquisition or a public stock offering of the company. This is done within three to seven years of their investment. Such provisions are discussed when you negotiate your long-term financial objectives with the investors.

Although the terms of the venture agreement can be negotiated, it is essential that you maintain a mutual relationship between your company and the investor; that is, you should both benefit by the relationship. Specifically, investors should be able to put you in touch with important contacts and should assist you in recruiting experienced managers. If you feel that the relationship is adversarial and that there is not a genuine sharing between the two parties involved, it is advisable to look elsewhere for funding. Certainly, you should cover yourself by seeking funding from several investors and comparing the provisions of their agreements to one another prior to accepting an investor's terms.

STRUCTURING THE DEAL

The final stage of the venture review process is the negotiation of the equity positions for the entrepreneurial team and the investor. Although, as mentioned earlier, the proposed deal structure should actually be included in the business plan itself, the final arrangement is subject to negotiation.

There are two key concerns in structuring the deal:

1. Determining the value of the business
2. Determining the return for the investor, which is actually dictated by the value of the business

The investor is interested in seeing what the company will be worth three to seven years down the road (i.e., at the time of a corporate acquisition or an initial public offering) in order to determine how an investment at this time will translate into a percentage of the ownership position of the company. Obviously, all investors are interested in maximizing the return on their investments. Thus the larger the ownership position, the greater the potential return.

What Is the Business Worth?

The first "piece of the puzzle" is the valuation of the business. There are three widely used approaches for valuing a business:

- Asset valuation
- Earnings valuation
- Cash flow valuation

Let's examine each of these.

Asset Valuation. Asset valuation involves the examination of the underlying worth of the assets of the business. This is a useful starting point for negotiations, as it constitutes the minimum value of the business. Assets can be valued as follows:

- Book value
- Adjusted book value
- Liquidation value
- Replacement value

Book value equals the total net worth or stockholders' equity of the company, as reflected on the balance sheet.

Adjusted book value adjusts for large discrepancies between the stated book value and the actual market value of such tangible assets as machinery and equipment—which have depreciated below—or land—which have appreciated above—their book value.

Liquidation value adjusts for the value of assets if the company had to dispose of those assets in a "quick sale."

Replacement value adjusts for the cost of replacing various assets of the company.

Earnings Valuation. This approach involves valuing the business based on:

- Historical earnings
- Future earnings

Historical earnings valuation assumes that we can extrapolate the future performance of the company based on how profitable it has been in the past.

Future Earnings valuation adjusts future earnings to reflect such new influences as sales potential of the product or service, economic factors, management capabilities, operating policies and strategies, and others.

Once you have decided on the time frame (i.e., historical versus future earnings) you must multiply the earnings figure by a factor to determine its value. Generally, a price–earnings (P/E) multiple is used. Assuming that the company will go public five years from now, you would incorporate the following factors into the valuation of the business:

- Projected earnings
- Nature of the industry and of similar companies
- Anticipated state of the stock market

For example, if the company is expected to have earnings of $1 million in five years and if similar companies are likely to go public at a P/E of 10 (i.e., 10 times earnings), the company is projected to be worth $10 million five years from now.

Cash Flow Valuation. This approach is concerned with the entrepreneur's personal return from the business rather than merely the return inherent in the business itself. Cash flow can accrue to the entrepreneur as follows:

- Operating cash flows
- Terminal value

Operating cash flows is a measure that takes into account cash flowing out of the business to the entrepreneur from:

- Perquisites [i.e., business-related expenses (e.g., company car, country club membership, etc.) charged to the company]
- Return of capital via debt repayment
- Interest
- Salary
- Dividends

Terminal value recognizes such sources of cash taken out of the business as:

- Return of capital via sale
- Capital gain via sale

The entrepreneurial team should also take into account such negative cash flows as:

- Deficient salary
- Additional paid-in capital

To arrive at a value, it is necessary to calculate the present value of the future cash flows of the business. This is based on the assumption that $1000 earned next year will be worth less than $1000 earned today, due to inflation and the opportunity for money earned today to be invested and to appreciate in value over the year.

Valuation is an extremely judgmental process involving trial and error. As suggested, there are several techniques of valuation, no single one of which can provide the "right" answer. Thus use a combination of methods that may be appropriate in a given situation.

What Is the Projected Return for the Investor?

Once a value is established for the business, the next concern is to use that information to project an appropriate return for the investor.

Assume that for the previous example, the business could be valued at 10 times projected earnings or $10 million in five years. If an investor invests $500,000 into the venture, he or she would expect that investment to grow by 5- to 15-fold, dependent on the risk of the investment over the next five years. If we assume that the risk is rather low (i.e., the company has a fairly established product and a capable management team), we can target a sixfold return (or a 40 percent compounded annual return) on the investment. Thus the $500,000 should be worth $3 million or 30 percent of the company.

WHEN TO RAISE CAPITAL

There is really never a right time (or a wrong time) to raise capital. For one thing it is always easiest to obtain funds when you do not need the funds; investors tend to be abundant when you are in a sound financial position, capable of managing your own growth, and tend to be unavailable at a time when your funds are scarce.

Furthermore, as your company grows, its value continually increases, thereby making it an attractive investment opportunity. At the same time, however, your personal equity stake is increasing, thereby tempting you to delay giving up part of your equity until a later time, when your company will be worth even more. Of course, as your business grows, it will continually require additional capital, thereby diluting your equity position in the company.

Thus it becomes important for you to strike a balance between the time that you need capital the most and the time that your company's market value is greatest. For that reason, most growth businesses attempt to raise capital in stages, thereby maximizing both.

Availability of Capital

Capital for funding small growth businesses becomes available when the stock market is experiencing an upsurge (i.e., a "bull market") and tends to be scarce when the market is experiencing a downswing (i.e., a "bear market"). Venture investors make their money when the public buys new stock issues, which occurs most often during bull markets. At that time, investors can liquidate some of their existing investments and can use the cash obtained for investments in other ventures, such as your own.

CONCLUDING REMARKS

We have attempted to provide some insight on how to prepare and package a business plan to enhance the likelihood of obtaining capital for your business. As noted, only a small percentage of venture proposals are funded. You can solidify your chances of obtaining funding, however, by preparing a business plan that is properly packaged and incorporates the following features discussed earlier:

1. Includes realistic financial projections with a provision for the investor to "cash out" within three to seven years
2. Demonstrates that you have an experienced and capable management team
3. Describes your competitive advantages that will benefit your customers

Such a plan will considerably enhance the likelihood of your company obtaining funding.

We present next a step-by-step guide for preparing a business plan that incorporates the key features noted in the preceding sections.

PART II

PREPARING THE BUSINESS PLAN: A STEP-BY-STEP GUIDE

Production Process
Quality Assurance/Quality Control
Contingency Plans

IV. Marketing
Marketing Orientation
Marketing Strategy
Contingency Plans
An Overview of the Marketing Section

V. Financial Data
Current Financial Position
Payables/Receivables
Cost Control
Break-Even Analysis
Financial Ratios
Financial Projections
An Overview of the Financial Data Section

VI. Organization and Management
Key Personnel
Other Personnel
Miscellaneous Issues
Contingency Plans

VII. Ownership
Structure of Business
Financing/Equity Considerations

VIII. Critical Risks and Problems
Description of Risks

IX. Summary and Conclusions
Summary
Scheduling

SECTION 3:   APPENDICES

This part presents a step-by-step guide for preparing a business plan. It contains a detailed explanation of each of the topics to be covered in the business plan and provides commentaries from the perspective of the investor on exactly what he or she is looking for when reading and evaluating the plan. In addition, there are three overview sections which provide more comprehensive information on the market analysis, marketing, and financial data sections of the business plan, three of the sections of the plan most carefully scrutinized by investors. A series of worksheets that parallel this part is included in Part III.

There is one caveat that you should consider as you go through these next two parts. Although we have presented a series of forms to follow and a set of questions to answer, keep in mind that preparing a business plan is more than a mere checklist. As we indicated earlier, the process of planning—that is, the sharing of ideas among members of the management team while preparing the plan, the ability to meet with customers or potential customers to gather information, and so on—is often more important than the plan. Do not lose sight of the fact that the business plan is a powerful tool in which to secure capital; yet it is more the process of developing the plan than the plan itself that will strengthen the strategic thinking capabilities of management, thereby enhancing the likelihood of long-term success.

Section 1

Preliminary Information

The preliminary information in the business plan includes:

- Cover page
- Table of contents
- Table of appendices
- Executive summary

Let's examine each of these.

COVER PAGE

The cover page should include the following:

- Company logo (if available)
- Name of company (as well as previous names of the company, if appropriate)
- Address
- Phone number
- Date business was established
- Name and position of contact person at your company
- Date of application
- Copy number of report (i.e., copy X of Y copies distributed)
- Nondisclosure statement

TABLE OF CONTENTS

The table of contents should list the titles and page numbers of each of the main sections and subsections of the business plan. As noted in the following sample table of contents, the body of the plan contains a section about each of the nine topics discussed previously.

TABLE OF CONTENTS

TABLE OF APPENDICES

Similar to the table of contents, the table of appendices should list the titles and page numbers of the financial statements and other appendix information. A sample format is provided below.

EXECUTIVE SUMMARY

Typically, an investor will spend only 5 or 10 minutes to review a business plan in order to determine if he or she should read it in detail or go on to another plan. Normally, if the investor will read any part of the plan, it will be the executive summary. If the business plan is the vehicle to get you in the door to speak to the investors, the executive summary is the vehicle to ring the door bell; if it does not ring loudly and clearly, the investor will not know that you are at the door.

Thus it is essential to prepare an appealing, convincing executive summary to capture the reader's attention and to make him or her more likely to read the remainder of the plan. In essence, the executive summary is the most important part of the business plan, as it will dictate whether or not the remaining pages are read.

Although the executive summary appears as the first part of the plan, it should actually be the last part of the plan that you write. The executive summary will also serve as a one- to three-page proposal to be submitted to investors prior to submitting the more lengthy formal business plan. (Some investors prefer to receive the business plan in a series of stages; others prefer to receive a complete package at one time.)

The executive summary should include the following information at the top of the page:

- Company name, address, phone number
- Name and position of contact person at your company
- Date of preparation of business plan

Following that, you should include the following summary information:

A. *Description of business.* Briefly describe the nature of your product or service, its unique features, and what you hope to accomplish over the next 5 to 10 years.

B. *Strategic direction.* Identify the stage (e.g., startup, development, turnaround) of the business. Briefly describe the overall strategic (or long-range) direction of the company for the next three to five years.

C. *Market/marketing.* Briefly describe the market segment that you are attempting to reach and how you plan to reach that segment. Demonstrate the benefits of the product or service to those users. How will you market your product or service? What are your sales projections for the next five years?

D. *Management.* Briefly describe the backgrounds and responsibilities of the founders and top managers of the company.

E. *Financial features.* State your expected revenues and profits for this year, next year, and for five years in the future. Provide similar information on your projected assets, liabilities, and net worth. Estimate how much capital you will need and how you intend to use the proceeds.

F. *Financial arrangements/exit.* For debt funding, what will be used as collateral? For equity funding, how much (as a percentage) equity are you prepared to give up in exchange for such an investment? What is the expected annual return for the investors? How many investors are sought? What is the minimum investment required per investor?

Explain how and when the investors will get their money out of the business (e.g., through buyback, acquisition, public offering, etc.). In the case of multiple sources of financing, summarize the sources and amounts of funding.

Body of the Report

I. BACKGROUND AND PURPOSE

IA. HISTORY

IA1. Briefly describe the history of your product(s) or service(s). This is extremely important if you are offering a new or unique product or service.

IB. CURRENT CONDITIONS

IB1. Briefly describe what your product(s) or service(s) is, where and how the product(s) or service(s) is or will be used, and who the customers are or will be. In essence, this is the definition of your business or the scope of your operations.

IB2. Discuss the potential for promising new products. This is often indicative of future increased returns, which are very attractive in the eyes of the investor.

IB3. (If this is a technology product or service) Provide a technically accurate description of what the product(s) and/or service(s) is and how the product(s) works or how the service(s) is used. If appropriate, include a drawing of the product(s) in the appendices.

IB4. (If this is a technology product or service) Outline the tests that have been made and provide their results. Outline future tests to be made and provide their objectives.

IC. THE CONCEPT

IC1. Describe the key factors that dictate the success of your product(s) or service(s) (e.g., price competitiveness, product or service quality, marketing capabilities, etc.). Have any competitors been successful due largely to any of these factors? Explain how your product(s) or service(s) also demonstrate(s) characteristics.

IC2. Describe the unique features of your product or service (i.e., competitive strengths) that distinguish it from those of your competitors. Discuss the benefit(s) of the product(s) or service(s) to the end user. Why will they need it? Does it save time? Save money? Make life easier? And so on. Many investors feel that this is the essence of the company's competitive strategy and therefore the essence of the business plan. As mentioned earlier, user benefit is one of the key investor turn-ons. You can further appeal to the investor by addressing the issue of what will happen to your potential customers if they *do not* buy your product or service.

IC3. Describe the unique aspects of your strategy if appropriate (i.e., how you will produce, distribute, and market your product or service).

ID. OVERALL OBJECTIVES

ID1. Briefly describe your overall objectives in very general terms.

ID2. Describe your strategic or long-range goals. Discuss how your company will grow over the next three to five years. Investors tend to have a three- to five-year perspective on their investments.

IE. SPECIFIC OBJECTIVES

Develop a list of specific (and quantifiable, if possible) objectives for the next two years as well as for five years in the future in as many of the following areas as possible:

IE1. Revenues/sales
IE2. Profitability
IE3. Market share/market standing
IE4. Product (service) quality
IE5. Innovation
IE6. Efficiency/productivity
IE7. Employee morale
IE8. Management development
IE9. Social concern/social responsibility (impact on community)

Include the corresponding tables of objectives in the appendices wherever possible.

II. MARKET ANALYSIS

IIA. MARKET RESEARCH

IIA1. What types of market research and industry studies have been conducted by your company as well as by others? Discuss future studies to be conducted. It is critical that you demonstrate to investors that you have received feedback on your product or service from potential customers. Perhaps the most convincing "evidence" of market research is to have a track record of satisfied customers. If you are at an earlier stage of development, investors will want to see letters of intent, presold units, advances, or some other indication of future sales.

IIB. OVERALL MARKET

IIB1. Describe the overall market—present and projected—in terms of location (international versus national versus regional versus local), sales, profits, growth rate, trends, and so on.

IIB2. List the leading companies in this industry and describe their financial success.

IIB3. Present a table of projected industry sales as well as your projected market share for the next five years. Present a best case, worst case, most likely case estimate of sales potential. Investors prefer to fund businesses with a previous operating history and in markets with a 25 percent or more annual growth rate; a smaller growth rate may be acceptable, however, if a company is a market leader. Investors particularly like to fund businesses that have entered growth-oriented markets in which established leaders have not yet become involved.

IIC. SPECIFIC MARKET SEGMENT

IIC1. Describe the *specific* target market or market segment—present and projected.

IIC2. List the leading companies selling to this target market and describe their financial condition.

IIC3. Present a table of projected industry sales for the segment. Include your projected market share for each of the next five years. Present a market survey analysis in the appendix, if available. You should present a best case, worst case, and most likely case estimate of sales potential for this target market.

IIC4. Explain how you will continue to assess your target market over the coming years to make the necessary strategic changes in your plan.

IID. COMPETITIVE FACTORS

Describe each of the following competitive factors and explain how they are expected to affect sales:

    IID1. Existing rivals (present competitors)
    IID2. Entrants (future competitors)
    IID3. Buyers or purchasers (clients/customers)
    IID4. Suppliers
    IID5. Substitute (alternative) products or services

From this section it should be very clear to the investor where your strengths and weaknesses fall relative to your competitors and how these competitive forces are likely to affect your future growth potential.

For your leading competitors, list the annual volume, market share, profitability, and so on, over the past few years. Compare your strengths and weaknesses in terms of economies of scale, profit margins, personnel, R&D capabilities, sales and distribution, and so on, to the market leader. This will demonstrate the riskiness of the investment.

List and describe your five largest customers. What percent of your sales do they represent? Has that changed over the past few years? Investors want to see customer loyalty. Do you have any promising prospective customers? Investors are interested in whether your company will be dominated by a few high-volume customers. Although such customers can generate a larger portion of sales, they can be very demanding. Moreover, if they take their business elsewhere, your company can suffer tremendously. In general, investors prefer having numerous smaller-volume customers to having relatively few larger-volume customers.

Similarly, investors prefer that a company not be solely dependent on one or two major suppliers.

IIE. OTHER MARKET INFLUENCES

    IIE1. Describe the impact of each of the following on present and projected sales:

- Economic factors (e.g., inflation, recession, etc.)
- Technological factors (e.g., new technologies, new products, etc.)
- Government influences (e.g., agencies affecting you, current and proposed legislation, etc.)
- Social factors (e.g., age, demographics, income, etc.)
- Seasonal fluctuations
- Random, unexpected disturbances (e.g., political instability, war, energy crisis, etc.)

Describe the key market indicators of any of these factors that may have a significant impact on sales.

IIF. SALES FORECASTS

IIF1. Present (in chart form) preliminary sales projections for your company over the next five years. Three sets of projections should be made—best case, worst case, most likely case—with the associated sales revenues in each case. (A graph of sales forecasts—in the appendices—is also helpful to demonstrate trends.) Provide an explanation of the reasons for the differences in the three sales projections.

———— **An Overview of the Market Analysis Section** ————

The Market Analysis section of the business plan is presented to convince the reader or investor that your product(s) or service(s) will have a substantial market in a growing industry and that sales can be achieved in the face of competition. All other sections of the plan are based on the sales estimates derived in this section.

One of the most important features of this section is that it should provide an indication of the demand for the product(s) or service(s) and, consequently, the funding requirements for the business. [Of course, the amount of capital necessary for the venture will be dictated not only by the market demand (i.e., the projected sales volume and revenues) for the product (or service) but also by the costs to develop and market the product.] How can you forecast demand? In this part of the business plan, you should develop the appropriate market forecasts. This involves:

1. Identifying a target market
2. Examining competitive forces affecting the business
3. Developing forecasts of the economic, technological, political, and social trends that are likely to influence the venture

You can then use those data to project the costs necessary to generate the expected sales revenues. That information, which is presented in financial statement form, is discussed in detail in Part V of the business plan, "Financial Data."

There is one overriding concern in marketing which should be taken into account when conducting your market analysis: Know your customer. Investors look for evidence that a company is market-driven rather than technology-driven. Simply stated, market appeal and sales potential are much more attractive to the investor than are technical factors. That should be evident in the "Market Analysis" section; moreover, it should be emphasized in the "Marketing" section (Part IV of the business plan).

IDENTIFYING A TARGET MARKET

Your market research should address two basic sets of questions.

1. What has been the trend in sales in your market area for your principal product(s) or service(s) over the last five years? What do you expect the trend to be five years from now?

2. What sales volume do you expect to reach with your product(s) or service(s)? What revenues can you expect?

Focus

How do you address these questions? Where do you begin your market research? It begins with a clear understanding of your business definition or "mission" (i.e., what business are you in?). Your business definition describes what product(s) and/or service(s) you provide and who is likely to purchase that product offering. For example, your company might develop computer software for small manufacturing businesses; or it might provide personnel recruitment services for accounting and law professionals.

Because your business venture is likely to have limited resources, it is critical that you develop a specific, targeted business definition. Thus rather than attempt to develop a product or service with mass appeal, identify and seek out a specific market. Investors will want to see that you have focused your efforts on what you do best and that you will concentrate on maximizing those strengths.

Gaining a Competitive Edge

Skis. Having a clear sense of a specific market segment can even provide you with an opportunity to launch a new product. William Kirschner developed a fiberglass and plastic ski and filled an important market niche. At the time, there were no fiberglass or medium-priced skis available (Head produced metal skis that were selling in the range $115 to $140 and Fischer produced wooden skis that cost around $50). So he developed a new market for his product, which eventually enabled his K-2 skis to become the leader in the industry, surpassing Head.

PCs. Newer, smaller businesses have realized tremendous benefits by targeting their efforts toward a specific market. For example, hundreds of new computer or computer-related companies have been formed over the past few years that cater to specific target markets. For example, Tandem sells mainframe computers with backup systems (i.e., two systems "in tandem" with one another) to businesses; Info Design Systems sells business software; Cray Research sells "supercomputers"; Activision sells computer game software; and so on.

Zs. Mark Smith, president of the small chain of Century Hotels, has been very successful competing against his larger counterparts such as Hyatt, Hilton, Sheraton, Ramada Inn, Marriott, and Holiday Inn. Smith acknowledges that Century

> can't get the main body of a convention to come to us...but we can get the top guys. We'll get the executives or the board of directors who don't want to stay at the convention hotels.

By differentiating its service from its competitors and by carefully targeting its sales efforts to a specific customer—in this case, top executives—the company has been quite successful in a very competitive industry.

Production and Profitability: The Case of Experience

In many industries, as you produce more units your costs to produce each unit decrease because the total labor, equipment, space, and overhead costs are spread out over more units. This is the essence of "economies of scale."

Strategic planners have developed a concept known as the "experience curve" which supports the foregoing notion. It suggests that as production doubles, costs per unit tend to decrease by approximately 20 to 30 percent. Naturally, this favors the large corporations with sizable production runs—they can produce more units, thereby lowering their costs per unit and can therefore either charge less for the same unit that a smaller company sells or realize a greater profit margin per unit.

Bud, P&G, and Avon.   There are several good examples of how companies have used the experience curve as a competitive tool. In the beer industry, Budweiser, which has maintained the highest level of sales in the industry, also has the lowest cost per unit and thereby the highest operating margin per unit among its competitors (Schlitz, Carling, Schaeffer, and Falstaff). The same holds true for Proctor and Gamble (P&G), which has been more profitable than its two leading competitors in the household products industry—Colgate-Palmolive and Lever Brothers—and for Avon, which has been the most profitable company in the cosmetics industry, which includes such companies as Gillette, Revlon, Fabergé, and Alberto Culver.

Segment, Segment, Segment! From the preceding discussion, we would expect only large companies with high levels of sales to be profitable. Recently, however, Michael Porter of the Harvard Business School demonstrated a very interesting relationship that exists between the number of units produced and the profitability of the company.[1] As suggested by the U-shaped graph below, Porter acknowledges that the large producers—such as Proctor and Gamble and Budweiser—can be profitable due to experience curve effects (or economies of scale). However, the small producers can be profitable if they have a well-differentiated product that competes in a specialized market. Inland Steel, for example, is far more profitable than many of its larger competitors in the steel industry. (Thus bigger is not necessarily better!) Companies that are neither

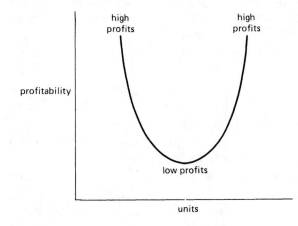

[1]See M. Porter, *Competitive Strategy* (New York: The Free Press, 1980).

differentiated nor possess a high market share—those at the bottom of the U, for example, Franklin Electric—tend to be very unprofitable.

Keep in mind, however, that although segmentation is generally the prescribed strategy for smaller, entrepreneurial companies, such companies should avoid targeting their market *too* narrowly. As noted in Section 1 of Part I, one of the appealing features to investors is "widespread marketability." Unless they see a potential market at least in the (tens or) hundreds of millions of dollars, they are unlikely to invest in such a venture.

How to Segment Your Market

The mass market can be segmented by age of consumer, geographic location, quality and price of product or service (i.e., economy versus luxury versus moderate models), and so on. Having segmented your market, you will be in a better position to demonstrate the user benefits of your product or service to investors that can be marketed to the appropriate target group.

There are three characteristics for a market segment:

1. *It should be measurable.* You should be able to measure the characteristics and size of the segment.
2. *It should be accessible.* The segment should be "reachable," that is, your advertising efforts should reach your potential customers.
3. *(Most important) It should have economic opportunity.* The segment must appeal to a large enough group of potential buyers to make it economically worthwhile for you to market the product or service.

By segmenting the market, you will not only be able to reach a "controlled" group in the population, but will be able to obtain information about the demand characteristics of that group. This is particularly true if you segment based on age, income, race, sex, geographic location, and so on.

Determining Customer Preferences

How do you market to a specific target segment? Recently, companies have placed a much greater emphasis on target marketing to determine consumer preferences. For example, Kroger Co. holds more than 250,000 consumer interviews annually to define customer attitudes more precisely. Other companies have made extensive use of focus groups to assess consumer attitudes prior to launching new products.

"Do It, Fix It, Try It." A trend among better managed entrepreneurial companies has been to adhere to a philosophy of developing a pilot product (or prototype), testing reactions, refining the product, and then getting it out to the market shortly thereafter. This will enable you to obtain some preliminary indication of customer appeal—something that investors will require—and to perfect the product or service when you will eventually market it on a larger scale. Moreover, this philosophy encourages innovation and action, two requisites for success. As noted by Robert Adams, head of research and development

for the tremendously successful 3M Corporation: "Our approach is to make a little, sell a little, make a little more."[2]

Win Ng of the multimillion-dollar Taylor & Ng household goods operation in San Francisco shares this philosophy. As he notes: "Developing a prototype early is the number one goal for our designers, or anyone else for that matter. We don't trust it until we can see it and feel it."

It is just such an attitude that can give small companies a tremendous competitive advantage over their larger counterparts. Charles Phipps of Texas Instruments, in describing the early success of the company, noted that

> they surprised themselves: as a very small company, $20 million, with very limited resources, they found they could outmaneuver large labs like Bell Labs, RCA, and General Electric in the semiconductor area because they'd just go out and try to do something with it, rather than keep it in the lab.

Thus, before making a full commitment to a new product or service, make sure that people will be receptive to it. This will be an attractive feature to investors. If people like the prototype, you can proceed as planned; if not, you should either make the necessary alterations or terminate the project.

For example, several years ago two students started a company—as a result of a class assignment—that would sell a mix for making hot spiced wine. As described by the two students:

> We went out into the kitchen and mixed up a batch, put some into a thermos bottle and drove to a supermarket. The store manager listened to our description of the product, then took a taste from the thermos. He told us that if we would package it to sell for under one dollar retail he would order a couple of cases and let us put it on the shelf. From there we went to some more stores and got similar reactions from the other managers. That convinced us we at least had a market for getting the product tried.[3]

After successfully launching the product, the company—Fireside Lodge Corporation—was selling $400,000 worth of the mix annually.

Demand for New Products or Services

Perhaps the most difficult task in conducting market research is in determining demand for new products or services. How do you forecast demand if there has been zero (measurable) demand up until this point? Typically, entrepreneurs will estimate demand by developing an arbitrary percentage of an arbitrary total market or market segment. Generally, such forecasts tend to be extremely inaccurate, as there is little basis for these estimates.

For example, I am familiar with a startup business which was planning to sell point-of-sale advertisements in retail grocery stores to such companies as

[2]These examples are discussed in Tom Peters and Robert Waterman, *In Search of Excellence* (New York: Harper & Row, 1982), pp. 136–137.

[3]See K. Vesper, *New Venture Strategies* (Englewood Cliffs, NJ: Prentice-Hall, 1980), p. 155.

Coca-Cola, General Mills, Lever Bros., and other companies which sell their products in those stores. Their estimates of demand for advertisements were based on a percentage of the total demand for grocery sales in this country. Unfortunately, there was no basis whatsoever for their forecasts. Demand should have been based on the benefits for the users (i.e., the foods and consumer goods companies) rather than on the capacity of the stores, which would merely have displayed the advertisements. Analogous to this example, let's assume that a company has the capacity of producing 10,000 units of a given product per week; should sales estimates be based on this capacity? Obviously not. Sales estimates should be based on a careful assessment of the target market. Production levels should then be established based on those sales estimates, rather than vice versa.

Test Marketing. Perhaps the best way to forecast demand is to test market the product or service on a trial basis; that is, go right to the potential users or customers and see if they will use it. Ask them what they think about its features, price, quality, and so on. Ask them if they know of anybody else who would use it. This information will not only give a preliminary indication of product or service demand—which is vital information for the investor—but it will provide immediate feedback on how to improve your prototype.

You can then follow up your test marketing efforts by administering a questionnaire or survey to a larger audience. Once again, the purpose of this follow-up is to determine how people feel about your prototype product or service and if they would be likely to purchase it.

Projections of demand for the product or service are of extreme importance to the investor. Moreover, it is crucial to support those projections with the results of your market research and with an explanation of the benefit of the product or service to the user. If you can quantify the benefits in terms of savings or earnings to the user—for example, a product that will result in either fewer rejects, fewer breakdowns in equipment, lower costs, or greater speed of operations for the user—investors will be more willing to provide funding for the venture.

In any event, evidence of satisfied customers provides the investor with the most convincing data that there is future demand for a product or service. Demonstrate that a target marketplace exists and that users have been pleased with your product or service, even if it is only in the prototype stage. Market research data, letters from users, and other documentation will certainly support your claim.

There is one more aspect of projecting market demand which is often overlooked—the distinction between number of potential customers versus sales to those customers. For example, 20 percent of your target customers may represent 80 percent of the demand for the product or service. Thus you must ask: (1) Is it possible to penetrate that 20 percent, and (2) if so, how can you penetrate that 20 percent? How costly will it be to do so? Investors must have satisfactory answers to these questions before they will provide funding.

COMPETITIVE FORCES AFFECTING YOUR BUSINESS

Once you have clearly targeted a specific market segment and have made a preliminary projection of demand for your product or service, your market research should examine the various competitive forces that affect demand. Specifically, investors will be interested in knowing the impact of each of the following factors on your business:[4]

- Existing competitors in your industry
- Potential entrants into your industry
- Buyers, customers, or clients
- Suppliers or distributors
- Substitute products or services

Each of the competitive forces noted above poses a threat to the firms competing in a given market or market segment. For example, G.D. Searle's commercialization of Nutrasweet—a natural sweetener (i.e., a substitute product)—posed a severe threat to the existing competitors in the artificial sweetener industry. Furthermore, suppliers can certainly exert power over a business because they control the supply of raw materials (remember the Arab oil embargo!); similarly, new entrants can pose a threat to companies because they can take market share away from existing businesses (as People Express Airlines had done initially); and so on.

Alternatively, any business—even a new venture—that carefully assesses its environment and operates in a market with relatively few competitors, can be very powerful. This has been Cray Research Corp.'s strategy in the supercomputer market. Thus you can exert power over new entrants if you have an established image; you will also have power over suppliers if there are many suppliers and if there are relatively few businesses competing with you. Having such power over suppliers, buyers, competitors, and so on, can certainly enhance the likelihood of obtaining funding.

What Threats Does a New Venture Face?

New ventures should be particularly sensitive to the following threats, which are commonly known as "barriers to entry":

- *Economies of scale*—the fact that costs decrease as production increases; thus existing competitors have a decided advantage over new businesses in terms of cost efficiency.
- *Product differentiation*—brand identification and customer loyalty enjoyed by established companies, stemming from product differences, customer service, or past advertising.

[4]See M. Porter, *Competitive Strategy* (New York: The Free Press, 1980).

- *Capital requirements*—requirements for large investments, such as expensive machinery, new plants, and costly inventory in the business.
- *Switching costs*—one-time costs when switching from one product to another (e.g., compatibility of computer hardware products).
- *Government policy*—for example, regulations (common in the trucking, rail, liquor, and retailing industries) that limit the number of new entrants.

Some industries have greater barriers to entry than do others. For example, in the automobile industry, there have been over 2500 attempts to start new companies in the United States in the last 80 years. Yet only General Motors, Ford, AMC, Chrysler, and a few smaller companies—such as Avanti and Checker—have remained. Clearly, the barriers to entry for John DeLorean's venture into this industry were rather great and the odds against him were high right from the start.

If, however, you are providing a unique or innovative product or service, the barriers to entry can often be minimized due to the absence of existing competitors. Furthermore, you are likely to pose a threat to established companies whose products or services do not have such distinguishing features.

How to Assess the Nature of Competition in Your Industry

When assessing the nature of competition in your industry, you should address the following general questions while preparing your business plan:

- Who are your principal competitors selling in your market area?
- What is their percentage of market penetration and dollar sales in that market?
- What are the strengths and weaknesses of each competitor? What is your opinion of their products, facilities, marketing characteristics, product development, adaptability to changing market conditions, and so on?
- Have any of your competitors withdrawn from your market area? Why?
- What advantages to you have over your competitors in terms of:
  —Price
  —Performance
  —Durability
  —Versatility
  —Speed or accuracy
  —Ease of operation or use
  —Ease of maintenance or repair
  —Ease or cost of installation
  —Size or weight
  —Styling or appearance
  —Other features

- What advantages do they have over you?
- What barriers to entry exist? How will they affect your business?
- What is unique about your product or service?
- (Most important) How will your product or service benefit its users?
- How can you enhance your competitive position by taking advantage of user benefit?

Answers to these questions will greatly assist your market research efforts and will enable you to develop an appropriate marketing strategy for your product or service that will appeal to investors. (This is discussed in greater detail in part IV of the business plan, "Marketing.")

Once you have taken the necessary steps to assess your market, you will be in a better position to make strategic decisions for your business. Naturally, conducting an accurate assessment will not ensure success—it has been noted that the Edsel was the most market researched car in American history. However, a careful analysis will alert you to the potential risks that may face you over the coming years.

HOW DO YOU DEVELOP FORECASTS OF FUTURE TRENDS?

Not only is it important to assess the nature of competitive and other environmental forces that are currently affecting the business, but it is crucial that you develop an understanding of how various environmental trends will affect your success five or ten years in the future. After all, if investors maintain a three- to seven-year time horizon, they will expect you to develop forecasts of the various economic, technological, political, and social trends that will affect your venture over that period.

There are several techniques of forecasting, many of which rely on sophisticated statistical techniques that are beyond the scope of this book. However, by using some less sophisticated techniques, you will still be able to develop fairly accurate forecasts that can be included in your business plan. One such technique involves isolating early signals or early indicators in the environment that *may* affect your business.

Economic Indicators

To determine the direction of the economy, for example, you should monitor such economic indicators as the following:

Gross national product (GNP) is the broadest measure of the nation's economic health. It is issued quarterly by the Department of Commerce and represents the best estimate of what has happened to the output of goods and services. By adjusting for inflation (i.e., by eliminating changes in prices so that what is being measured is the actual volume of production) we obtain the "real GNP." Real GNP should grow nearly 4 percent annually to provide jobs for new workers entering the labor force.

Industrial production measures the output of factories, mines, and utilities and is a guide to the economy's position between reports on GNP. It is issued monthly by the Federal Reserve Board.

Wholesale Price Index (WPI) is a guide to prices charged by producers for their goods. It is issued monthly by the Department of Labor. This index often foreshadows trends in consumer prices. (The index, however, often misses many discounts and exaggerates rising trends.) Particular attention should be paid to the changes in prices of finished goods, which do not fluctuate as much as farm and food prices and therefore are a better measure of inflationary pressure.

Consumer Price Index (CPI) provides an indication of the changes in the cost of living. It is issued monthly by the Department of Labor. This index is arrived at by tracking prices in a "market basket" of about 100 items.

Retail sales indicate consumer attitudes toward spending. These are issued weekly and monthly by the Department of Commerce. A long slowdown in spending usually leads to cutbacks in output.

Unemployment rate is the percentage of the civilian work force that lacks jobs and is looking for work. However, to determine whether business is getting better or worse, the number of jobs (i.e., the rate of employment) is a better measure. Both figures are reported monthly by the Labor Department. Workers are constantly entering or leaving the labor market and changing jobs. Thus the economy reaches "full employment" when the unemployment rate is somewhere between 4 and 5 percent.

Housing starts (similar to building permits, which is a leading economic indicator; see below) provide some indication of possible trouble ahead. The reason is that recent recessions have been preceded by a period of tightening credit and rising interest rates which tend to take money out of the mortgage market, thereby depressing home building before the rest of the economy turns downward. These figures are provided by the Department of Commerce.

Leading economic indicators are a composite measure of many of the indicators that generally move in advance of the GNP. It is issued monthly by the Department of Commerce. Included in the index are stock prices, the money supply, number of hours worked by the average factory worker, the rate of layoffs, new orders for plants and equipment, and building permits. If the index moves in the same direction for more than three months in a row, it generally indicates that total output will move in that direction within a year or so.

Keep in mind that economic projections, which tend to be quantitative and objective, can generally be made for a maximum of one or two years in the future; this is considerably shorter than for technological, political, or social projections, which are, of course, much less quantitative and more subjective in nature.

Technological Indicators

Technological change is generally long in the making and therefore probably the easiest of all future "uncertainties" to forecast. Before a new technology (such as computers, robotics, lasers, biotechnology, etc.) makes a significant impact on the economy (i.e., 1 percent of the GNP), it goes through a series of stages as follows:

1. Scientific findings
2. Laboratory feasibility
3. Operating prototype
4. Commercial introduction
5. Widespread adoption
6. Diffusion to other areas
7. Significant social and economic impact

Thus there is a long time span—often 20 years or more—from the time an idea is first developed until it makes an impact on society. Although the time span from stage to stage may vary, most technological changes or innovations follow this basic sequence. You will therefore be able to monitor technological innovations at various points along this sequence to determine the "new" technologies of tomorrow.

Some good technological indicators include:

• Patents applied for and awarded
• Technical papers delivered at conferences
• Attendance at technology conferences
• Financial support through the National Science Foundation (NSF) or corporate foundations for technological research

This information can be obtained by contacting the Federal Patent Office, the National Science Foundation (NSF), trade associations, or universities.

Social Concerns. You must recognize, however, that technological trends are closely linked to social trends. Thus a company might have the capability to develop a new technology within the next few months. However, society might not be willing to accept that technology. For example, many significant developments in biotechnology took place 20 to 30 years ago. Yet the commercialization of most biotechnology products has been hampered due to society's fears and lack of awareness of this new technology.

Political Indicators

Political change seems like it is exceedingly difficult to forecast due to the dramatic changes that take place from week to week or even from day to day in our country. Political changes, however, generally go through stages in a similar manner to technological changes (partly because technology has been the impetus for much political action). Specifically, before a law goes into effect at the national level, it will have been an issue for interest groups as well as for local legislators for many months or years. Therefore, you can monitor various early political indicators such as the following:

- State and local laws (especially in such bellwether states as California, Florida, Colorado, Washington, and Connecticut)[5]
- Legislation in other countries (see below)
- Development of congressional committees
- Local election returns
- Past legislation
- Political appointments
- Changes in polls, public opinion, etc.
- Development of public interest groups
- Development of new government agencies
- Regulatory activity
- Changes in the tax structure
- New technologies

Thus, rather than monitor existing laws, you should monitor precipitating events that will often result in new laws. One of the best ways to forecast legislation likely to take place in the United States is to monitor legislation currently taking place in other countries, especially European nations. For example, FDA approval of selected pharmaceutical products in this country has often taken place three to eight years after such approval has been granted in Switzerland and Germany. Similarly, workplace legislation in France and sociopolitical trends in Scandinavian countries have often preceded the identical legislation in the United States by five to ten years.

There is a bill status office that will provide you with the current status of any legislation and will inform you if legislation has already been introduced in a given topic. You can contact the office at

> 3669 HOBA #2
> The LEGIS office
> Washington, DC 20515
> (202) 225–1772

Social Indicators

Social trends tend to be either socioeconomic or sociopolitical. For example, demographic trends are social in nature but are best thought of as socioeconomic in their ramifications. Thus you should monitor the economic indicators discussed earlier to project such socioeconomic trends. Public policy trends are also social but have sociopolitical ramifications. Thus a careful monitoring of political indicators—for example, local regulations, public interest group activity, and so on—will give you some indication of the sociopolitical trends that are emerging.

[5]See J. Naisbitt, *Megatrends* (New York: Warner Books, 1982).

What Results Are Likely?

Naturally, I have made it seem like it is quite easy to develop accurate forecasts. However, despite the abundance of forecasting techniques, most of us have been rather unsuccessful in forecasting the future. Thus, recognize that we are not attempting to control future uncertainty, but rather to gain some understanding of *possible* future conditions. You should, therefore, attempt to develop two or three scenarios of the future—for example, a best case, a worst case, and a most likely case—and to develop alternative strategies based on these scenarios. As long as you have considered various alternative future conditions, you will have a decided advantage over those competitors that have not examined them.

When All Else Fails

Finally, there are a few "sure-fire" techniques that will improve your forecasting record considerably when all other techniques fail:

- *Hemline indicator.* As women's hems go up, so does the stock market (which is a leading economic indicator).
- *Bad guess theorem.* Do not go along with the crowds; when everybody is "bullish," you should be "bearish," and vice versa.
- *Boston snow index.* If there is snow on the ground in Boston on Christmas Day (regardless of when the snow fell), the stock market will go up the following year (over 70 percent accurate!).
- *Super Bowl indicator.* If a former NFL team wins the Super Bowl, the stock market will go up the following year (over 95 percent accurate!).

CONCLUDING REMARKS

We have just examined several ways to assess your target market and to develop forecasts of environmental uncertainties that could affect the success of your business. The techniques described will help you considerably in projecting the demand for your product or service over the coming years, a factor that is carefully scrutinized by investors.

Perhaps the most important feature of market research is that you should examine the potential demand for the product or service not only from your own viewpoint, but from the viewpoint of the potential customers as well. Thus the fundamental question to ask when conducting research on demand is: What unique feature about your product or service will benefit your customers? Will it save money? How long will it take to pay for itself? Will it give the customer power, status, or something else that he or she values?

After determining your market projections for the coming years, your next task is to use those projections as a basis for determining how much funding will be necessary for your venture. That is best accomplished by developing a set of financial statements that will clearly demonstrate to investors your cash needs and your present and projected financial position. That is the subject of part V of the business plan, "Financial Data."

Endnote: What Information Do You Need?

How do you monitor environmental factors that affect the venture? Numerous sources of industry trends exist, many of which can be obtained (for little or no charge) from county or university libraries, from associations, or from various government offices such as the Small Business Administration (SBA).

Let's examine some of the sources of information that will assist you in preparing the market research section of the business plan.

PERIODIC READING

As a starting point, there are several popular business magazines and journals (which are available in most libraries) that can keep you up to date with information that may affect the business. These references, which are also excellent sources of innovative product and service ideas, include:

- *Advertising Age* (excellent articles on trends in advertising)
- *Business Horizons* (published by the Indiana University School of Business)
- *Business Week* (generally geared to big business and the economy, but a valuable reference nonetheless)
- *Entrepreneur* (emphasis on retailing, published by the American Entrepreneur's Association)
- *Forbes* (excellent publication, similar to *Business Week* in its focus on big business)
- *Fortune* (also geared to big business)
- *Future* (good source of information on trends)
- *Futurist* (published by the World Future Society)
- *Harvard Business Review* (an excellent reference for top-level management planning; refer especially to the section on entrepreneurship entitled "Growing Concerns")
- *In Business* (originally devoted much attention to "nature" businesses but now has some excellent articles on other new ventures)
- *Inc.* (this is a *must* for learning how to build a growth business)
- *Journal of Small Business Management* (academic journal with interesting research findings)
- *Management Review* (published by the American Management Association)
- *Planning Review* (published by the North American Society of Corporate Planners)
- *Sales and Marketing Management* (good articles on marketing)
- *Savvy* (an excellent source for women entrepreneurs)
- *Sloan Management Review* (similar to the *Harvard Business Review* in emphasis)
- *Small Business Report* (good source of information on small business)

- *Technology Illustrated* (a nontechnical magazine describing the latest technologies)
- *Venture* (this is an excellent source for learning how to get started in a business)
- *Wall Street Journal* (this should be "required reading"; refer especially to the columns entitled "Small Business" and "Enterprise" which appear periodically)
- *Working Woman* (especially designed for women entrepreneurs)

GENERAL INFORMATION

There are also some very good directories and general references about businesses that will provide important statistics about your market. These directories, most of which can be found in county or university libraries, include:

- Fortune directories (from *Fortune* magazine)
  —500 Largest U.S. Industrial Corporations (May issue)
  —Second Largest 500 Corporations (June issue)
- 200 Largest Foreign Industrial Corporations (August issue)
- *Forbes* Annual Report on American Industry (January issue)
- Standard & Poor's *Industrial Surveys* (quarterly)
- *U.S. Industrial Outlook,* U.S. Department of Commerce (annual)
- *Funk and Scott's Index of Corporations and Industries*
- Moody's Industrial Manual (annual)
- Dun and Bradstreet's *Reference Book of Corporate Managements* (annual)
- Standard and Poor's *Register of Corporations, Directors, and Executives in Canada and the United States* (annual)
- Dun and Bradstreet's *Million Dollar Directory and Middle Market Directory* (annual)
- Thomas Register (good source of information on suppliers and manufacturers)

In addition, there are several references which provide indexes of valuable business information. These include:

- L. Daniells, *Business Forecasting for the 1980's—and Beyond* (Cambridge, MA: Harvard Business School)
- L. Daniells, *Business Intelligence and Strategic Planning* (Cambridge, MA: Harvard Business School)
- L. Daniells, *Business Information Services* (Berkeley, CA: University of California Press)
- P. Wasserman (Ed.), *Encyclopedia of Business Information Sources* (Detroit, MI: Gale Research Co.)
- *The Future: A Guide to Information Sources* (Washington, DC: World Future Society)
- D. Gumpert and J. Timmons, *The Insider's Guide to Small Business Resources* (New York: Doubleday)

The federal government can provide you with further information. The National Referral Center will be able to tell you which organizations provide free information on any topic. You can contact them at

> National Referral Center
> Library of Congress
> 10 First Street, SE
> Washington, DC 20540
> (202) 426–5670

You can also contact the Federal Information Center for information on government services:

> Federal Information Center
> General Services Administration
> 7th and D Streets, SW
> Washington, DC 20407
> (202) 755–8660

ECONOMIC DATA

To monitor economic activity, you should obtain one or more of the following sources of economic data:

- *Survey of Current Business* (Washington, DC: U.S. Government Printing Office) (monthly, with weekly and biannual supplements)
- *Statistical Abstracts of the United States* (Washington, DC: U.S. Government Printing Office) (annual)
- *Handbook of Basic Economic Statistics* (Washington, DC: Economic Statistics Bureau of Washington, DC)

These will often be available in county and university libraries.

CENSUS DATA

Census data can be particularly useful to the business in assessing demand for the product or service and in establishing various industry trends; this information will certainly strengthen your business plan. There is an abundance of census data available that can be obtained by contacting the Bureau of the Census of the U.S. Department of Commerce. This agency can provide you will the following reports:

- Bureau of Census Catalog of Publications (index of all Census Bureau data)
- Census of Agriculture
- Census of Retail Trade
- Census of Wholesale Trade

- Census of Manufacturers
- Census of Selected Services
- Census of Population
- Census of Housing

HOW THE SBA CAN HELP YOU

The U.S. Small Business Administration (SBA) is a federal agency whose purpose is to help people begin and remain in business. The SBA advocates programs and policies that will help small businesses and provides them with financial assistance (discussed in Part III of this book), management counseling and training, procurement assistance on government contracts, publications, and so on. The SBA provides special assistance to women, minorities, the handicapped, and veterans.

The SBA employs several thousand professionals in over 100 district field offices throughout the nation. They can assist you with special problems related to small business and can provide you with specific publications that will strengthen your business plan.

You can obtain information by contacting the SBA Answer Desk at (800) 368–5855.

Management Assistance. The SBA provides management assistance to small businesses through the following:

- Business counseling by the Service Corps of Retired Executives (SCORE) and Active Corps of Executives (ACE)
- Small Business Institutes (SBIs)
- Small Business Development Center (SBDCs)
- Business management courses
- Publications

Information obtained from any of these sources will be important when preparing your business plan.

SCORE and ACE. SCORE and ACE provide one-on-one counseling to both successful and unsuccessful small businesses. Many of these counselors are well equipped to assist entrepreneurs in preparing a business plan. The SBA attempts to match the needs of a specific business with the expertise available. (Special counseling is also provided by the SBA on matters of international trade and overseas markets.) An SBA district field office will put you in touch with a SCORE or ACE representative.

SBIs. The SBA has organized SBIs in about 500 universities and colleges throughout the nation. At each SBI, seniors and graduate students in management programs, who are guided by a faculty advisor and SBA management assistance experts, provide on-site management counseling to small businesses. Contact the school of management at a university in your area to see if they offer such assistance.

SBDCs. SBDCs are university-based centers that provide individual counseling and practical training, research studies, and other types of specialized assistance for small businesses. SBDCs are found at universities throughout the nation.

Business Management Courses. The SBA—along with educational institutions, chambers of commerce, and trade associations—sponsors courses, conferences, workshops, and clinics in preparing business plans, obtaining capital, financial management, administration, marketing, forecasting, management control, and so on, for small businesses. Contact your local SBA district field office for further information.

Publications. The SBA also has several publications available to assist you in starting and managing a business and in preparing your business plan. There are three types of publications:

- *Management aids (MAs):* deal with techniques for handling management problems and business operations
- *Small business bibliographies (SBBs):* provide reference sources for selected topics in management
- *Starting Out Series (SOSs):* one-page fact sheets that describe the financial and operational requirements for selected business

The following MAs are available:

Financial management and analysis

MA 1.001	The ABC's of Borrowing
MA 1.002	What Is the Best Selling Price?
MA 1.003	Keep Pointed toward Profit
MA 1.004	Basic Budgets for Profit Planning
MA 1.005	Pricing for Small Manufacturers
MA 1.006	Cash Flow in a Small Plant
MA 1.007	Credit and Collections
MA 1.008	Attacking Business Decision Problems with Breakeven Analysis
MA 1.009	A Venture Capital Primer for Small Business
MA 1.010	Accounting Services for Small Business
MA 1.011	Analyze Your Records to Reduce Costs
MA 1.012	Profit by Your Wholesalers' Services
MA 1.013	Steps in Meeting Your Tax Obligations
MA 1.014	Getting the Facts for Income Tax Reporting
MA 1.015	Budgeting in a Small Business Firm
MA 1.016	Sound Cash Management and Borrowing
MA 1.017	Keeping Records in Small Business
MA 1.018	Check List for Profit Watching
MA 1.019	Simple Breakeven Analysis for Small Stores
MA 1.020	Profit Pricing and Costing for Services

Planning

MA 2.002	Locating or Relocating Your Business
MA 2.004	Problems in Managing a Family-Owned Business
MA 2.005	The Equipment Replacement Decision
MA 2.006	Finding a New Product for Your Company
MA 2.007	Business Plan for Small Manufacturers
MA 2.008	Business Plan for Small Construction Firms
MA 2.009	Business Life Insurance
MA 2.010	Planning and Goal Setting for Small Business
MA 2.011	Fixing Production Mistakes
MA 2.012	Setting Up a Quality Control System
MA 2.013	Can You Make Money with Your Idea or Invention?
NA 2.014	Can You Lease or Buy Equipment?
MA 2.015	Can You Use a Minicomputer?
MA 2.016	Check List for Going into Business
MA 2.017	Factors in Considering a Shopping Center Location
MA 2.018	Insurance Checklist for Small Business
MA 2.019	Computers for Small Business-Service Bureau or Time Sharing
MA 2.020	Business Plan for Retailers
MA 2.021	Using a Traffic Study to Select a Retail Site
MA 2.022	Business Plan for Small Service Firms
MA 2.024	Store Location "Little Things" Mean a Lot
MA 2.025	Thinking about Going into Business?

General management and administration

MA 3.001	Delegating Work and Responsibility
MA 3.002	Management Checklist for a Family Business
MA 3.004	Preventing Retail Theft
MA 3.005	Stock Control for Small Stores
MA 3.006	Reducing Shoplifting Losses
MA 3.007	Preventing Burglary and Robbery Loss
MA 3.008	Outwitting Bad-Check Passers
MA 3.009	Preventing Embezzlement

Marketing

MA 4.003	Measuring Sales Force Performance
MA 4.005	Is the Independent Sales Agent for You?
MA 4.007	Selling Products on Consignment
MA 4.008	Tips on Getting More for Your Marketing Dollar
MA 4.010	Developing New Accounts
MA 4.012	Marketing Checklist for Small Retailers
MA 4.013	A Pricing Checklist for Small Retailers

MA 4.014   Improving Personal Selling in Small Retail Stores
MA 4.015   Advertising Guidelines for Small Retail Firms
MA 4.016   Signs in Your Business
MA 4.018   Plan Your Advertising Budget
MA 4.019   Learning about Your Market
MA 4.020   Do You Know the Results of Your Advertising?

Organization and personnel

MA 5.001   Checklist for Developing a Training Program
MA 5.004   Pointers on Using Temporary-Help Services
MA 5.005   Preventing Employee Pilferage
MA 5.006   Setting Up a Pay System
MA 5.007   Staffing Your Store

Legal and governmental affairs

MA 6.003   Incorporating a Small Business
MA 6.004   Selecting the Legal Structure for Your Business
MA 6.005   Introduction to Patents

Miscellaneous

MA 7.002   Association Services for Small Business
MA 7.003   Market Overseas with U.S. Government Help

The following SBBs are available:

SBB 1   Handcrafts
SBB 2   Home Businesses
SBB 3   Selling by Mail Order
SBB 9   Marketing Research Procedures
SBB 10   Retailing
SBB 12   Statistics and Maps for National Market Analysis
SBB 13   National Directories for Use in Marketing
SBB 15   Recordkeeping Systems—Small Store and Service Trade
SBB 18   Basic Business Reference Sources
SBB 20   Advertising-Retail Store
SBB 31   Retail Credit and Collection
SBB 37   Buying for Retail Stores
SBB 72   Personnel Management
SBB 75   Inventory Management
SBB 85   Purchasing for Owners of Small Plants
SBB 86   Training for Small Business

SBB 87   Financial Management
SBB 88   Manufacturing Management
SBB 89   Marketing for Small Business
SBB 90   New Product Development
SBB 91   Ideas into Dollars (Inventors' Guide)
SBB 92   Effective Business Communication

The following SOSs are available:

SOS 0101   Building Service Contracting
SOS 0104   Radio-Television Repair Shop
SOS 0105   Retail Florist
SOS 0106   Franchised Businesses
SOS 0107   Hardware Store or Home Centers
SOS 0111   Sporting Goods Store
SOS 0112   Drycleaning
SOS 0114   Cosmetology
SOS 0115   Pest Control
SOS 0116   Marine Retailers
SOS 0117   Retail Grocery Stores
SOS 0122   Apparel Store
SOS 0123   Pharmacies
SOS 0125   Office Products
SOS 0129   Interior Design Services
SOS 0130   Fish Farming
SOS 0133   Bicycles
SOS 0135   Printing
SOS 0137   The Bookstore
SOS 0138   Home Furnishings
SOS 0142   Ice Cream
SOS 0145   Sewing Centers
SOS 0148   Personnel Referral Service
SOS 0149   Selling by Mail Order
SOS 0150   Solar Energy
SOS 0201   Breakeven Point for Independent Truckers

To obtain copies of any of the publications above, contact either your local SBA office or the SBA publication center:

U.S. Small Business Administration
P.O. Box 15434
Ft. Worth, TX 76119

Procurement Assistance.   The SBA assists small businesses in obtaining a fair share of federal government contracts by:

- Helping federal agencies to direct government subcontracts to small businesses

- Helping private contractors to direct federal subcontracts to small businesses

- Referring qualified small businesses to federal prime contractors

- Monitoring the strategy of federal contracts to small firms by federal agencies

The SBA has developed a computerized data base of small businesses interested in bidding on government contracts. The data base, known as Procurement Automated Source System (PASS), is available at the 10 regional offices of the SBA as well as at about 100 regional offices of federal procurement officials and private prime contractors.

Federal procurement specialists in SBA offices can assist you in preparing bids and in obtaining such contracts by providing you with leads in R&D projects, new technology, and so on.

Minority/Women Assistance.   The SBA provides special assistance to minority-owned businesses. There is an office of Minority Small Business and Capital Ownership Development that directs programs for such businesses. The SBA also provides special management and financial assistance to any woman-owned business, which is defined as a "business that is at least 51 percent owned by a woman or women who also control and operate it." Contact your local SBA district field office for assistance.

How to Get Help from the SBA.   There are three levels of the SBA:

1. *Central office:*

    1111 18th Street, NW
    6th Floor
    Washington, DC 10417
    (202) 634–1818

2. *Regional offices:* Located in

Boston	Kansas City	Chicago
New York	Dallas	Seattle
Philadelphia	Denver	San Francisco
Atlanta		

3. *District offices:* There are over 100 district field offices located throughout the country. Following is a list of their locations:

Alabama
  Birmingham

Alaska
  Anchorage
  Fairbanks

Arizona
  Phoenix
  Tucson

Arkansas
  Little Rock

California
  Fresno
  Los Angeles
  Oakland
  Sacramento
  San Diego
  San Francisco
  Santa Ana

Colorado
  Denver

Delaware
  Wilmington

District of Columbia
  Washington, DC

Florida
  Jacksonville
  Coral Gables
  Tampa
  West Palm Beach

Georgia
  Atlanta
  Statesboro

Guam
  Agana

Hawaii
  Honolulu

Idaho
  Boise

Illinois
  Chicago
  Springfield

Indiana
  South Bend
  Indianapolis

Iowa
  Des Moines
  Cedar Rapids

Kansas
  Wichita

Kentucky
  Louisville

Louisiana
  New Orleans
  Shreveport

Maine
  Augusta

Maryland
  Towson

Massachusetts
  Boston
  Holyoke

Michigan
  Detroit
  Marquette

Minnesota
  Minneapolis

Mississippi
  Biloxi
  Jackson

Missouri
  Kansas City
  St. Louis
  Sikeston
  Springfield

Montana
  Helena

Nebraska
  Omaha

New Jersey
  Camden
  Vineland

New Mexico
  Albuquerque

New York
  Albany
  Buffalo
  Elmira
  Melville
  New York
  Rochester
  Syracuse

North Carolina
  Charlotte
  Greenville

North Dakota
  Fargo

Ohio
  Cincinnati
  Cleveland
  Columbus

Oklahoma
  Oklahoma City
  Tulsa

Oregon
  Portland

Pennsylvania
  Bala-Cynwyd
  Harrisburg
  Wilkes-Barre

Puerto Rico
  Hato Rey

Rhode Island
  Providence

South Carolina
  Columbia

South Dakota
  Sioux Falls

Tennessee
  Knoxville
  Memphis
  Nashville

Texas
  Austin
  Corpus Christi
  Dallas
  El Paso

Harlingen
Houston
Lubbock
San Antonio

Utah
  Salt Lake City

Vermont
  Montpelier

Virginia
  Richmond

Virgin Islands
  St. Thomas

Washington
  Seattle
  Spokane

West Virginia
  Charleston
  Clarksburg

Wisconsin
  Eau Claire
  Madison
  Milwaukee

Wyoming
  Casper

SPECIFIC INFORMATION ABOUT THE INDUSTRY

There are numerous sources from which to obtain specific information about an industry that will be valuable in preparing your business plan. Stanford Research Institute (SRI), Arthur D. Little, Frost & Sullivan, and various Wall Street research houses typically conduct industry studies. Although their services are often costly, they generally do a very comprehensive analysis of the environmental opportunities and threats facing an industry. You can also obtain valuable information on the industry from trade associations (see below) or from a local office of the SBA.

Informal Sources of Information. You should not, however, overlook the importance of collecting industry data informally—for example, from salespersons, suppliers, investors, customers, focus groups, newly hired employees from similar companies, attendees at conferences, and other business contacts. I am familiar with one entrepreneur who has found out more about his chief competitor simply by purchasing his products than he could have by hiring a consultant to conduct a formal competitive analysis. Often, an informal discussion with a business associate during a round of golf or during lunch or cocktails will give you more reliable and more timely information on industry trends than will a lengthy, costly consultant's report.

General Information on Associations. An excellent reference which provides general information (e.g., names, addresses, phone numbers, purposes, dates and locations of conferences, publications, fees, etc.) about most trade associations in this country is the *Encyclopedia of Associations* (Gale Research Co., Detroit, MI):

Publications of Associations. Most trade associations publish newsletters or magazines for their members as well as for other interested parties. Such publications, which will provide you with valuable information on trends and new developments in the industry, include:

- *Appliance* (Dana Chase Publications, Elmhurst, IL)
- *Broadcasting* (Broadcasting Publications, Washington, DC)
- *Chain Store Age* (Lebhar-Friedman Books, New York)
- *Computerworld* (Computerworld, Inc., Newton, MA)
- *Discount Merchandiser* (McFadden-Bartell Publishing, New York)
- *Discount Store News* (Lebhar-Friedman Books, New York)
- *Drug and Cosmetic Industry* (Drug Markets, Inc., New York)
- *Drug Topics* (Litton Publications, Oradell, NJ)
- *Editor & Publisher* (Editor & Publishing Co., New York)
- *Men's Wear* (Fairchild Publications, New York)
- *Merchandising Week* (Billboard Publications, Cincinnati, OH)
- *National Petroleum News* (McGraw-Hill, New York)
- *Product Management* (Litton Publications, Oradell, NJ)
- *Sales Management* (Bill Communications, New York)
- *Vending Times* (Vending Times, New York)

ADDITIONAL SOURCES OF INFORMATION

You can also contact several of the following sources to obtain valuable information to be incorporated into the business plan on the external opportunities and threats facing the business:[6]

General

American Planning Association	(202) 872-0611
The Boston Consulting Group	(617) 722-7800
The Conference Board	(212) 759-0900
Marketing Research Services	(404) 393-1010
North American Society of Corporate Planners (NASCP)	(513) 223-0419

International

Business International	(212) 750-6300
International Bank for Reconstruction and Development (World Bank)	(202) 477-1234

[6]Compiled by Dick Levin and associates at the University of North Carolina; see D. Levin, *The Executive's Illustrated Primer of Long-Range Planning* (Englewood Cliffs, NJ: Prentice-Hall, 1980).

U.S. Government

U.S. Department of Agriculture	(202) 655-4000
U.S. Department of Commerce	(202) 377-2000
U.S. Department of Labor	(202) 655-4000
U.S. Department of State	(202) 655-4000
U.S. Department of Transportation	(202) 655-4000
U.S. Department of the Treasury	(202) 566-2000

The Economy

The Brookings Institution	(202) 797-6000
Chase Econometrics	(212) 269-1188
Committee for Economic Development	(212) 688-2065
Data Resources, Inc. (DRI)	(617) 861-0165
Predicasts, Inc.	(216) 795-3000
Stanford Research Institute (SRI)	(415) 326-6200
Wharton Economics Forecasting Associates, Inc.	(215) 243-6451

Technology

Batelle Memorial Institute	(614) 424-6424
The Hudson Institute	(914) 762-0700
Office of Technology Assessment	(202) 224-6019

The Future

Applied Futures, Inc.	(203) 661-9711
The Committee for the Future, Inc.	(202) 966-8776
Congressional Clearing House for the Future	(202) 224-3121
The Futures Research Group	(202) 426-6698
The Future Group, Inc.	(203) 633-3501
World Future Society	(301) 656-8274

"WE ARE DROWNING IN INFORMATION BUT STARVED FOR KNOWLEDGE"

One thing should be very clear from the preceding discussion—there is *plenty* of information available that could be used in conducting your market research. As John Naisbitt recently noted in his recent best-selling book *Megatrends:* "We are drowning in information but starved for knowledge." It is unlikely that the business owner will suffer from not having enough information available, but rather from either:

- Having *too much* information (i.e., information overload)
- Not knowing where to look for the information that is available
- Using poor managerial judgment based on the available information

I am familiar with one entrepreneur, for example, who has been unsuccessful in launching three new ventures over the past four years, primarily because he has spent so much time reading up on industry trends that he has missed the opportunity in each situation to get his product out to his target market. Certainly this can be avoided by being selective in obtaining the references just described and by using your management team wisely when making critical long-term decisions.

III. DEVELOPMENT AND PRODUCTION

This section should highlight the various features related to researching, developing, and producing your basic product. As you prepare this section, keep in mind that investors would much rather fund late-stage projects (i.e., manufacturing or marketing) than early-stage projects (i.e., research).

IIIA. RESEARCH AND DEVELOPMENT (R&D)

In most cases the R&D portion should be rather brief, as investors assume that the company has already completed its basic research efforts.

IIIA1. Describe your competitive technologies. Identify the specific competences of your engineering staff. Describe the advantages of maintaining an engineering unit in house as compared to subcontracting out the work, if appropriate.

IIIA2. Describe the patents that your company holds.

IIIA3. How do you protect your competitive technologies?

IIIA4. Describe the regulatory considerations affecting your research and development efforts.

IIIA5. Describe the new research activity of your firm and that of your competitors. What obstacles do you face?

IIIA6. Describe the new products planned by your firm. What obstacles do you face?

IIIB. PRODUCTION REQUIREMENTS

Investors will often fund engineering efforts related to manufacturing, as this can enhance production efficiency and profitability.

IIIB1. Describe the following features of production along with the expected costs associated with buying, leasing, or simply expensing them:

- Materials/supplies
- Labor (including skills, unionization, availability of local labor, number of shifts, etc.)
- Plant facilities (including location, space, zoning, storage, capacity, etc.)
- Equipment (including maintenance, depreciation, insurance, lease versus buy decisions, etc.)
- Transportation/shipping
- Seasonal effects

In the appendices present in chart form cost–volume information at various levels of production. (This can be described in the context of break-even analysis; see section VD.) Describe the trends in this section.

IIIB2. Describe the competitive advantages in terms of production. Are your production facilities and production process state of the art? Do you have access to superior quality or lower-priced materials? Investors want to see a cost or quality advantage.

IIIC. PRODUCTION PROCESS

IIIC1. Outline the basic stages (or steps) of the development and production process—in list or flowchart form—that your company utilizes, along with a brief explanation of each stage. In addition, allocate the time and money (in amounts and percentages) that are required at each stage of production. Identify the difficulties and risks associated with the various stages. Keep in mind that the longer the stage, the more vulnerable you are to fluctuations in supply of materials. Investors like to see a simple step-by-step overview of the production process.

IIIC2. Provide rationale for producing as compared to subcontracting at the various stages of production.

IIID. QUALITY ASSURANCE/QUALITY CONTROL

IIID1. Describe the quality assurance (quality control), inspection, production control, and inventory control features of your product or service along with the costs and manpower allocated to these control mechanisms. What percent of your units are defective? What has been the trend in recent years? Remember, even an extremely effective marketing effort will not offset a poor-quality product.

IIIE. CONTINGENCY PLANS

IIIE1. Present contingency plans for the production aspects of your business. Include such features as alternative sources of material, provisions for additional workers, overtime, and the like. Also, describe how you intend to expand your production capabilities as you grow.

IV. MARKETING

IVA. MARKETING ORIENTATION

IVA1. Provide a brief introduction to your marketing orientation. Regardless of the type of product or service that you provide it is essential that you develop an orientation to the customer. This section will demonstrate your commitment to the marketing effort.

IVB. MARKETING STRATEGY

IVB1. Provide some rationale for why you have selected the particular segment in which you will compete. Demonstrate that there are various environmental opportunities in that segment and that you possess the competitive strengths (e.g., product or service features) to enable you to take advantage of such opportunities. You may provide some information regarding why you did not choose other segments in which to compete. Make sure, however, that you emphasize the specific target market that you are pursuing.

IVB2. Describe the overall marketing strategy that you will use to attract the targeted market. Demonstrate how this strategy will support your own strengths and capitalize on the weaknesses of your competitors.

IVB3. Describe the image that you wish to portray. Demonstrate how the services that you will provide to your customers and the marketing strategy that you will undertake will be consistent with your image.

IVB4. Provide a detailed explanation of your pricing strategy, including how you will arrive at the given price (e.g., percent markup; cost plus; competitive bidding; margins to retailers, wholesalers, etc.) Describe your profit margin per unit under various scenarios. What price discounts (e.g., for quantity purchases) will you offer? Remember, there is a price–quality relationship; if the quality of your product or service is so outstanding, you cannot expect to provide it for too low a price. In addition, provide some information—in chart form, if possible—on the prices of your competitors and what they actually provide for that price.

IVB5. What credit policy (e.g., 2/10 net 30) will you be using?

IVB6. Describe in detail the channel(s) of distribution (i.e., jobbers, retail, wholesale, brokers, door-to-door, mail order, etc.) and the personnel (i.e., your own sales force, sales representatives, distributors, etc.) that you plan to use to reach your target market and the costs associated with reaching your target market by this channel. Describe the geographic location—local, regional, national—in which you will market your product or service.

IVB7. Describe in detail the promotional or selling tactics (i.e., trade shows, trade magazines, direct calling, telephone, mail, radio, television, brochures, etc.) that you will use to attract customers. Investors will generally want to see that you have explored various alternative advertising tactics. Be prepared to use a combination of techniques. Describe the costs associated with the selling tactics that you will use, broken down by cost per person reached. You should not allocate much more than 10 percent of your sales to cover the costs of selling the product. Present data to support the use of a particular form of advertising. Also, discuss your plans for the production of your advertisement(s) and press release(s).

IVB8. What warranties or guarantees will you be providing to your customers?

IVB9. What features related to branding, packaging, labeling, and so on, will make your product unique? This is especially important for consumer products. Discuss costs. If possible, include a photograph of the package in the appendices.

IVC. CONTINGENCY PLANS

IVC1. Provide contingency plans for your marketing effort.

An Overview of the Marketing Section

It is not enough for a market to exist; there must be people to sell and support the product or (service) and a strategy to shape the marketing effort for the next three to five years. The Marketing section discusses the alternative strategies that can be used to reach the potential market described in part II of the plan, "Market Analysis." Because marketing is a later-stage function than either research and development or market research, investors will generally be eager to fund marketing efforts, provided that a prototype has been developed and there are early indicators of acceptance of the product.

As you prepare this section, keep in mind one key caveat, which was discussed to some extent earlier: The important issue in marketing is not your product or service, but how your customers view your product or service. To take a marketing orientation, you must therefore demonstrate to investors that you can look at your business through the eyes of your customers or potential customers and can market your product or service to them.

HOW TO ATTRACT CUSTOMERS

The investor's first concern is how you will attract customers to your business. Often, this issue is how to pull customers away from your competition. This will generally involve:

- Developing and maintaining the proper image
- Establishing the optimal marketing strategy

Although I am describing them individually, these considerations are interrelated and often overlap. Thus you must treat your marketing effort as a "package" and demonstrate to investors that your advertisements are consistent with the image that you wish to convey for your product or service. Too often I have seen companies use low-quality advertising efforts in attempting to promote their high-quality offerings. Such advertising efforts detract considerably from their intended image.

DEVELOPING THE PROPER IMAGE

Every action that you and your employees take has an impact on your image. If people come to your place of business for your service, the cleanliness of the floors, the manner in which they are treated, and the quality of your work will help form your image. McDonald's, for example, has successfully developed and maintained an image of "QSCV": quality, service, cleanliness, and value.

If you take your business to the customer, the conduct of your employees will influence your image. Pleasant, prompt, and courteous service before and after the sale will help develop a positive image for your business. Your image should be concrete enough to promote in your advertising. For example, "service with a smile" is an often-used slogan to enhance a company's image.

How you position your products or services should be consistent with the image you wish to portray. For example, a retailer positioned at the high end of a market should provide amenities and an atmosphere that reinforces such an image in the eyes of the potential customers. Make sure that you know what image you would like to convey to your customers and be prepared to make that image consistent with your product or service and with your marketing strategy.

Sy Syms, for example, has developed an image of providing good-quality clothing at a reasonable cost at his factory retail outlets. The advertising and distribution strategy as well as the layout of his stores support the image that he has successfully attempted to convey to his customers.

Providing Customer Services

One way to enhance your image is to provide various services or conveniences (e.g., parking) to customers. These services may be "free" to the customer, but not to you. Plan for these expenses and be certain to account for them in the financial projections portion of your business plan.

First, consider the services that your competitors offer and estimate the cost of each service. You might have to provide many of these services just to be competitive with them. Then consider other services that would attract customers which your competitors are not offering and obtain estimates of the cost of such services. After you compile a list of all services with their associated costs, you will need to determine how you can add these costs to your prices without pricing your goods or services out of the market. As noted earlier, these services should be consistent with the image you wish to portray to your customers.

Small businesses often possess a decided advantage over their larger, established competitors in that they can provide special services to their customers and can do so at a "justifiably" higher price than can larger companies.

YOUR MARKETING STRATEGY

There are three major components of your overall marketing strategy which are directly tied to your image:

- Pricing
- Distribution
- Promotion

As noted, you must show investors how these features are consistent with one another in order to strengthen your overall marketing strategy.

Pricing

In establishing a pricing policy, there are several important factors to consider:

- Materials and supplies
- Labor
- Operating expenses
- Planned profit
- Competition

Generally, the only (successful) way that a business can have low prices is to sell low-cost products or services. Your pricing policy will depend largely on your cost of goods and on your various operating expenses. In addition, you should consider what your competitors charge for similar products or services. (You can obtain average selling prices or service fees from a trade association.) If your prices are higher than those of your competitors, make sure that you offer the necessary services to justify your prices.

Your overriding concern in pricing is the perceived value of the goods or services to the purchaser. One thing is very clear, however. Customers are willing to pay premium prices for goods or services if they perceive premium value, especially if the products or services are unique. This is certainly seen in the case of Tandem, ROLM, Bloomingdale's, and Nieman-Marcus.

Price Competitiveness. It is generally difficult for new businesses to be price competitive because they are not in a position to experience the economies of scale of their larger competitors. In some situations, however, new ventures, have been able to charge lower prices than their competitors and thereby use such a pricing strategy as the basis of their competitive advantage. People Express Airlines had considerable success using this strategy in its earliest stages. The company was able to allow its passengers to fly at a price "lower than driving" (as it suggested in its advertisements) because their own costs were substantially less than those of its competitors. People Express, which was able to cut its costs by flying to secondary" airports (e.g., Newark rather than Kennedy or Laguardia), maintaining a small number of personnel per passenger, providing "no frills services" (i.e., no meals or complimentary beverages), and paying low salaries—however, with excellent profit sharing and employee ownership benefits—to its personnel, was realizing tremendous profits by passing these cost savings along to its customers, thereby ensuring high levels of volume (which had reached over 80 percent capacity on average on its flight).

People Express, however, tends to be the exception. They were initially successful because they were an exceptionally well-managed company that had taken advantage of a tremendous environmental opportunity—price deregulation—to offer an alternative service to their customers. Their competitors had not been able to match their prices, as they feared such a tactic would alter their image considerably. (As I have indicated, the entire marketing effort must mesh.)

Of course, the later years of People Express were quite different. Eventually, their obsession with growth and their unrelenting expansion activity caught up with them, and they eventually failed.

Most new businesses, however, will have to compete based on service or based on the innovative nature of their product or service, rather than based primarily on price. It is recommended that new businesses identify a market segment and develop an appropriate marketing strategy for that segment based on product or service quality without pricing themselves out of the market.

Many new businesses introduce products at low prices with the idea that they will be able to raise prices as they develop a group of loyal customers. Unfortunately, this does not happen; companies that do so quickly begin to lose their loyal customers. Generally, it is easier to lower prices than it is to raise prices. Many new businesses—especially technology manufacturing businesses (e.g., calculators, computers, VCRs, etc.) which can benefit greatly from economies of scale as production increases—have introduced products at moderate to high prices in order to reach the "early adopter," the people who enjoy being the first ones to buy new products, who are not very sensitive to price. Ultimately, these companies have lowered the prices of their products to enable others who are more sensitive to price to try them.

A basic relationship holds for pricing: many small businesses can charge higher prices while still generating fairly high levels of sales, due to the personalized nature of their services (i.e., a competitive advantage).

Pricing for Retail and Service Businesses. In retail businesses, companies often use a credit or a credit card system. There are costs associated with the use of credit cards, so plan for them. If you use a credit card system, what will it cost you? Can you add this cost to your prices without hurting sales?

Pricing for professional service businesses does not necessary follow the same rules as for product businesses. Of course, people want value. However, they will often perceive greater value (i.e., be more willing to listen to advice) if they are dealing with a $150 an hour professional, rather than a $50 an hour professional, even though their work might be comparable. That does not mean that you should charge as high rate as possible for your services, as your service fees should be in line with your experience and qualifications. However, do not expect to attract more business by offering high-quality services at a budget rate. Keep your pricing strategy consistent with the image that you want to convey.

As an example, a few years ago a child psychologist started her own business after spending several years as a counselor in a high school. She was able to keep her overhead costs down because she operated out of her house. So she passed the cost savings along to her customers, thereby establishing hourly fees of about half the prevailing rate. The problem that she encountered was that her clients viewed her advice as "cut rate" service.

If your customers feel that they "get what they pay for," your pricing policy should be based on their perceptions of value rather than merely on your costs to provide them with the service. Naturally, it is not necessarily advisable to charge premium rates for your services. If customers have readily available alternatives—for example, if they can get the *same* thing "around the corner" for less money or if there are adequate "substitutes" for your service—your service fees might have to be more competitive. Some trade associations have a schedule of fees or service charges for businesses. You should consult your trade association for these to ensure that your prices are competitive.

Pricing for Construction Businesses.[7] Success in the construction industry is based largely on competitive bidding practices. It is essential that you develop careful and complete cost estimates in order to make competitive bids. Use that information to develop realistic financial projections for your business plan.

Estimating. Many successful contractors attribute their success to their estimating procedures. They build the job on paper before they submit a bid. In doing this, they break the job down into work units and pieces of material. Then they assign a cost to each item. The total of these costs will be the direct construction cost. There are also indirect costs of a job (such as overhead expense—i.e., the cost of maintaining an office, automobiles, license fees, etc.). Other expenses that should also be considered when bidding include interest charges that must be paid on money borrowed to get the job under way, insurance, surety bond premiums, travel expenses, advertising costs, office salaries, lawyer's fees, and so on.

Trade associations, as one of their services, can provide you with a package of business forms. A cost estimate form would be included in this package. The obvious advantage in using these forms is that they are specifically designed for estimating construction projects.

Bonding. The practice of bonding has been a traditional way of life for anyone engaged in contract construction. Bonding companies provide bonds for a certain percentage of the contract price. There are three main types of bonds:

- *Bid bonds* assure that the bidder is prepared to perform the work according to the terms of the contract if successful in the bid.
- *Performance bonds* assure completion of the job according to plans and specifications.
- *Payment bonds* assure anyone dealing with the bonded contractor that they will be paid.

The effect that bonding companies have had on contractors is evident in the area of competition. The customer, by requiring that the contractor be bonded, is more or less assured of adequate completion of the job. Therefore, contractors are compared on a basis of price. Bonding also looks attractive in the eyes of a banker or investor.

[7]SBA Management Aid 2.008.

The SBA has a surety bond program designed to help small and emerging contractors who previously might have been unable to get bonding. The SBA is authorized to guarantee up to 80 percent of losses incurred under bid, payment, or performance bonds on contracts up to $1.25 million. Application for this assistance is available from any SBA field office.

Distribution

In developing a distribution policy, and in describing the distribution policy in your business plan, you should consider:

- The location in which you are (or will be) situated.
- How you get (or will get) your product or service to the ultimate consumer. (Will you sell it directly through your own sales division or indirectly through manufacturer's agents, brokers, wholesalers, and so on? This is a distribution as well as a promotion concern.)
- What this method of distribution costs (or will cost) you.

Distribution Strategy for Retail Stores. In retail businesses, your sales potential depends largely on location. In most cases you will draw your customers from the surrounding areas. The following questions should help you work through the problem of selecting and maintaining a profitable location, a factor that is very important to the investor.[8]

First, you should consider the general location. In what part of the city or town should you be located:

- In the downtown business section?
- In the area right next to the downtown business area?
- In a residential section of the town?
- On the highway outside town?
- In the suburbs?
- In a suburban shopping center?

Two major factors for retailers to consider in selecting site locations are cost and traffic flow. Generally, low-cost, low-traffic locations require greater expenditures on advertising to build traffic.

You should then narrow down a specific place in your location:

- What is the competition in the area you have picked?
- How many of the stores look prosperous?
- How many look as though they are barely getting by?
- How many similar stores went out of business in this area last year?
- How many stores opened up in the last year?
- What price line does the competition carry?
- Which store or stores in the area will be your biggest competitors?

[8]See SBA Management Aid 2.0220.

Assuming that you have found an appropriate building, consider the following:

- Is the neighborhood starting to get run down?
- Is the neighborhood new and on the way up?
- Are any superhighways or throughways planned for the neighborhood?
- Is street traffic fairly heavy all day?
- How close is the building to bus lines and other transportation?
- Are there adequate parking spaces convenient to your store?
- Are the sidewalks in good repair? (You may have to repair them.)
- Is the street lighting good?
- Is your store on the sunny side of the street?
- What is the occupancy history of this store building? Does the store have a reputation for failures? (Have stores opened and closed after a short time?)
- Why have other businesses failed in this location?
- What is the physical condition of the store?
- What service does the landlord provide?
- What are the terms of the lease?
- How much rent must you pay each month?
- What is your estimate of the gross annual sales you expect in this location?
- Will you have enough room if and when your business grows?

Distribution Strategy for Other Service Businesses.[9] In service businesses, demand is often a function of the area you serve. That is, how many customers in the area will need your services? Will your customers be industrial, commercial, consumer, or all of these?

When selecting a site to locate or expand your business, consider the nature of your service. If you pick up and deliver, you will want a site where the travel time will be low and you may later install a radio dispatch system. Or if customers must come to your place of business, the site must be conveniently located and easy to find.

In selecting an area to serve, you should first consider the following:

- Population and its growth potential
- Income, age, occupation of population
- Number of competitive services in and around your proposed location
- Local ordinances and zoning regulations
- Type of trading area (commercial, industrial, residential, seasonal)

For additional help in choosing an area, contact the local chamber of commerce and the manufacturer and distributor of any equipment and supplies you will be using.

[9]See SBA Management Aid 2.022.

After deciding on a general area, you should then consider the specific site for your service business. You should determine the following:

- Will the customer come to your place of business?
- How much space do you need?
- Will you want to expand later?
- Do you need any special features required in lighting, heating, or ventilation?
- Is parking available?
- Is public transportation available?
- Is the location conducive to drop-in customers?
- Will travel time be excessive?
- Will you prorate travel time for service calls?
- Would a location close to an expressway or main artery cut down on travel time?
- If you choose a remote location, will savings in rent offset the inconvenience?
- If you choose a remote location, will you have to pay as much as you save in rent for advertising to make your service known?
- Will the supply of labor be adequate and the necessary skills be available?
- What are the zoning regulations of the area?
- Will there be adequate fire and police protection?
- Will crime insurance be needed and be available at a reasonable rate?
- Is the area in which you plan to locate supported by a strong economic base? For example, are nearby industries working full time? Only part time? Did any industries go out of business in the past several months? Are new industries scheduled to open in the next several months?
- What is the competition in the area?
- Does the area appear to be saturated?
- How many businesses look as though they are barely getting by?
- How many similar services went out of business in the area last year? Why did they fail?
- How many new services opened up in the last year?
- How much do your competitors charge for your service?
- Which firm or firms in the area will be your biggest competition?

Finally, you might consider some specific issues regarding the building itself:

- Will you build? What are the terms of the loan or mortgage?
- Will you rent? What are the terms of the lease?
- Is the building attractive? Does it need repairs? What will repairs cost?
- What services does the landlord provide?

Direct Selling. As noted in Section 1 of Part I of this book, perhaps the most essential characteristic of a successful entrepreneur is his or her ability to sell.

Too many entrepreneurs fail simply because they lack the skills to get the product to the market. Victor Kiam (Remington Products), Ross Perot (Electronic Data Systems), and Lee Iacocca (Chrysler) all illustrate the importance placed on sales.

Initially, the entrepreneur may be quite successful in selling his product locally to various customers. For example, Jerome Schulman, a chemist who developed Shane toothpaste, singlehandedly began selling the specialized aloe gel product in the Chicago area for two years. After getting a few major food and drug chains to carry his product, sales grew to close to 100,000 tubes a month, or about three times what he sold in his entire first year of business. Shortly thereafter, however, Schulman hired his first assistant to help him market his product.

Eventually, the entrepreneur will need to hire salespersons to ensure that the sales function receives the attention that it deserves. Ideally, salespersons should be motivated, self-confident, possessed of good speaking and listening skills, and experienced in sales—yet not be "floaters" (i.e., having worked for three or more companies over the past five years). Investors will be quite interested in the qualifications of your sales personnel and, more important, of your director (or vice-President) of sales.

Developing a Budget for Direct Selling. How much money should you allocate per sales call? As a rough guideline, you should allow for a maximum of 10 percent of the selling price of the product to cover all costs associated with the salesperson (including salary, commission, and travel expenses) for a given sale. For example, if you are selling precision instruments at a single unit price of $10,000, you can budget $1000 (i.e., 10 percent of $10,000) per sale for the salesperson. Assuming that one in ten prospects purchases the equipment, you should allocate $100 (i.e., 1/10 × $1000) per sales call. Typically, in-house sales calls cost a minimum of $100. Using sales agents (or "sales reps")—which give you less control because the reps sell various other products (see below)—will often reduce this cost by 50 to 75 percent.

Use of Sales Agents. An important consideration in distribution is whether to use direct selling to your customers or to employ sales agents who represent several clients on a commission basis. If you hire your own salespersons, you incur certain costs—such as social security payments, fringe benefits, insurance, office expenses, and so on—yet you have more control of your accounts. If you utilize sales agents, however, you tend to have lower costs but have less control. Thus there are advantages and disadvantages associated with each:

Advantages of using sales agents include:

- They provide immediate entry into a territory.
- They make regular calls on potential and existing customers.
- They often provide high-quality salesmanship.
- Cost is a predetermined selling expense (i.e., commissions are a percentage of sales).

You should, however, also consider the following disadvantages prior to deciding on the use of sales agents:

- There is less control over your product or service.
- Selling expenses on large-volume orders may be excessive.
- Allegiance is not to your company because other clients are served by the same sales reps.
- You can lose your customers if contact with the sales rep is canceled.

Several organizations assist businesses in finding competent sales reps. Among them are:

- Direct Selling Association
  Suite 600
  1776 K Street, NW
  Washington, DC 20006
  (202) 293–5760

- United Association of Manufacturers Representatives
  P.O. Draw 6266
  Kansas City, KS 66106
  (913) 258–9466

- L.H. Simmonds, Inc.
  60 East 42nd Street
  New York, NY 10017
  (212) 889–1530

- Manufacturers Agents National Association (MANA)
  Box 3467
  Laguna Hills, CA 92654
  (714) 859–4040

- New England Manufacturing Exchange (NEMEX)
  10 Moulton Street
  Cambridge, MA 02138
  (617) 354–1150

Promotion

We are treating promotion as the last aspect of your marketing strategy because you have to have something to say before your advertising efforts can be effective. When you have an image, customer services, a price range, and a means of distribution, you are ready to tell prospective customers why they should buy your products or services. Too often, small businesses invest in advertising and other forms of promotion, such as personal selling, contests, and discount offerings, without having a clear sense of the target market they hope to reach or the image they want to convey.

Tough Chickens. Advertising is certainly a necessary and worthwhile expense for your business. However, the key to your success will be the quality or the distinguishing features of your product or service, more than how you promote it. Thus advertising is meant to *support* the beneficial attributes of your offering rather than to serve as a substitute for them.

Frank Perdue, chairman and principal owner of Perdue Farms Inc. of Salisbury, Maryland, has guided his company to a billion-dollar enterprise that realizes margins severalfold above the industry average and maintains a 50 percent market share in various urban markets. Perdue, who has become quite a celebrity in the northeast, appears personally in radio and television ads to tell his potential buyers: "It takes a tough man to make a tender chicken" or "My chickens eat better than you do. If you want to start eating as good as my chickens, take a tip from me. Eat my chickens." Yet Perdue insists that advertising is not the key to his company's success. As he notes:

> The quality of the product is number one, our advertising is number two....Too many people take a mediocre product and fail. Eighty percent of all newly advertised products fail. The manufacturer decides the consumer is a fool. That's why it fails. They think advertising is a cure-all. But when you advertise something, you stick it in the consumer's mind that your product is better. They expect something a little more.[10]

What Should Your Advertising Do for Your Business? Before you can think about how much you can or want to spend on advertising, you should determine what you want your advertising to do for your business. You should consider:

- The strengths of your business
- How your business is different from your competitors
- What message you want your advertising to get across to your existing and potential customers
- To whom (i.e., to which market segment) you want to convey this message

Develop an Advertising Budget. You should then determine a budget for advertising for the next few years to be included in your business plan. Compare the budget to that of other similar businesses. You can obtain estimates of average advertising expenses as a percentage of sales from trade associations. If your estimated costs for advertising are substantially higher than the average for your industry, you might reevaluate your budget. No single expense item—such as advertising—should get so out of line as to affect profits significantly. Your task is to determine how much you can afford to spend and still do the job that needs to be done. In other words, how much "bang can you get for the buck"?

You are looking for the most effective means to convey your message to those most likely to use your product or service. Ask the local media (newspapers, radio, and television, and printers of direct-mail pieces) for information about their services.

[10]See *Inc.*, February 1984, p. 22.

Then, when selecting the appropriate form of advertising (i.e., newspapers, posters, radio, mail, etc.) you should consider:

- The size of the audience
- The frequency of use of the particular form of advertisement
- The cost of a single advertisement
- The total cost of advertising (i.e., cost of a single ad multiplied by the frequency of use)
- The cost of the advertisement per person reached (i.e., the total cost divided by the size of the audience)

The cost of advertising will certainly vary considerably from business to business and from location to location. However, as a general rule, an expenditure of 5 to 10 percent of your sales (revenues) on advertising should not be considered excessive. In the earliest stages of your venture you may even have to spend more than that in order to familiarize customers with your offering and to establish the appropriate image.

Advertising Options. There are numerous ways to advertise your product or service. Some examples are:

Classified ads in newspapers and magazines: cost will depend on readership of publication.

Yellow Pages: allows you to run an ad as big as that of your largest competitors; a *must* for most businesses. Typically, a 1-inch ad will cost a few hundred dollars per year.

Telephone calls: a low-cost but often time-consuming way to develop and maintain a customer orientation.

Circulars or brochures: low cost per item; an effective way to promote your products or services to a concentrated area—in some cases, for many years.

Personal letters: an excellent way to reach clients in service businesses. Cost and time can be reduced significantly by the use of a word processor or a personal computer with a word processing software program. You can purchase mailing lists to assist you in target marketing.

Poster and signs: a low-cost way to attract customers in retail businesses; reaches a great many people over a long period of time.

Radio advertising: enables you to reach a fairly large group of potential customers over a large geographic area for just a few hundred dollars. This medium allows you to target by age of consumer (see below).

Television advertising: a high-cost but often effective way to reach a very large group of potential customers; advantageous in that it provides both an audio and a visual message.

Newspaper advertising: can be quite costly if you place weekly ads in a newspaper over an extended period, yet it enables you quickly to reach a very large target market.

Business cards: an inexpensive and necessary way to maintain contact with customers.

Billboards: an effective advertising technique for hotels, restaurants, and various other businesses.

Sampling: an expensive way to advertise your product, but can be effective if a one-time use will result in repeat sales.

Magazine advertising: not as expensive as you would expect. Surprisingly, it can cost just a few thousand dollars to run a full-page ad in a regional edition of a national magazine.

Trade shows and exhibits: a very effective way to exhibit your product to an interested group of potential customers (see below).

Unique ads: T-shirts, skywriting, shopping bags, Little League sponsorships, and the like, can all be very effective advertising tools.

Public relations: an extremely effective and low-cost way to reach your audience. For example, by inviting a reporter to your place of business during a grand opening, a community event, and so on, you might receive "free" one-time advertising in the form of a newspaper article or a press release.

Speeches or articles: a very effective way to make yourself known in a community and to enhance your credibility; especially effective for doctors, lawyers, consultants, accountants, and other professionals.

Establishing contacts: getting involved with the local chamber of commerce, service clubs, regional development agency, local branches of various associations, universities, and similar agencies is an effective way of developing new clients.

Seminars: an effective but sometimes costly way to advertise financial and other consulting services.

You should discuss which methods you are currently using or plan to use in your business plan and should provide estimates of their costs and impact.

Which Methods Work Best? Clearly, a combination of the techniques noted above can strengthen your advertising message. However, certain advertising options are more appropriate for some businesses than for others. For example, if you have a very narrow target market segment which is difficult to reach—as in the case of specialty products—you would probably want to allocate more of your promotion budget to the use of sales persons, free samples, gifts to store clerks, and advertisements in trade publications than to the use of advertisements in popular magazines. In short, you want to select the advertising method that can effectively reach the most people in your target market in an affordable manner.

Advertising by Retailers. Retailers will generally rely most heavily on newspapers, radio, and direct mail. Newspapers, in particular, can account for two-thirds or more of their advertising budget. However, other media forms—magazines, television, billboards, transportation signs, and so on—will enable the retailer to reach a wider market. And, of course, good Yellow Pages advertising is essential for small retailers.

Newspapers are especially effective because they lend themselves very well to promotional tie-ins such as the use of coupons. Radio advertising can also be effective because radio follows the listener everywhere. Rates for radio advertising vary depending on the number of commercials for which you contract, the time periods, and the station itself. Direct mail is especially useful if the store offers charge accounts; mail will enable the business to reach its charge customers by an effective, low-cost technique.

The Power of Radio.   Radio advertisements can be an effective low-cost way of reaching your target market. The cost of radio advertising (based on the cost to reach 1000 listeners) has risen only half as much as newspaper advertising and only two-thirds as much as television advertising over the past 15 years. Costs of radio advertising, however, vary considerably due to the nature and size of the listening audience as well as the negotiating skill of the parties involved in the advertising agreement; thus it can cost anywhere from $15 to $500 or more for a 60-second spot on a local radio station.

Although radio advertisements are used predominantly for retail and consumer goods businesses, companies in other industries—for example, banks, which use radio to relay current interest-rate information; high-technology businesses, which use it for recruitment purposes; and newspaper and magazine companies, which use this medium to attract advertisers and subscribers—have recently used radio successfully to reach their markets. And why not? More than half of the population gets their first news in the morning listening to radio.

A few years ago, Sau-Sea Foods, Inc., of Yonkers, New York, was able to increase its New York sales by almost 50 percent largely due to its radio advertisements. The company, which decided to reposition its shrimp cocktail product from an appetizer to a low-calorie snack that appeals to women between the ages of 20 and 45, has advertised on nine radio stations that play predominantly adult contemporary music to reach this audience.

Trade Shows.   Recently, companies have begun using trade shows as an effective advertising technique. For example, ACCO International, a $150 million manufacturer of office products, sold close to $3 million to $4 million of its products in three days at a recent trade show of the National Office Products Association (NOPA). Trade shows, when combined with other promotional practices, can be particularly useful for small, growing businesses as they allow them to demonstrate their products to suppliers, customers, and investors in a cost-effective fashion. As noted by a recent study by the Trade Show Bureau, the average cost of a trade show contact is about $70, compared to as much as $250 for an average field sales call. In addition, it takes an average of less than one field sales call to book an order from a trade show lead as compared to over five sales calls to close an industrial sale.[11]

Trade shows are particularly effective in introducing a new product to the marketplace. This is extremely important for high-technology companies that want to get initial reactions from customers. Customers are not very likely to

[11] See *Inc.*, May 1984, p. 66.

spend $50,000 or more on a piece of electronic or medical equipment without seeing it in operation ahead of time.

Trade shows can be advantageous to small businesses because they put all displayers on somewhat equal footing. As noted by Graham Miller, chairman of LTX Corp., a semiconductor test equipment maker in Westwood, Massachusetts:

> I can create a company image that is, shall we say, "anticipatory." We can, quite simply, look bigger than we are.[12]

A few of the notable trade shows in the country include:

- International Consumer Electronics Show (Summer and Winter)
- National Hardware Show
- NHMA/International Housewares Exposition (January and July)
- COMDEX (Fall)
- RVIA/Recreational Vehicle Industrial Association Annual National RV Show

Advertising Slogans. Do not overlook the importance of advertising slogans. Advertising slogans—such as "IBM Means Service" or "Progress Is Our Most Important Product" (GE)—often become more than just a means to sell a product or service; they reinforce the shared values (or culture) of the members of the organization. Certainly, Dana Corporation's people benefit by its slogan "Productivity Through People," and Wal-Mart's people benefit by its slogan "We Care About Our People," as do their customers.

Chappell's Department Stores in New York uses an effective slogan in its advertising efforts—"Personally Yours." A large part of the company's success is that it attempts to maintain a closeness with its customers and to live up to the slogan every day.

Guidelines for Advertising. A couple of basic guidelines for advertising, which will enable you to inject some "selling punch" into your ads, are as follows:

You will need a consistent, well-planned advertising effort. Do not expect instant success with your advertisements. In fact, you probably will not realize the impact of your effort until you have given your customers close to one dozen impressions of an advertising message. Thus promote your effort actively and consistently.

Advertise products or services that have merit in themselves.

Make your advertisements believable. Do not turn off customers due to a lack of credibility.

Emphasize the benefits (i.e., the image of what the product or service *provides* to your customers) of your offering. People do not buy "products"; they buy power, style, beauty, wealth, value, and so on. When demonstrating the

---

[12] See *Inc.*, May 1984, p. 65.

benefits, give one or two primary reasons; do not "pack" the ad with *all* of the reasons to purchase the offering.

You will be competing with thousands of advertisements each day to attract customers; thus you must do something to make your advertisements stand out. Be unique, without detracting from your message; make the ads easy to recognize.

If a retail business, include store name, address, telephone number, store hours, and price of item.

Get your customers motivated to act now; for example, use phrases such as "Call today!"

Use words in your advertisements that motivate your customers. Examples are:

- free
- sale
- you
- new
- improved
- quality
- value
- economy
- service
- style

However, do not abuse these words; you are likely to get excellent results if you use just two or three (but no more) of these words in an advertisement.

Evaluating Your Advertising Efforts. It is important for you to know how effective your advertising efforts are. You can generally get a good feel for this by:

- Monitoring sales of a particular item
- Monitoring store traffic (in retail stores)
- Monitoring the number of coupons brought in (for food or drug items)
- Monitoring requests made that refer to the ad
- Using two different ads and monitoring the effectiveness of each one

You should also monitor the marketing efforts of your competitors. Be aware of their prices (especially for "sale" items) and of the types of advertisements that they use to convey their messages to their customers. Because advertising efforts of competitors are meant to be made public—whereas R&D and production efforts are often confidential—you will be able to gain an edge in marketing if you attempt to monitor and remain one step ahead of your competitors' marketing efforts.

Some Useful Advice: An Ad Maker's Advice on Attracting Customers. Jay Conrad Levinson, who has spent over 20 years as a professional ad maker and has begun several small ventures of his own, has developed a list of 10 common mistakes made by advertisers.[13]

Mistake   1.   Doing your advertising yourself without the help or advice of a pro

Mistake   2.   Making a marketing plan as you go along rather than ahead of time

Mistake   3.   Switching from one advertising medium to another

Mistake   4.   Being impatient with your advertising and changing it often

Mistake   5.   Expecting miracles of advertising—instant results and huge sales

Mistake   6.   Being cute and clever in your advertising; being funny just to be funny

Mistake   7.   Letting the radio station or TV station write your copy and plan your commercial

Mistake   8.   Letting the newspaper or magazine write and design your advertisements

Mistake   9.   Stopping advertising to save money

Mistake 10.   Skimping on advertising production so that you will have money to run more ads

In addition, Mr. Levinson has developed a list of 10 "secrets" to help businesses in their advertising efforts:

Secret   1.   Be prepared to invest properly in this conservative investment.

Secret   2.   Pinpoint your audience and direct your ads right to them, and to no one else.

Secret   3.   Involve your audience by gaining access to their unconscious minds.

Secret   4.   Consider using a pro to make your ads.

Secret   5.   Stick with the niche you have selected for yourself.

Secret   6.   Newspapers are best for news ads; TV is best for ads that demonstrate; radio is best for intimate copy; magazines are best for personally involving and longer-copy ads.

Secret   7.   If you run an ad once in a regional edition of a nationally respected magazine, you can use reprints of that ad for years and gain the same credibility for your business the original ad brought.

Secret   8.   Consistency will be your greatest advising ally: consistency in exposure, media, message, look, sound, identity, and format.

Secret   9.   Judge your advertising against your strategy to be sure all points are covered. Then judge it by how interesting and desirable it makes your product or service.

Secret 10.   Advertising is a fancy name for selling.

[13]See J. Levinson, *555 Ways to Earn Extra Money* (New York: Holt, Rinehart and Winston, 1982), pp. 388–389.

CONCLUDING REMARKS

You must demonstrate to investors that you have adhered to a marketing orientation. To do so, it is essential that you have a good relationship with your customers; seek their advice for ideas on new products and services and then get feedback from them after the sale. For many successful technology companies, 50 percent or more of their sales are from products that were a direct result of customers' suggestions; naturally, these companies are devoting a good portion of their marketing efforts to meeting with their customers to seek additional ideas on new products.

Certainly, it is extremely difficult to sell products or services without making your customers aware of them through your advertising efforts. However, consumers today are educated enough to buy only those goods that they want. It is a better investment to find out what it is that your customers are seeking than to advertise goods or services which they are unlikely to purchase or with which they will be unhappy. Remaining close to your customers before and after the sale should be the essence of your marketing effort; be sure to convey this message to investors in your business plan.

V. FINANCIAL DATA

VA. CURRENT FINANCIAL POSITION

VA1. Summarize the highlights of the following financial statements:

- (Audited, if possible) profit and loss statement and balance sheet for the past two years
- Startup costs
- Current profit and loss statement
- Current cash flow statement
- Current balance sheet

In this section you should provide explanations and conclusions about your financial statements. The actual statements—audited financial statements for the past two to three years as well as your financial projections for the next three to five years (see Part VF)—should appear in the appendices.

VA2. Describe any unusual items on the financial statements. For example, will there be major expenditures on capital equipment (e.g., plant, equipment, machinery), research and development, or advertising over the next three to five years? These expenditures divert cash from short-term operating expenses and can hamper the cash flow position of the company. Yet they are critical for the firm's long-term growth.

VB. PAYABLES/RECEIVABLES

VB1. Describe the debts of the company. List delinquent accounts and their amounts. List accounts payable that are over 90 days overdue. How long does it take for accounts payable to turn over?

VB2. Describe your receivables. List receivables that are uncollectible and those that are more than 90 days overdue (questionable). List your customers that have receivables that represent 10 percent or more of your total of accounts receivable. There is major uncertainty if you lose such accounts. How long does it take for receivables to turn over? How does this compare to the industry average? What is the average age of your receivables?

VC. COST CONTROL

VC1. Describe how you will monitor and control funds and explain who will have responsibilities in this area. Investors look very adversely upon companies with sloppy cost control techniques which do not effectively monitor their cash flow position, especially at the earliest stages of development. A negative indicator is when general and administrative expenses (e.g., expenditures on office supplies, rent, travel and entertainment, salaries of officers, etc.) are disproportionately high. Such expenditures should be kept at a minimum for companies in their development and growth stages.

VD. BREAK-EVEN ANALYSIS

VD1. Briefly describe your break-even estimates; that is, how many units (or dollars worth) of the product or hours of the service must be sold to cover your costs? You can also describe the minimum market share needed to break even if appropriate. Present a table of break-even points in the appendices.

VE. FINANCIAL RATIOS

Summarize the past and present performance of your company by providing a detailed summary of the following ratios:

VE1. Liquidity
VE2. Profitability
VE3. Leverage
VE4. Activity

Compare your present performance to your past performance and to that of your competitors. You can obtain industry averages from a trade association or from Robert Morris Associates.

One ratio that is of particular interest to many investors is gross profit margin (per unit), that is, selling price − (direct material + direct labor) divided by selling price. Due to the staggering costs of overhead and nondirect costs, it is often difficult for a small business to be successful without attaining a minimum of 40 percent (and preferably 50 percent) gross profit margins. Many investors will not even fund businesses unless they can demonstrate such margins.

Investors will also be extremely interested in other profitability measures. They evaluate investments based on potential returns on their investment. If they do not envision significant returns (i.e., 35 to 65 percent compounded annual returns or 5 to 15 times their investment in three to seven years), they will be unlikely to invest in the venture.

VF. FINANCIAL PROJECTIONS

VF1. Describe the assumptions underlying your projected financial statements.

VF2. Summarize the highlights of your projected financial statements:

• Startup costs
• Profit and loss statement (monthly for the first year, then quarterly for the next three years, then annually thereafter)
• Cash projections (monthly for the first year, then quarterly for the next three to five years)
• Balance sheet (quarterly for the first year, then annually thereafter)

In this section, provide the explanations and conclusions of your financial statements. The actual financial statements should appear in the appendices.

———— **An Overview of the Financial Data Section** ————

The Financial Data section is basic to the evaluation of an investment opportunity by an investor. It also serves as an operational plan for the financial manager of the company. In this section you should describe your financial needs and your financial position. To many investors, this section is the heart of the business plan. It is presented in a "numbers-oriented" format. Give the investors the "columns and rows" that they want to see.

Once you have an idea of the size of your target market and of the potential revenues that you could generate from your product or service—which was the basis of part II of the business plan, "Market Analysis"—as well as the costs to develop and market your product or service, you must then incorporate that information into a series of projected financial statements.

STARTUP COSTS

If your business is at a very early stage of development, investors will require you to prepare a statement of projected startup costs.

Preparing Startup Cost Projections

Some startup costs involve large capital expenditures and can either be paid for in full prior to beginning operations or in installments. These costs include the following:

- *Beginning inventory.* Suppliers will assist you in estimating your start-up inventory.
- *Furniture and fixtures.* You should obtain this information from contractors and suppliers. For a retail establishment, these costs would include:
  —Storage shelves
  —Display stands
  —Shelves and tables
  —Window display fixtures
  —Special lighting
  —Counters
  —Outside sign
  —Installation costs
  —Other decorating and remodeling costs

  For a retail store the above expenses are likely to be $35 to $75 per square foot—or $35,000 to $75,000 for a 1000-square foot store.

- *Other assets:*
  —Safe
  —Cash register
  —Land
  —Building
  —Office equipment
  —Automotive equipment
  —Other equipment and machinery

Other startup costs generally involve smaller expenditures (often under $2500) and will need to be paid for in full prior to beginning operations. These include the following:

- *Deposits with public utilities.* (You should contact utility companies to determine expected costs.)
- *Legal and other professional fees.* (You should contact your lawyer, accountant, consultants, and so on, to determine these costs.)
- *Licenses and permit.* (You should contact city, county, state, and federal offices to find out which ones you will need.)
- *Advertising and promotion for opening.* (You can obtain this information from advertising and public relations firms.)
- *Accounts receivable.* (This represents additional inventory that you will need to buy until your credit customers pay.)
- *Prepaid items.* (These include rent, insurance, and similar items.)
- *Cash.* (This is needed for unexpected expenses, losses, special purchases, and so on.)
- *Other expenses.*

In addition, you will have numerous expenditures throughout the course of the year. As a buffer, you should have enough cash on hand initially to cover three to four months of the following recurring expenses:

- Salary of owner-entrepreneur
- Other salaries
- Rent
- Telephone
- Other utilities
- Advertising
- Professional fees
- Travel and entertainment
- Delivery expense
- Repairs and maintenance
- Office supplies
- Taxes
- Interest
- Miscellaneous expenses

Simply project your monthly expenses for each of the above and multiply by 3 or 4 to determine how much cash you will need to cover these expenses.

A financial statement should be prepared to indicate the startup costs for the business. These costs should also be included in the statement of cash projections (discussed later).

In addition to an analysis of startup costs, investors will want to see, at a minimum, the following three financial statements:

- Projected profit and loss statement
- Statement of cash projections
- Projected balance sheet

PROFITS AND LOSSES

The profit and loss statement (or statement of income or earnings statement) measures current and projected revenues, expenses, and income. Although attention to the "bottom line" is extremely important, the bottom line provides an incomplete measure of a company's performance, as it says nothing about the cash flow position of the business. Thus, merely realizing a profit will not guarantee success; all it means is that your expenses are lower than your revenues. (See the later section on "Cash Flows.")

In preparing an income statement, it is useful to express expenses as a percentage of sales. In so doing you will be better able to:

- Compare your results to industry averages.
- Track your performance accurately (e.g., your profits may be increasing in dollars, yet decreasing as a percentage of sales).

You can obtain industry averages for costs and net profits from Dun & Bradstreet, Robert Morris Associates, and trade associations.

Cash Versus Accrual Basis Accounting

There are two alternative methods of accounting for operations, the choice of which can affect significantly the earnings of a business.

Cash Basis Accounting. Under this method, revenues are not realized until the cash is actually received, and expenses are not realized until the payments are actually made. Thus accounts receivable, prepaid expenses, and accounts payable do not show up on the financial statements of the company.

Accrual Basis Accounting. This is the preferred method of accounting for transactions since it recognizes revenues at the time when they are earned, regardless of when the payments are received and recognizes expenses at the time an obligation to pay for the expense is made. Thus revenues, expenses, gains, and losses are all recorded during the time periods in which they affect the performance of the company.

Preparing Profit and Loss Projections

The general format for developing profit and loss projections is as follows:

1. Revenues	Total sales
2. Cost of sales	Total cost of (raw) materials or other items for sale
3. Gross profit	Subtract line 2 from line 1

4. Expenses:

a.	Salary expense	Wages plus overtime, bonuses, etc.
b.	Payroll expenses	Benefits (e.g., health insurance), paid sick leave or vacation, etc.
c.	Other services	Subcontract labor
d.	Office supplies	Items used in business and not resold
e.	Maintenance and repairs	Routine repairs and maintenance including redecorating, painting, etc.
f.	Advertising	Cost of all forms of advertising
g.	Automobile	All costs associated with automobiles
h.	Travel and entertainment	All travel and entertainment costs
i.	Consulting services	Accounting, legal, and other consulting
j.	Rent	Only leased property
k.	Telephone	Local plus long distance phone charges
l.	Utilities	Electricity, heat, water, etc.
m.	Insurance	Property, worker's comp, etc.
n.	Taxes	Real estate, sales tax, excise tax
o.	Interest	Interest on loans
p.	Depreciation	Amortization of capital assets
q.	Other expenses	Other expenses not included above

5.	Total expenses	Add lines 4a through 4q
6.	Operating profit	Subtract line 5 from line 3
7.	Other income	Other sources of income, not part of operations
8.	Other expenses	Other sources of expenses, not part of operations
9.	Pretax profits	Add lines 6 plus 7 minus line 8
10.	Income tax provision	Estimate taxes you will pay
11.	Net income after tax	Subtract line 10 from line 9

CASH FLOWS

The statement of cash projections (or cash flow statement or cash flow analysis) highlights cash inflows and outflows during the period resulting from operations and/or investment and financing activities. You should not necessarily be alarmed if your cash outflows exceed your cash inflows on occasion. However, if this is a regular occurrence, it might indicate that you are undercapitalized, which can be a serious problem. Monitor your cash flows and develop a forecast of your cash flows for the next two years of operation to ensure that you will have adequate funding to operate effectively. Investors will carefully scrutinize your cash flow position for this reason.

If you are managing a high-growth company, your cash demands (i.e., cash outflows) will generally be greater than they would be for a low-growth company. Naturally, there are greater risks involved with a growth business, and accordingly, there are greater potential returns with such a venture. For growth businesses it becomes even more important to monitor your cash flow position continually.

Cash flow is often a more important indicator of survival for small growth-oriented businesses than is profitability. Numerous companies realize substantial profits only to have continual problems in paying their bills.

An important feature of cash projections from the perspective of the investor is that it can indicate a flow of recurring revenue streams for a company. Such recurring revenues—for example, monthly maintenance charges, retainer fees, subscription charges, management fees, etc.—enhance the accuracy (or predictability) of the cash projections, thereby reducing the downside risk of the investment.

From the investor's perspective, cash flow projections will demonstrate how long it will be until the business breaks even. Therefore, it is important to present your cash flows at least until the business goes from a negative cash flow position to a positive position.

Optimizing Cash Flows

Cash Management. Sound cash management involves keeping a sufficient amount of cash on hand (in a checking account) for normal operations and prudently investing the excess. Investors will want to see that you manage your cash in a professional, businesslike manner. It is therefore advisable to take the following steps to manage your cash:

- Deposit payments immediately into interest-bearing accounts.
- "Play the float." For example, transfer funds from your interest-bearing account to your checking account a day or two after you pay your employees or pay your bills.
- Keep only minimum balances in your noninterest-bearing accounts at most times.
- If available, open up an interest-bearing checking account.
- Pay employees bimonthly rather than weekly.
- Consider alternative inventory valuation methods.

Inventory Valuation. Selecting the appropriate inventory accounting practice can be a very effective way of optimizing your cash flow. The use of last-in, first-out (LIFO) rather than first-in, first-out (FIFO) inventory valuation during inflationary periods results in a lower reported profit and thus a lower level of income taxes and a higher level of cash flow. Amtrol, Inc. (discussed earlier) noted that such a practice reduced its annual taxes by over $1 million. Keep in mind, however, that stockholders may be unhappy with the net income figure when LIFO is used because such an inventory valuation provides a more conservative profit for the company.

Your Receivables, Their Payables. When you have an account receivable, you have, in essence, become a "banker" for your customer; you have given the customer a loan, often at no interest, for at least a month. Thus the customer has leverage over you. You should therefore develop an appropriate credit policy to ensure efficient collection of your receivables (e.g., 2/10 net 30; i.e., a 2 percent discount if the bill is paid within 10 days; otherwise, the payment is due in full in 30 days). The policy might be effective in encouraging speedier payment of invoices, a factor that gains favor in the eyes of the investor.

You should view your receivables, however, as a "double-edged sword"—if they get too high, your customers, rather than you, have the funds, thereby preventing you from making the best use of your money. If, on the other hand, your receivables are too low, your credit policy may be overly restrictive, which may hurt your sales. Continually monitor your average collection period to assess the position of your receivables.

Aging Your Receivables: Aging your accounts receivable is a way of determining what percentage of your receivables are current and past due. Assume that you are aging them on 15-day intervals (and I would suggest a 15-day rather than a 30-day interval); then you can chart your accounts to determine the amount and percent of your receivables in a given category, as demonstrated by the following example.

	Age (Days)	Amount Receivable	
		Dollars	Percent
Current	0–15	25,000	12.5
	16–30	43,000	21.5
Overdue	31–45	47,000	23.5
	46–60	31,000	15.5
	61–75	26,000	13.0
	76–90	12,000	6.0
	More than 90	16,000	8.0
		200,000	100.0

Such a chart will highlight whether your accounts are past due and should alert you to the necessity of using techniques to speed up your collections.

Your Payables, Their Receivables. Your accounts payable are what you owe your suppliers (or creditors). In this case you have taken a loan from your creditors and you have leverage over them.

One effective way to enhance your cash flow position through the use of your payables is to arrange for your suppliers to bill you after your monthly peak in receipts. This will allow the payment to coincide with your strongest cash position.

Like receivables, payables have two sides to them. If your payables are too high, you may be taking unnecessary risks; if they are too low, you may not be taking advantage of the opportunity to use debt to finance your growth. Monitor the extent of your leverage to assess the position of your payables and include this information in your business plan.

When suppliers ship goods to you, they give you, in effect, an "interest-free loan"—generally for a period of 30 days. Take advantage of this. Do not pay for the goods before the schedule requires you to do so; but do not pay late because suppliers are likely to assess a substantial interest penalty and to take away this "privilege" with subsequent deliveries.

Collect Early, Pay Late. The rule of thumb regarding receivables and payables is to collect as early as possible and to pay as late as possible. Naturally, if you collect too early or pay too late, you will likely be penalized.

The following suggestions can help you maintain a solid cash flow position simply by improving your collections and payment practices.

To reduce your receivables and speed up your collections:[14]

- Have periodic phone contacts and visits with customers in order to maintain contact with them and accelerate collections.
- Enclose stamped, self-addressed envelopes with large invoices.
- Establish a minimum purchase for the use of credit cards.
- Offer discounts for advance payments or cash payments.
- Hire a professional credit manager to assist you with collections.
- Adjust salespersons' commissions based on the amount of overdue accounts that they service. (This will also encourage salespersons to do more than just "sell.")
- Charge interest on payments that are late.
- Send invoices out weekly or biweekly rather than monthly.
- Age accounts regularly, preferably on 15-day rather than 30-day intervals.
- Do not deliver new orders until previous bills have been paid.
- Establish the invoice date, rather than the shipping date, as the date when the order is completed.
- Require periodic payments for large jobs rather than one payment after completion of the job.

To increase your payables and slow down your payments:

- Negotiate credit terms based on the date of billing rather than on the date of shipping.
- Negotiate for installment payments to suppliers.
- Join a buyers group to obtain lower finance charges and possibly to allow for longer payment periods.
- Obtain a credit guarantee from your bank to enable your suppliers to give more favorable credit terms.
- Date checks on bank holidays.

"Diddling." Dick Levin, associate dean of the School of Business Administration at the University of North Carolina, has suggested that entrepreneurs

[14]Adapted from B. Bradway and R. Pritchard, *Projecting Profits during Inflation and Recession* (Reading, MA: Addison-Wesley, 1981).

should "diddle" to enhance their cash flow position.[15] Diddling, which is legal, might involve, for example, taking a pessimistic view of the collectibility of your receivables by charging them off as bad debts if they are overdue. When—and if—the accounts are ultimately paid, they will be reported as income; however, you have deferred the tax on that income by initially charging them off as bad debts.

Other examples of "diddling" involve:

- Delayed invoicing, which defers income to a future time period (that is how you can diddle the IRS).
- Early invoicing—billing before the goods are received (if your customers agree to it; they are likely to agree to it if you sweeten the deal with a price discount), which enables you to report income in an earlier period (that is how you can diddle your banker).

Levin warns that diddling without proper records, however, is a big mistake!

Preparing Cash Flow Projections

The general format for developing cash flow projections is as follows:

1. Cash balance (beginning of month) — Cash on hand at the end of previous month
2. Cash receipts:
   a. Cash sales — Cash sales only
   b. Credit collections — Cash collected from credit sales
   c. Loan proceeds — Cash received by you from loans
   d. Other cash receipts — Cash received from other sources
3. Total cash receipts — Add lines 2a through 2d
4. Total cash available — Add line 1 plus line 3
5. Cash paid out:
   a. Expenses:
      (1) Purchases — Merchandise for sales or for use
      (2) Gross wages — Wages plus overtime, bonuses, etc.
      (3) Payroll expenses — Benefits (e.g., health insurance), paid sick leave or vacation, etc.
      (4) Other services — Subcontract labor
      (5) Office supplies — Items used in business and not resold
      (6) Maintenance and repairs — Routine repairs and maintenance including redecorating, painting, etc.
      (7) Advertising — Cost of all forms of advertising
      (8) Automobile — All costs associated with automobiles
      (9) Travel and entertainment — All travel and entertainment costs

[15]See D. Levin, *Buy Low, Sell High, Collect Early, and Pay Late* (Englewood Cliffs, NJ: Prentice-Hall, 1983).

(10)	Consulting services	Accounting, legal, and other consulting services
(11)	Rent	Only leased property
(12)	Telephone	Local plus long-distance phone charges
(13)	Utilities	Electricity, heat, water, etc.
(14)	Insurance	Property, worker's compensation, etc.
(15)	Taxes	Real estate, sales tax, excise tax
(16)	Interest	Interest on loans
(17)	Other expenses	Other expenses not mentioned

b. Total expenses — Add lines 5a1 through 5a17

c. Other expenditures:

(1)	Loan principal payment	Payment on loans
(2)	Capital purchases	Building, equipment, vehicle, leasehold improvements
(3)	Startup costs	Startup costs not included above
(4)	Reserve/escrow	Any escrow amounts
(5)	Owners withdrawal	Wages, health and life insurance, etc.

d. Total other expenditures — Add lines 5c1 through 5c5

6. Total cash disbursements — Add line 5b plus line 5d
7. Cash balance (end of month) — Subtract line 6 from line 4

KEEPING YOUR FINANCES IN BALANCE

The balance sheet (or statement of financial position) provides a listing of your assets, liabilities, and net worth (or equity) at a given time. You will be able to monitor your financial position by calculating various financial ratios based on these figures. (This is discussed in detail in the portion on "Ratio Analysis" later in this section.)

Preparing Balance Sheet Projections

The general format for developing balance sheet projections is as follows:

1. ASSETS:
2. Current assets:

a.	Cash	Cash in checking account
b.	Cash in investments	Savings, certificates of deposit, etc.
c.	Accounts receivable	Amount owed to you from previous sales
d.	Inventory: raw materials	Materials bought from others
e.	Inventory: work in progress	Cost of materials and labor for merchandise you are working on

f. Inventory: finished goods | Finished products ready for sale

g. Prepaid items | Prepaid rent, insurance, etc.

h. Other current assets | Other current assets not included above

3. Total current assets | Add lines 2a through 2h

4. Fixed assets:

    a. Furniture and fixtures | Cost of all furniture/furnishings

    b. Leasehold improvements | Cost of renovations, etc., which add value to property

    c. Machinery and equipment | Cost of all machinery and equipment

    d. Land and building | Cost of property and buildings

5. Total fixed assets | Add lines 4a through 4d

6. Accumulated depreciation | Depreciation on all items on lines 4a through 4d

7. Net fixed assets | Subtract line 6 from line 5

8. Other assets:

    a. Goodwill | The value in excess of the cost of the assets

    b. Miscellaneous | Other items not included above

9. Total other assets | Add line 8a plus line 8b

10. TOTAL ASSETS | Add lines (3 + 7 + 9)

11. LIABILITIES:

12. Current liabilities:

    a. Accounts payable | Bills or amounts you owe to others

    b. Taxes payable | Payroll taxes, real estate taxes, income taxes you owe

    c. Interest payable | Interest payments that you owe

    d. Current portion of long-term debt | Principal portion of any long-term debts

    e. Short-term debt | Lines of credit from bank or short-term debts

    f. Miscellaneous payables | Other items not included above

13. Total current liabilities | Add lines 12a through 12f

14. Long-term liabilities:

    a. Long-term loans | All loans that are over 12 months in term

    b. Less current portion | Subtract out current portion of long-term loans

    c. Total long-term loans | Subtract line 14b from line 14a

    d. Convertible debentures | Amount of any convertible debentures

15. Total long-term   Add line 14c plus line 14d
    liabilities

16. TOTAL LIABILITIES   Add line 13 plus line15

17. EQUITY:
    a. Preferred stock   Amount of preferred stock
    b. Convertible   Amount of convertible preferred stock
       preferred stock
    c. Common stock   Amount of common stock
    d. Paid-in surplus   Amount in excess of par value
    e. Retained earnings   Total earnings achieved over the years

18. TOTAL EQUITY   Add lines 17a through 17e

19. TOTAL LIABILITIES   Add line 16 plus line 18
    AND EQUITY

Note: Line 19 must equal line 10.

Merrill Lynch Pierce Fenner & Smith, the prominent brokerage firm, offers an excellent publication entitled "Understanding Financial Statements" which can help you develop and understand the three financial statements noted above. You can obtain the publication free of charge by contacting your local Merrill Lynch office.

GIVING THE INVESTORS WHAT THEY WANT

Here's where you can gain a substantial advantage over other entrepreneurs seeking funding. It has been said that although all entrepreneurs are not created equal, all venture capitalists are. Typically, venture capitalists and other professional investors in private companies are graduates of the Harvard Business School (or Stanford, Wharton, Northwestern, Columbia, etc.) who have spent two to three years working at a major bank, then two to three years with a management consulting firm, before joining a Small Business Investment Company (SBIC), venture capital company, or investment banking firm. They have been similarly trained in financial analysis and feel most at home when they are examining financial data on the Robert Morris Associates financial forms upon which they have been trained. Why not give them what they know best—prepare your financial projections on Robert Morris (or some similar) forms.

As you can see from the forms on the following pages, the Robert Morris forms[16] present the three key financial statements—earnings statement, cash projections, and statement of financial position—on a single page.

Although the rule of thumb is that professional investors prefer the Robert Morris Associates forms, there are many others who prefer separate statements; furthermore, a very small number of investors do have a positive bias toward computerized spreadsheet (i.e., Lotus, VisiCalc, SuperCalc, etc.) printouts.

It is your responsibility to determine the type of presentation preferred by potential investors in your company. You will be able to learn about their preferences through informal talks with entrepreneurs of companies in their investment portfolio, other investors, and business associates.

[16]Used by permission of Robert Morris Associates,© 1984 RMA.

SUBMITTED BY

DATE

PERIOD

SPREAD IN HUNDREDS ☐
SPREAD IN THOUSANDS ☐

ACTUAL | PROJECTIONS

P R O F I T and L O S S	1	NET SALES	
	2		
	3		
	4	Less Materials Used	
	5	COST OF GOODS SOLD	
	6	GROSS PROFIT	
	7	Less Sales Expense	
	8	General & Administrative Expense	
	9	Depreciation	
	10		
	11	OPERATING PROFIT	
	12	Less Other Expense	
	13	Add Other Income	
	14	PRE TAX PROFIT	
	15	Income Tax Provision	
	16	NET PROFIT	
C A S H P R O J E C T I O N	17	CASH BALANCE (Opening)	
	18	Add Receipts Cash Sales & Other Income	
	19	Cash Sales Plus Receivable Collections	
	20		
	21		
	22	Bank Loan Proceeds	
	23	Other Loan Proceeds	
	24	TOTAL CASH AND RECEIPTS	
	25	Less Disbursements Trade Payables	
	26	Direct Labor	
	27	OPERATING & OTHER EXPENSES	
	28		
	29	Capital Expenditures	
	30	Income Taxes	
	31	Dividends or Withdrawals	
	32	Bank Loan Repayment	
	33	Other Loan Repayment	
	34	TOTAL CASH DISBURSEMENTS	
	35	CASH BALANCE (Closing)	
B A L A N C E S H E E T	36	ASSETS Cash and Equivalents	
	37	Receivables	
	38	Inventory (Net)	
	39		
	40	CURRENT ASSETS	
	41	Fixed Assets (Net)	
	42		
	43		
	44	TOTAL ASSETS	
	45		
	46	LIABILITIES Notes Payable Banks	
	47	Notes Payable Others	
	48	Trade Payables	
	49	Income Tax Payable	
	50	Current Portion L T D	
	51		
	52	CURRENT LIABILITIES	
	53	Long Term Liabilities	
	54		
	55	TOTAL LIABILITIES	
	56		
	57	NET WORTH Capital Stock	
	58	Retained Earnings	
	59		
	60	TOTAL LIABILITIES AND NET WORTH	

© 1984 Robert Morris Associates. Form No. 117 Rev. B 84
Surveyor (Controller) & Johnson
These forms are intended for use in common or lending transactions.
Where any other use is contemplated it is suggested that a careful review
be made to ensure compliance with applicable laws and regulations.
ORDER FROM Banker Systems, Inc., St. Cloud, MN 56302

rma

BALANCE SHEET

Line No.	Title	Instructions
(36 through 44)	**ASSETS**	
36	Cash and Equivalents	Enter cash and readily marketable securities--current year only. For subsequent years use the closing cash balance (line 35).
37	Receivables	Enter actual receivables in the first column. To project, use previous receivables figure plus projected net sales (line 1), minus projected cash sales and receivables collections (line 19).
38	Inventory	Enter actual inventory in the first column. To project, add purchases to beginning inventory. Then, subtract materials used to calculate the ending inventory amount (lines 2 through 4). If the inventory purchase figure is not available, balances can be calculated based on historic turnover ratios.
40	Current Assets	Enter sum of lines 36 through 39.
41	Fixed Assets (Net)	Enter fixed assets. To project, add previous year's fixed assets and any fixed asset additions. Then, deduct estimated accumulated depreciation.
42 through 44		Enter other non-current assets (stockholder's receivables, intangibles, etc.)
45	TOTAL ASSETS	Add lines 40 through 44.
(46 through 56)	**LIABILITIES**	
46	Notes Payable-Banks	Prior period balance plus loan proceeds (line 22), less repayments (line 32).
47	Notes Payable-Others	Prior period balance plus note proceeds (line 23), less repayments (line 32).
48	Trade Payables	Prior period balance plus purchases less payments (line 25). If the inventory purchase figure is not available, balances can be projected based on historic payables turnover.
49	Income Tax Payable	Add prior period balance to income tax provision (line 14) and deduct income taxes paid (line 30).
50	Current Portion Long-Term Debt	Estimate current maturities by entering the sum of prior period debt's maturities and additional bank loan proceeds scheduled repayments.
51		Enter the sum of any other current liabilities.
52	CURRENT LIABILITIES	Enter the sum of lines 46 through 51.
53 through 55	Long-Term Liabilities	Enter long-term liabilities here. Calculate long-term debt by adding previous period long-term debt (line 53) to loan proceeds (line 22 & 23), and subtracting current maturities (line 50).
55	TOTAL LIABILITIES	Enter sum of lines 52 through 55.
(57 through 59)	**NET WORTH**	
57	Capital Stock	Enter current capital stock figure. An increase will occur if capital stock is sold, a decrease will occur if existing stock is repurchased or retired.
58	Retained Earnings	Add prior period retained earnings to projected net profit (line 16), and deduct dividends or withdrawals (line 31).
59		Enter other equity items.
60	TOTAL LIABILITIES AND NET WORTH	Enter sum of lines 56 through 59.

HOW TO USE THIS FORM

RMA's Projection of Financial Statements, Form C-117, may be completed by the banker, the customer, or both working together. It is designed to be flexible and may be used as a:

1) **Projection tool** to provide a picture of the customer's present and future financial condition. Actual and estimated financial data form the basis of the calculations.
2) **Tool for analysis** of the customer's borrowing needs and debt repayment ability.
3) **Budget** to aid in planning for the customer's financial requirements and repaying the banker's credit accommodation.

INSTRUCTIONS: In the first column, enter the actual PROFIT AND LOSS STATEMENT and BALANCE SHEET of the date immediately prior to projection period. Then, in each subsequent column, covering a projection period (e.g., month, quarter, annual).
- Enter on the "date" line, the ending date of each projection period (e.g., 1/31, 3/31, 19____)
- Enter on the "period" line the length of each projection period (e.g., 1 mo., 3 mos., 12 mos.)
- Then, follow the line-by-line instructions below.

Line No.	Title	Instructions
		PROFIT AND LOSS STATEMENT
1	NET SALES	Enter actual or beginning net sales figure in the first vertical column. We suggest you project future net sales based upon a % sales increase or decrease. Estimate acceptable % figure and record here ____%. (This % is generally calculated based on historical changes in net sales. However, consideration must also be given to factors, such as general business conditions, new products and services, and competition.)
2 through 5	COST OF GOODS SOLD	Enter all relevant components of customer's cost of goods sold calculation. Project future cost of goods sold based upon % increase or decrease. Estimate acceptable percentage figure and insert here ____%. (This figure is generally estimated as a percentage of sales based on prior years.)
6	GROSS PROFIT	Line 1 minus line 5.
7 through 10	Sales Expense, General and Administrative Expenses, Other	Enter all items. Project future expenses based on an increase or decrease. Estimate acceptable percentage figure and insert here ____%. (This figure is generally estimated as a percentage of sales based on prior years. Anticipated increases in major expenses, such as lease, officers' salaries, etc., should also be considered.)
11	OPERATING PROFIT to Operating Profit	Line 6 minus the sum of lines 7 through 10.
12 through 13	Various adjustments	Enter all items and estimate future adjustments.
14	PRE-TAX PROFIT	Line 11 minus the sum of lines 12 through 13.
15	Income Tax Provision	Common methods used for calculating Income Tax Provision include the most current year's tax as a % of the Pre-Tax Profit.
16	NET PROFIT	Line 11 minus the sum of lines 12 through 15.
		CASH PROJECTION CALCULATION
17	CASH BALANCE	Enter opening cash balance. For subsequent periods, enter the closing cash balance (Line 35) from previous period. Or enter an adjusted amount to reflect a desired cash balance.
18 through 21	Receipts	Enter total cash sales & other income plus receivables collected. Receivable collections must be calculated separately. This requires an analysis of the customer's sales and collection patterns.

(1) Estimate the portion of each month's sales collected in that month and subsequent months.
(2) From the sale's figure last month and the previous month(s), calculate how much of the existing receivable figure will be collected in the current month.
(3) Deduct the collected receivables balance calculated in (2) above from the month-end balance of accounts receivables.
(4) Add this month's sales figure to the remainder of receivables calculated in (3) above. This figure is the new accounts receivable figure for the end of the current month.

EXAMPLE Assumptions:
Projection calculation - monthly

Monthly Net Sales	9/30	$250M
	10/31	$300M
	11/30	$150M
Accounts Receivable balance:	9/30	$250M
	10/31	$367M

To determine receivable collections for November --

Accounts Receivable balance, 10/31		$367M
Deduct: 66% of 10/31 sales	200M	
33% of 9/30 sales	83M	283M
		84M
Add 11/30 sales		150M
Accounts Receivable Balance, 11/30		$234M

The average collection period is 45 days. This means that 66.7% (30 days ÷ 45 days) of each month's sales will be collected the following month and the remaining 33.3% in the second month.

Line No.	Title	Instructions
22 through 23	Bank Loan Proceeds/ Other	Enter actual or projected bank loan proceeds on line 22. Enter any other receipts on line 23.
24	TOTAL CASH AND RECEIPTS	Enter sum of lines 17 through 23.
25 through 33	Disbursements	Enter actual or estimated cash disbursements on these lines.
34	TOTAL DISBURSEMENTS	Enter sum of lines 25 through 33.
35	CASH BALANCE (Closing)	Line 24 minus line 34. Note: The closing cash balance on line 35 may be entered on line 17 in the next column. However, if the closing cash balance is negative, or below the desired opening cash balance, then bank loans (line 22) may be needed to raise the closing cash balance to zero, or to the desired opening cash balance. The bank loan necessitates planning for repayment (line 31 and 32) in subsequent columns.

EFFECTIVE CONTROLS

Financial statements provide a system of controls that will enable business owners to prevent potential problems *before* they occur. As businesses grow, one of the biggest problems facing them is inadequate controls. Investors will want to see that you have taken steps to monitor and enforce controls wherever appropriate.

Philip Edelstein, who runs Danbury Plumbing Services in Danbury, Connecticut, has developed a unique way to impress on his employees the importance of cost controls. Edelstein posts a chart of the company's revenues and expenses every month. He also allocates 15 percent of the firm's profits for a "minibonus" pool which are distributed to the company's 20 employees each month, based on their salary level and seniority. The company paid out $100,000 in minibonuses last year while experiencing a level of sales per employee of $400,000, twice the industry average.

Be Specific about Your Costs

If you sell more than one product or service, you will need to organize your costs to determine which lines are profitable and which are not. This will assist you considerably in cost control and in managerial decision making.

If you refer to the projected earnings statement presented earlier, you will notice that some of the expenses (e.g., raw materials) are directly associated with a product, while other expenses (e.g., rent) must be allocated to several products. The allocation can be based on square footage of plant space, number of people per department, capital cost of machinery per product, percentage of sales, and so on. Such an allocation will enable you to develop an accurate cost per unit for the various products that your company offers. You will then be able to use those cost figures to provide a basis for pricing, to estimate the costs of expended production, or to modify or expand a product line.

Numerous small businesses fail because they do not utilize any system of cost control and thus do not have any idea of their costs for *each* product line. I know of one manufacturing company that was under the impression that it was operating profitably, yet 50 percent of its product lines were unprofitable to maintain. Without knowing which products are the most profitable, you are likely to make improper decisions regarding your product mix.

It is highly advisable that you work with an accountant to establish a system of cost controls for your business. In addition, an excellent reference in management cost control is William Rotch et al., *The Executive's Guide to Management Accounting and Control Systems* (Houston: Dame Publications, 1982).

Good record keeping is essential for any business. You should speak to an accountant about developing a system of records that will keep track of your:

- Revenues and expenses
- Receivables and payables
- Inventory (so that you will always have enough on hand for your customers, but not more than you can sell)
- Payroll

In addition, the system should be set up in a way that will allow you to prepare your income taxes as easily as possible.

The National Association of Accountants (NAA), which has over 300 chapters nationwide, provides assistance on these matters to persons who are starting a business. You can contact them at the following address for assistance:

> National Association of Accountants
> 919 Third Avenue
> New York, NY 10022
> (212) 354-9700

CAPITAL ACQUISITIONS

An important financial consideration that directly affects the amount of funding that you will require is the acquisition of long-term fixed assets. These can be acquired through leasing or buying.

A lease is a long-term agreement to rent any asset, such as buildings, land, or equipment. The user (or lessee) makes periodic payments to the owner of the asset (or lessor).

Advantages and Disadvantages of Leasing

Is it advisable to lease, rather than buy, the asset? There are several advantages to leasing fixed assets. These include:

- There is no need for a large initial cash outlay or for a down payment. (This is one way to reduce the likelihood of undercapitalization.)
- There are no restrictions on a company's financial operations.
- The payments are often spread out over a longer period and can be lower than they are for loans.
- There is protection against the risk of equipment obsolescence. (This is especially important in the case of leasing computer or other high-technology equipment.)
- There may be tax benefits in leasing. Lease payments are tax deductible as operating expenses, whereas purchase payments are not. (Make sure, however, that your lease is a "true lease" and not an installment purchase.)

However, there are some major disadvantages of leasing assets:

- Leasing generally costs more than purchasing.
- You lose the use of the asset at the end of the term of the lease.
- You lose the benefit of price appreciation of the asset.
- You cannot cancel a lease agreement; it is a long-term legal obligation.

The Lease Agreement

If you decide to lease an asset, examine the lease agreement carefully, paying particular attention to:

- The nature of the financing
- The payment amounts and terms
- The disposition of the asset at the end of the term
- Who gets the investment tax credit
- Who is responsible for maintenance and taxes
- Renewal options and cancellation penalties
- Other special provisions

An accountant will be able to assist you in determining whether or not you should lease a particular asset. Furthermore, you should have an attorney review the lease agreement before you accept its terms.

BREAK-EVEN ANALYSIS

Break-even analysis is a simple mathematical model that provides answers to many important "what if" questions. For example: (1) If prices increase by 5 percent, what is the effect on profits? (2) If fixed costs decrease by 10 percent, what happens to the break-even point? (3) If fixed costs decrease by 10 percent, prices increase by 5 percent, and we want to increase profits at the rate of 10 percent, how many units must we sell?

In addition, break-even analysis is an important concern to the investor, since he or she will be interested in the downside risk of the business venture. For the investor the question becomes how few units need to be sold without suffering a loss. Specifically, at the break-even point, the total expenses are equal to the total revenues. Revenues above that point constitute profits, whereas revenues below that point constitute losses. If a company projects sales of 10,000 units but needs to sell only 5000 units to break even, it will be profitable with all sales above 50 percent of its projected volume.

To determine break-even estimates, the following data must be available:

- *Variable costs.* Costs that vary directly with the number of units sold; they include materials plus labor plus a percentage of overhead directly allocated to the sale of a given number of units.
- *Fixed costs.* Costs that remain unchanged with the number of units sold; they include rent, utilities, insurance, administrative salaries, etc.
- *Total costs.* Variable costs plus fixed costs.
- *Selling price per unit.*

Break-even is calculated by using the following formulas:

$$\text{break-even point (in units)} = \frac{\text{total fixed costs}}{\text{selling price (per unit)} - \text{variable cost (per unit)}}$$

$$\text{break-even point (in dollars)} = \text{break-even point (in units)} \times \text{selling price (per unit)}$$

As an example, assume that Ice Creamery, Inc. produces ice cream at a cost of $1 per gallon. They sell the ice cream in 5-gallon tins for $10 apiece to retailers. The firm's fixed costs are $40,000 per year. Thus the break-even point in units is

$$\frac{\$40,000}{\$10/\text{unit} - \$5/\text{unit}} = 8000 \text{ units}$$

Furthermore, the company will reach its break-even point in revenues when they sell

$$8000 \text{ units} \times \$10/\text{unit} = \$80,000$$

Another valuable use of break-even analysis is in making decisions regarding pricing. For example, assume that Ice Creamery wants to lower their price to their retailers by $1/unit without any changes in fixed costs or variable costs per unit. The break-even volume would then be increased as follows:

$$\frac{\$40,000}{\$9/\text{unit} - \$5/\text{unit}} = 10,000 \text{ units}$$

Also, the company would be required to sell $10,000 more of their ice cream to break even:

$$10,000 \text{ units} \times \$9/\text{unit} = \$90,000$$

RATIO ANALYSIS: ASSESSING YOUR FINANCIAL POSITION

Ratio analysis is a rigorous approach to evaluate the financial condition and performance of a company. The ratios can be calculated from figures on the earnings statement and balance sheet. Current and projected ratios should be compared to the past performance of the company and to the past or present performance of similar firms in the industry. The ratios should be discussed in your business plan.

There are four types of financial ratios that you should monitor regularly:

1. Liquidity ratios
2. Profitability ratios
3. Leverage ratios
4. Activity ratios

Liquidity ratios indicate the amount of cash or short-term assets available to the firm. If the liquidity position gets too high, the firm is sacrificing profitability; if the liquidity position gets too low, the firm may not be able to meet its current obligations.

Examples:

a. Current ratio $\quad = \quad \dfrac{\text{current assets}}{\text{current liabilities}}$

(measures the extent to which the claims of the short-term creditors are covered by the firm's current or short-term assets)

b. Quick ratio $= \quad \dfrac{\text{current assets} \ - \ \text{inventory}}{\text{current liabilities}}$
(acid test ratio)

(measures the extent to which the claims of the short-term creditors are covered by the firm without it having to sell its inventory)

c. Inventory to
net working
capital $\quad\quad = \quad \dfrac{\text{inventory}}{\text{current assets} \ - \ \text{current liabilities}}$

(measures the extent to which the company's working capital is tied up in inventory)

Profitability ratios indicate how well the company has performed.

Examples:

a. Gross profit margin $\quad = \quad \dfrac{\text{sales} \ - \ \text{cost of sales and services}}{\text{sales}}$

(measures the margin available to cover a company's operating expenses and yield a profit)

b. Net profit margin $\quad = \quad \dfrac{\text{net income}}{\text{sales}}$

c. Return on assets $\quad = \quad \dfrac{\text{net income}}{\text{total assets}}$
(return on investment)

(measures the return on investment of both the stockholders and creditors)

d. Return on equity $\quad = \quad \dfrac{\text{net income}}{\text{total equity}}$

(measures the return on investment of the stockholders)

e. Earnings per share $\quad = \quad \dfrac{\text{net income}}{\text{number of common shares outstanding}}$

(measures the profitability of the company, adjusted for the number of shares the company has issued)

Leverage ratios indicate how the company finances its operations. If a firm's leverage (debt) is too high, it may be taking great risks; if it is too low, it is not taking advantage of opportunities to use long-term debt to finance growth.

Examples:

a. Debt to assets $= \dfrac{\text{total debt}}{\text{total assets}}$

(measures the extent to which a firm borrows money to finance its operations)

b. Debt to equity $= \dfrac{\text{total debt}}{\text{total equity}}$

(measures the creditor's funds as a percentage of stockholders' funds)

c. Long-term debt to equity $= \dfrac{\text{long-term debt}}{\text{total equity}}$

(measures the balance between a firm's debt and its equity)

Activity ratios indicate the productive efficiency of the firm: Generally, higher activity ratios are associated with higher profitability (due to high productive efficiency).

Examples:

a. Inventory turnover $= \dfrac{\text{sales}}{\text{inventory}}$

(measures the amount of inventory that a firm uses to generate its sales)

b. Fixed-asset turnover $= \dfrac{\text{sales}}{\text{net plant}}$

(measures how efficiently the plant is utilized by the company to generate its sales)

c. Average collection period $= \dfrac{\text{accounts receivable}}{\text{average daily sales}}$

(measures the average time period to receive payment from customers)

Sources of Information on Financial Ratios

You will be able to obtain information on financial ratios for most industries from the following sources:

- *Almanac of Business and Industrial Financial Ratios* (Englewood Cliffs, NJ: Prentice-Hall) (annual)

- *Annual Statement Studies* (Philadelphia: Robert Morris Associates) (annual)
- *Dun's Review* (New York: Dun & Bradstreet) (annual)
- Various trade associations

CONCLUDING REMARKS

We have just discussed how to determine your financial needs. Clearly, two of the biggest errors made by entrepreneurs are that they tend to underestimate their costs while they overestimate the demand for their product or service. My own general rule regarding this is: Once you have developed your cost and sales estimates for the coming years, double your cost projections and divide your sales projections by a factor of 2 to 3 to obtain more realistic estimates. If, after working through the calculations, the projections still look attractive, you can begin to get excited. As noted by one perceptive banker after reviewing an entrepreneur's projected financing needs: "Now that you've told me how much money you'll need to get yourself into trouble, how much will you need to get out of trouble?"

Perhaps the most ironic fact regarding financial projections is that although they are one of the most carefully scrutinized portions of the business plan, they are rarely achieved. In fact, over the past 12 years in which I have been reading business plans, I have seen only a handful of companies that have surpassed their financial projections. (Lotus Development, for example, after forecasting first-year sales of $6 million, posted revenues of $53 million, much to the pleasure of one of their investors, Sevin Rosen Management Co.) True, several ventures have achieved levels of 70, 80, or 90 percent of their projections, thereby earning extremely attractive returns for their investors, but few have achieved the levels that they projected. For that reason, a best case, worst case, and most likely case set of projections will paint a more realistic picture for the investor.

Once you know how much money your venture will require, your next task is to obtain the necessary funding. From where will you obtain these funds? How will you convince investors that your venture warrants their investment? In Part IV of this book we discuss various sources of funding.

VI. ORGANIZATION AND MANAGEMENT

The quality of management is, perhaps, the single most important factor considered by the investor. In fact, this is often the first item that he or she will examine. Most investors prefer a mediocre product with a first-rate management team to a first-rate product with a mediocre management team. Also recognize that investors prefer to fund management teams rather than individual entrepreneurs. It is essential that you demonstrate that you have a management team that is committed to your business and with the necessary skills to ensure that the plan will be carried out properly.

VIA. KEY PERSONNEL

VIA1. Provide an organization chart that clearly delineates the responsibilities of the managers. Indicate if any of the managers have already worked together and what the experiences were. Your goal is to demonstrate to investors that you have a management team with expertise in marketing, finance, and operations.

VIA2. Provide a chart of the key executives/managers of the company along with their primary (and secondary) responsibilities. Include a brief statement of their career highlights that demonstrates their ability to perform these responsibilities. You should also include their ages, experience in the industry, and experience with the company. Also include in the appendices the résumés of key executives as well as financial information about them and character references.

VIA3. Establish the initial salaries, bonuses, pensions, and other benefits for the key managers. In general, salaries should be in line with industry averages; yet salaries should be modest if you expect to obtain financing for an emerging growth business. Deferred compensation, however, in terms of stock options is desirable, as it demonstrates long-term commitment.

When issuing stock, it is highly advisable that it be made available to key executives over a period of perhaps three or four years. This encourages the executives to think strategically and enhances the likelihood that they will remain with the company for an extended period of time.

VIA4. Describe the key executive positions that must be filled over the next two to three years. What unique skills and experience will be necessary? You must demonstrate an ability to plan for the growth of your business and to attract and maintain personnel. In addition, provide information on potential candidates and on areas of responsibility.

VIA5. Provide a list of the current and proposed members of the board of directors along with a few sentences describing their backgrounds. Include the names, ages, corporate affiliations, compensations, ownership, and contribution of each of the directors. Also, provide a rationale for the choice of these directors. Investors want to see a board of directors that can provide contacts, expertise, and experience to the company.

VIA6. State the legal, accounting, banking, and advertising organizations that will work with you and discuss the value that they serve. What are the costs associated with their services? Also, demonstrate how these people will assist you in business decisions and in making contacts. Investors recognize that experienced professional help will enhance the likelihood of success of the company. In addition, these professionals can serve as an important source of contacts.

VIB. OTHER PERSONNEL

VIBI. How many employees have you hired over the past five years? How many do you plan to hire over the next few years? For which positions? Describe their responsibilities. What percentage are skilled versus unskilled? How will they be compensated?

VIB2. Provide some information on how you will staff the organization.

VIB3. How will employees share in the wealth of the company? What provisions are there for employee ownership, profit sharing, and so on? What is the rationale for such programs?

VIC. MISCELLANEOUS ISSUES

VICI. Describe the extent of insurance coverage for the company and its officers. List policies that are presently in effect. Keep in mind that although insurance premiums reduce cash flow, they limit contingent downside liability.

VIC2. Discuss any other key issues of concern regarding organization and management.

VID. CONTINGENCY PLANS

VID1. Provide some information on your contingency plans in organizing and managing the company.

VII. OWNERSHIP

VIIA. STRUCTURE OF BUSINESS

VIIA1. Describe the legal form of business—sole proprietorship, partnership, corporation—that you have selected and the rationale for the choice. Discuss any special features related to legal structure, such as limited partnerships, S status, 1244 stock, foreign corporation, and so on.

VIIA2. Explain all mergers, consolidations, and reorganizations that the company has gone through. Merger activity will indicate growth potential to the investor.

VIIA3. Describe all franchise, royalty, licensing, and working agreements currently in effect and planned over the coming years.

VIIB. FINANCING/EQUITY CONSIDERATIONS

VIIB1. Describe the following features of the stock of your corporation:

- The number of shares of stock authorized and issued. (*Note:* The number of shares authorized is the maximum number of shares that may be issued. The company is not obligated to issue all the shares that it authorizes.)
- The price per share of stock.
- The average price paid for a share of stock by officers and directors.
- Voting rights, dividend payments, and conversion features (e.g., debt with warrants, convertible debentures, etc.) of the stock.

VIIB2. List all owners (individuals, corporations, and trusts) and their share of stock owned or available under warrants or conversion privileges. How will the ownership change after receiving financing? For example, assume that investor A owns 250,000 shares of the original 500,000 shares issued by the company. If the company issues an additional 500,000 shares, investor A's ownership position will be reduced from 50 percent (250,000/500,000) to 25 percent (250,000/1,000,000). What percentage of stock is owned by employees? Also, what changes in ownership have taken place in recent years? Frequent changes are often indicative of instability.

VIIB3. How much of an investment have you and the other officers made in the business? Is it debt or equity? Explain the rationale. Investors will want to see that the owners are making a contribution to the business and are committed to the long-term success of the company.

VIIB4. Briefly describe the funding that will be necessary, in both the form of debt and equity, for your business over the next three to five years. When will you need the funds? Investors prefer to disburse cash in stages rather than in one lump sum. How do you intend to use the money? Investors generally feel that expenditures for R&D are more risky than are expenditures for capital acquisitions or for marketing. You should include a chart of projected capital requirements in the appendices.

VIIB5. Describe the financing arrangement that you propose. Although the terms are negotiable, investors generally wish to see a well-structured deal. If debt, what will be used as collateral? Personal guarantees look very attractive to the investor because they reduce the risk of his or her investment; however, such a financial arrangement is far less attractive to the entrepreneur (or any other guarantor) who takes on increased personal risk. If equity, how much ownership in the company will be given up? What are the projected annual returns for the investors? How many investors are sought? What is the minimum investment required by each investor? How will the investors get their money out (i.e., buyback, acquisition, initial public offering, etc.)?

VIII.   CRITICAL RISKS AND PROBLEMS

It is important that you identify the potential risks (i.e., "show-stoppers") to the company; if an investor discovers any unstated negative factors, it can undermine the credibility of the entire plan. Furthermore, by identifying risks, you demonstrate some very good managerial skills and show the investor that you are prepared for contingency events.

VIIIA.   DESCRIPTION OF RISKS

Identify the key risks in the following areas and determine their potential impact on the company:

VIIIA1.   Cost overruns in R&D and production
VIIIA2.   Failure to meet production deadlines
VIIIA3.   Problems with suppliers and distributors
VIIIA4.   Sales projections not attained
VIIIA5.   Unforeseen industry trends
VIIIA6.   Competitive price cutting
VIIIA7.   Unforeseen economic, political, social, and technological developments
VIIIA8.   Capital shortages
VIIIA9.   Cyclical fluctuations
VIIIA10.   Other risks

Discuss the steps you intend to take to manage these critical risks.

IX. SUMMARY AND CONCLUSIONS

IXA. SUMMARY

Briefly summarize the key features of the report, paying special attention to:

IXA1. The unique features of your company, stressing the importance of user benefit.

IXA2. Your overall strategic direction—how you will coordinate all aspects of the company to achieve and sustain your long-term goals.

IXA3. Your expected sales and profits and the amount and length of time necessary to attain the projected level of sales and profits.

IXA4. Your capital requirements. Also include the amount of investment that you have personally made in the business and the percentage of ownership for yourself and for the investors.

IXB. SCHEDULING

Develop—in chart form—a planned schedule or timetable for your business. This will let the investor know when you will need the funding and in what amounts. For a startup business, you should include the expected dates for the following (only for those applicable to your business):

- Seeking legal counsel
- Filing the necessary documents for establishing the desired legal structure of the business
- Completion of research design and development
- Completion of prototype
- Purchase/lease of plant and equipment
- Selection of production personnel
- Ordering of production materials
- Beginning of production
- Selection of sales personnel
- Receipt of first orders
- Beginning of sales
- Receipt of first cash or payments of first accounts receivables
- Other critical dates (e.g., when important legislation becomes effective, etc.)

Create slack in the schedule whenever appropriate.

Section 3

Appendices

At a minimum, the appendices should include the basic financial statements of the company: profit and loss statement, cash projections, and balance sheet. More complete appendices would include the following:

- Photographs of product
- Sales and profitability objectives
- Market surveys
- Production flowcharts
- Price lists or catalogs
- Sample advertisements or press releases
- Financial statements:
  - —Historical financial statements
  - —Startup costs
  - —Projected profit and loss statement
  - —Projected statement of cash projections
  - —Projected balance sheet
- Fixed-asset acquisition schedule
- Break-even analysis
- Résumés and character references
- Individual and organizational tax returns

PART III

WORKSHEETS FOR DEVELOPING THE BUSINESS PLAN

COVER PAGE
TABLE OF CONTENTS
TABLE OF APPENDICES
EXECUTIVE SUMMARY
    I.   Background and Purpose
   II.   Market Analysis
  III.   Development and Production
  IV.   Marketing
   V.   Financial Data
  VI.   Organization and Management
 VII.   Ownership
VIII.   Critical Risks and Problems
  IX.   Summary and Conclusions
APPENDICES

The worksheets in this part parallel the material in Part II of this workbook. The worksheets will help you organize and outline your thoughts as you prepare the business plan.

(Logo—if available)

BUSINESS PLAN

(Name of Company)

(_____Address_____)

(_____)

(Phone Number)

Established: (_____Date_____)

Contact person: (_____Name_____); (_____Position_____)

(Date of Application)

Copy _____ of _____ copies distributed

This business plan contains proprietary information that is not to be shared, copied, disclosed, or otherwise compromised without the consent of (Name of Company).

TABLE OF CONTENTS

TABLE OF APPENDICES

EXECUTIVE SUMMARY

(Name of Company) _____

(Address) _____

_____

(Phone Number) _____

Contact person: (Name) _____ ; (Position) _____

Date: _____

_____

A. Description of Business

Nature of product(s)/service(s):

Unique features of product(s)/service(s):

Objectives; expected accomplishments (in terms of revenues, growth rate, market share, etc.)

i

B. Strategic Direction

Stage of business (i.e., startup, growth, turnaround, etc.):

Long range direction:

C. Market/Marketing

Market segment(s) sought:

Benefits of product(s)/service(s) to this market segment:

Summary of advertising/pricing/distribution policy:

Sales projections:

ii

129

D. Management

    Backgrounds:

    Responsibilities:

E. Financial Features

	Actual 19____	Actual 19____	Actual 19____	Projected 19____	Projected 19____	Projected 19____
Revenues						
Net income						
Assets						
Liabilities						
Net worth						

    Capital needed; how it will be used:

iii

F. Financial Arrangements/Exit:

Terms of the deal (i.e., debt/collateral arrangement; alternatively, how much equity will be given up in exchange for capital):

Expected annual return for investor:

Number of investors sought; minimum investment required by each investor:

How investors will get their money out (i.e., buyback, acquisition, public offering, etc.):

Summary of Financing:

	Current Amount	Amount Needed
Debt	$_____	$_____
Debt with warrants	$_____	$_____
Convertible debentures	$_____	$_____
Preferred stock	$_____	$_____
Common stock	$_____	$_____

iv

I. BACKGROUND AND PURPOSE

IA. History

   IA1. Brief synopsis:

IB. Current Conditions

   IB1. Description of product(s)/service(s):

         Nature of product(s)/service(s)

         Principal applications of product(s)/service(s)

         Nature of industry/target market

   IB2. Planned new products:

1

IB. Current Conditions (continued)

    IB3. Technical description of product:

    IB4. Technical tests performed:

        Description of tests

        Results of tests

        Future tests to be conducted

2

I. BACKGROUND AND PURPOSE (continued)

IC. The Concept

IC1. Key success factors of such a product(s)/service(s) (e.g., price competitiveness, quality, marketing capabilities, etc.):

Competitors demonstrating such factors

Which of these factors are demonstrated by your company?

3

IC.   The Concept (continued)

IC2.   Unique features of product(s)/service(s) (i.e., distinct competences or competitive advantages):

Benefit of the product(s)/service(s) to the customer (i.e., Will it save money? Improve quality? etc.)

IC3.   Unique aspects of your strategy [i.e., how you will produce, distribute, and/or market your product(s)/service(s)]:

4

ID.   Overall Objectives

    ID1.   Objectives:

    ID2.   Strategic (long-range) goals:

IE.   Specific Objectives

    IE1.   Revenues/sales:

    IE2.   Profitability:

    IE3.   Market standing:

I. BACKGROUND AND PURPOSE (continued)

IE. Specific Objectives (continued)

  IE4. Product (service) quality:

  IE5. Innovation:

  IE6. Efficiency/productivity:

  IE7. Employee morale:

  IE8. Management development:

  IE9. Social concern/social responsibility:

6

II. MARKET ANALYSIS

IIA. Market Research

    IIA1. Results of market research studies:

        Reaction to prototype

        Market research studies to be conducted

7

II. MARKET ANALYSIS (continued)

IIB. Overall Market

    IIB1. Description of overall market (present and projected):

        Location

        Size in dollars/units

        Trends

        Characteristics

        Buying habits of clients/customers

II. MARKET ANALYSIS (continued)

IIB.   Overall Market (continued)

IIB2.   List of leading companies in industry:

IIB3.   Projected industry sales:

			Present Year		
	19___	19___	19___	19___	19___
Revenues—best case					
Percent growth					
Revenues—most likely case					
Percent growth					
Revenues—worst case					
Percent growth					
Projected market share					

9

II. MARKET ANALYSIS (continued)

IIC.   Specific Market Segment

    IIC1. Description of specific target market (present and projected):

        Location

        Size in dollars/units

        Trends

        Characteristics

        Buying habits of clients/customers

10

II. MARKET ANALYSIS (continued)

IIC. Specific Market Segment (continued)

IIC2. List of leading companies in specific target market:

IIC3. Projected industry sales for this segment:

	19___	19___	Present Year 19___	19___	19___
Revenues— best case					
Percent growth					
Revenues— most likely case					
Percent growth					
Revenues— worst case					
Percent growth					
Projected market share					

IIC4. Means of assessing target market in future:

11

IID.   Competitive Factors

    IID1.   Description and assessment of leading competitors:

        Current business focus

        Annual revenues

        Market share

        Profitability

        Other factors

12

IID. Competitive Factors (continued)

IID1. Description and assessment of leading competitors (continued):

Nature of Competition

Relative
Strengths

Relative
Weaknesses

Competitor A:

_____

Competitor B:

_____

Competitor C:

_____

Competitor D:

_____

Competitor E:

_____

II.   MARKET ANALYSIS (continued)

IID.   Competitive Factors (continued)

   IID1.   Description and assessment of leading competitors (continued):

Advantages over Competitors

Price:

Performance:

Durability:

Versatility:

Speed or accuracy:

Ease of operation or use:

Ease of maintenance:

Ease and cost of installation:

Size or weight:

Styling or appearance:

Other features:

14

II. MARKET ANALYSIS (continued)

IID. Competitive Factors (continued)

IID1. Description and assessment of leading competitors (continued):

Advantages of Competitors over You

Price:

Performance:

Durability:

Versatility:

Speed or accuracy:

Ease of operation or use:

Ease of maintenance:

Ease and cost of installation:

Size or weight:

Styling or appearance:

Other features:

II. MARKET ANALYSIS (continued)

IID. Competitive Factors (continued)

    IID2. Description and assessment of potential competitors:

        Current business focus

        Annual revenues

        Market share

        Profitability

        Barriers to entry

        Other factors

16

IID.   Competitive Factors (continued)

    IID3.   List and description of largest clients/customers:

        Amount and percentage of sales represented by largest client/customer

        Amount and percentage of sales represented by five largest clients/customers

        Credit terms offered to leading clients/customers

        Promising prospective clients/customers

II. MARKET ANALYSIS (continued)

IID. Competitive Factors (continued)

    IID4. Description and assessment of largest suppliers:

        Amount and percentage of purchases represented by largest supplier

        Amount and percentage of purchases represented by five largest suppliers

        Credit terms offered by leading suppliers

        Promising prospective suppliers

    IID5. Description and assessment of substitute (alternative) products/services:

18

II.   MARKET ANALYSIS (continued)

IIE.   Other Market Influences

IIE1.   Impact of the following:

Economic factors

Indicators

Technological factors

Indicators

Government influences

Indicators

19

IIE. Other Market Influences (continued)

IIE1. Impact of the following (continued):

Social/demographic factors

Indicators

Seasonal fluctuations

Indicators

Other factors

Indicators

20

II. MARKET ANALYSIS (continued)

IIF. Sales Forecasts

IIF1. Sales projections for your company (in dollars and units)

	19___	19___	19___	19___	19___
Best case					
Dollars					
Units					
Most likely case					
Dollars					
Units					
Worst case					
Dollars					
Units					

III. DEVELOPMENT AND PRODUCTION

IIIA. <u>Research and Development</u>

    IIIA1. Description of competitive technologies:

        Competences of engineering staff

        In-house versus subcontract R&D activity

    IIIA2. Patent or copyright position:

    IIIA3. Measures to protect competitive technologies:

22

III. DEVELOPMENT AND PRODUCTION (continued)

IIIA. Research and Development (continued)

IIIA4. Regulatory considerations:

IIIA5. New research and development activities to be undertaken in coming years:

Obstacles (costs, widespread acceptance, etc.)

IIIA6. New products planned:

Obstacles (costs, widespread acceptance, etc.)

III. DEVELOPMENT AND PRODUCTION (continued)

IIIB. Production Requirements

    IIIB1. Description of production requirements (including costs at different levels of volume):

        Materials/supplies (including availability)

        Labor (including skills, availability, unionization, etc.)

        Facilities/plant location (including zoning, storage space, parking, capacity, etc.)

24

IIIB. Production Requirements (continued)

    IIIB1. Description of production requirements (continued):

        Equipment (including maintenance, depreciation, insurance, etc.)

        Transportation/shipping

        Seasonal effects

    IIIB2. Competitive advantages in production:

        Quality

        Costs

25

III. DEVELOPMENT AND PRODUCTION (continued)

IIIC.   Production Process

   IIIC1.   Description of production process:

   Stages of process

   Costs at various stages

   Difficulties and risks at various stages

   IIIC2.   Rationale for producing as compared to subcontracting:

26

IIID.   Quality Assurance/Quality Control

Description of quality assurance/quality control procedures:

Defect rate

Trend in defect rate

IIIE.   Contingency Plans

IV. MARKETING

IVA. Marketing Orientation

    IVA1. Description of marketing philosophy:

IVB. Marketing Strategy

    IVB1. Specific target market sought:

        Environmental opportunities

        Company strengths

        Ability to capitalize on the weaknesses of competitors

    IVB2. Overall marketing strategy:

28

159

IVB.   Marketing Strategy (continued)

IVB3.   Image you want to portray:

IVB4.   Pricing strategy:

List prices

Profit margins

Discount prices

Competitors' prices

IVB5.   Credit policy:

29

IVB.   Marketing Strategy (continued)

IVB6.   Channels of distribution (e.g., direct sales, wholesalers, brokers, mail order, etc.):

Costs

Geographic location

IVB7.   Advertising/promotion (e.g., radio, TV, newspapers, telephone, mail, trade journals, point-of-purchase promotions, giveaways, personal endorsements):

Costs of advertising

30

IV. MARKETING (continued)

IVB. Marketing Strategy (continued)

IVB8. Warranties/guarantees:

IVB9. Branding/packaging/labeling:

Costs of branding/packaging/labeling

IVC. Contingency Plans

31

162

V. FINANCIAL DATA

VA. <u>Current Financial Position</u>

    VA1. Summarize highlights of financial statements:

        Startup costs

        Profit and loss statement

        Cash flow analysis

        Balance sheet

    VA2. Unusual items on financial statements:

32

VB.   Payables/Receivables

VB1.   Debts:

Current lines of credit

Accounts payable over 90 days past due

Turnover of accounts payable

VB2.   Receivables:

Uncollectibles

Accounts receivable over 90 days past due

Customers with receivables of 10 percent or more of total accounts receivable

Turnover of accounts receivable

Average age of receivables

33

VC. Cost Control

    VC1. Monitoring of funds:

        Responsibility

VD. Break-Even Analysis

    VD1. Break-even estimates:

        Units

        Dollars

        Market share needed for break-even

34

VE. Financial Ratios

VE1. Liquidity:

Current ratio

Quick ratio

Inventory to net working capital

Implications of liquidity ratios

VE2. Profitability:

Gross profit margin

Return on assets

Return on equity

Implications of profitability ratios

35

VE. Financial Ratios (continued)

VE3. Leverage/debt:

Debt to assets

Debt to equity

Long-term debt to equity

Implications of leverage ratios

VE4. Activity:

Inventory turnover

Fixed-asset turnover

Average collection period

Implications of activity ratios

VE5. Summary of performance:

V. FINANCIAL DATA (continued)

VF. Financial Projections

    VF1. Assumptions:

    VF2. Projections:

        Summarize highlights of projected financial statements

VI.   ORGANIZATION AND MANAGEMENT

VIA.   Key Personnel

VIA1.   Organization chart:

VIA2.   Executive team:

Name	Position	Age

Descriptions, responsibilities and backgrounds of key managers

38

VIA.   Key Personnel (continued)

VIA3.   Compensation (including stock and other incentive bonuses) of key managers:

Name	Compensation	Stock Options Granted	Options Avg. Price	Options Exercised

VIA4.   Key managers needed:

Unique skills and experience necessary

VIA5.   Members of board of directors and their affiliations:

Current

Proposed

39

VI. ORGANIZATION AND MANAGEMENT (continued)

VIA. Key Personnel (continued)

   VIA6. Other firms assisting you:

   Legal

   Accounting

   Consulting

   Banking

   Insurance

   Advertising

   Other

VIB.   Other Personnel

    VIB1.   Employees hired:

        Current

        Proposed

        Skilled versus unskilled

        Compensation

    VIB2.   Staffing/training:

41

VI. ORGANIZATION AND MANAGEMENT (continued)

VIB.   Other Personnel (continued)

   VIB3.   Profit sharing for employees:

VIC.   Miscellaneous Issues

   VIC1.   Insurance coverage:

   VIC2.   Other issues:

VID.   Contingency Plans

42

VII. OWNERSHIP

VIIA. Structure of Business

VIIA1. Legal form of business:

Where corporation is chartered

Where corporation is licensed to do business as a foreign corporation

Special features (e.g., issuance of 1244 stock, S status, etc.)

43

VII.   OWNERSHIP (continued)

VIIA.   Structure of Business (continued)

VIIA2.   Mergers, consolidations, reorganizations:

VIIA3.   Franchise, royalty, licensing, and working agreements:

Currently in effect

Planned for the future

44

VII.   OWNERSHIP (continued)

VIIB.   Financing/Equity Considerations

    VIIB1.   Financial features:

        Total shares of stock authorized/issued

        Price per share of stock

        Average price per share paid by officers and directors

        Voting rights, dividend payments, conversion features, etc.

45

VII.   OWNERSHIP (continued)

VIIB.   Financing/Equity Considerations (continued)

VIIB2.   Names and descriptions of owners/percentage of ownership held by each:

Name	# of Shares	% Ownership before Financing	% Ownership after Financing	Price Paid for Ownership

Employee ownership

Changes in ownership

VIIB3.   Amount of investment by officers and directors:

46

VIIB.   Financing/Equity Considerations (continued)

VIIB4.   Funding needed:

	Current Amount	Amount Needed	Percent Total Financing
Common stock:			
Preferred stock:			
Debt with warrants:			
Convertible debentures:			
Debt:			

Purpose of funding:

Amount Needed	When Needed	Purpose

VIIB.   Financing/Equity Considerations (continued)

VIIB5.   Financing arrangement:

Collateral for debt issuance

Amount of equity to be given up in exchange for funds

Expected annual return for investor

Number of investors sought

Minimum investment required by each investor

How investors will get their money out (i.e., buyback, acquisition, public offering, etc.)

48

VIII.   CRITICAL RISKS AND PROBLEMS

VIIIA.   Description of Risks

   VIIIA1.   Cost overruns in R&D and production:

   VIIIA2.   Failure to meet production deadlines:

   VIIIA3.   Problems with suppliers and distributors:

49

VIIIA.   Description of Risks (continued)

      VIIIA4.   Sales projections not attained:

      VIIIA5.   Unforeseen industry trends:

      VIIIA6.   Competitive price cutting:

      VIIIA7.   Unforeseen economic, political, social, and technological developments:

VIIIA.   Description of Risks (continued)

VIIIA8.   Capital shortages:

VIIIA9.   Cyclical fluctuations:

VIIIA10.   Other risks:

51

IX. SUMMARY AND CONCLUSIONS

IXA. Summary

IXA1. Unique features of company/user benefit:

IXA2. Overall strategic direction:

IXA3. Expected revenues and profits:

IXA4. Capital requirements and ownership:

52

IX. SUMMARY AND CONCLUSIONS (continued)

IXB. Scheduling

Timetable:

Event   Target Date

184

APPENDIX A: PHOTOGRAPH OF PRODUCT

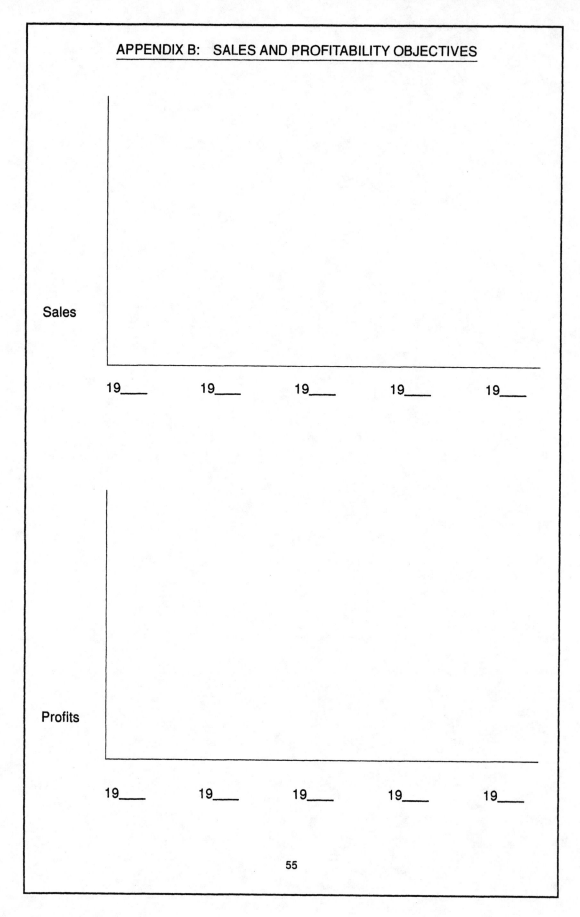

APPENDIX B: SALES AND PROFITABILITY OBJECTIVES

Sales

19____   19____   19____   19____   19____

Profits

19____   19____   19____   19____   19____

55

APPENDIX C: MARKET SURVEY

APPENDIX D: PRODUCTION FLOWCHART

Stage 1:

Stage 2:

Stage 3:

Stage 4:

Stage 5:

57

188

APPENDIX E: PRICE LIST/CATALOG

Item	Price	Quantity Price

58

APPENDIX F: SAMPLE ADVERTISEMENT

59

APPENDIX G: SAMPLE PRESS RELEASE

60

APPENDIX H: HISTORICAL FINANCIAL STATEMENTS

61

192

APPENDIX I: TABLE OF STARTUP COSTS

Items		Costs
Beginning inventory		_____
Furniture and fixtures:		
Storage shelves	_____	
Display stands	_____	
Window display fixtures	_____	
Special lighting	_____	
Counters	_____	
Outside sign	_____	
Installation costs	_____	
Other decorating and remodeling costs	_____	_____
		_____
Other assets:		
Cash register	_____	
Safe	_____	
Land	_____	
Building	_____	
Automotive equipment	_____	
Other equipment and machinery	_____	_____
		_____
Deposits with public utilities	_____	
Legal and other professional fees	_____	
Licenses and permits	_____	
Advertising and promotion for opening	_____	
Accounts receivable	_____	
Prepaid items	_____	
Cash	_____	
Other expenses	_____	_____
		_____
Monthly expenses (allowing for three to four months cash on hand)		
Salary of owner-entrepreneur	_____	
Other salaries	_____	
Rent	_____	
Telephone	_____	
Other utilities	_____	
Advertising	_____	
Professional fees	_____	
Travel and entertainment	_____	
Delivery expense	_____	
Repairs and maintenance	_____	
Office supplies	_____	
Taxes	_____	
Interest	_____	
Miscellaneous expenses	_____	_____
TOTAL STARTUP COSTS		_____

62

APPENDIX J: CURRENT AND PROJECTED PROFIT AND LOSS STATEMENT

	Year 1—Months:	Year 2—Qtrs:	Year 3—Qtrs:
	1 ... 12	1 ... 4	1 ... 4
Revenues	____ ... ____	____ ... ____	____ ... ____
Less: Cost of sales	____ ... ____	____ ... ____	____ ... ____
Gross Profit	____ ... ____	____ ... ____	____ ... ____
Less: Salary expense	____ ... ____	____ ... ____	____ ... ____
Payroll expenses	____ ... ____	____ ... ____	____ ... ____
Other services	____ ... ____	____ ... ____	____ ... ____
Office supplies	____ ... ____	____ ... ____	____ ... ____
Maintenance and repairs	____ ... ____	____ ... ____	____ ... ____
Advertising	____ ... ____	____ ... ____	____ ... ____
Automobile	____ ... ____	____ ... ____	____ ... ____
Travel and entertainment	____ ... ____	____ ... ____	____ ... ____
Consulting services	____ ... ____	____ ... ____	____ ... ____
Rent	____ ... ____	____ ... ____	____ ... ____
Telephone	____ ... ____	____ ... ____	____ ... ____
Utilities	____ ... ____	____ ... ____	____ ... ____
Insurance	____ ... ____	____ ... ____	____ ... ____
Taxes	____ ... ____	____ ... ____	____ ... ____
Interest	____ ... ____	____ ... ____	____ ... ____
Depreciation	____ ... ____	____ ... ____	____ ... ____
Other expenses	____ ... ____	____ ... ____	____ ... ____
Total Expenses	____ ... ____	____ ... ____	____ ... ____
Operating Profit	____ ... ____	____ ... ____	____ ... ____
Add: Other income	____ ... ____	____ ... ____	____ ... ____
Less: Other expenses	____ ... ____	____ ... ____	____ ... ____
Pretax Profit	____ ... ____	____ ... ____	____ ... ____
Income Tax Provision	____ ... ____	____ ... ____	____ ... ____
Net Income after Taxes	____ ... ____	____ ... ____	____ ... ____

(*Note*: Profit and loss projections should be prepared for years 1-5.)

63

APPENDIX K: STATEMENT OF CASH PROJECTIONS

	Year 1—Months:				
	1	2	3	4	... 12
Cash Balance (opening)	_____	_____	_____	_____	... _____
Add: Cash sales	_____	_____	_____	_____	... _____
Credit collections	_____	_____	_____	_____	... _____
Bank loan proceeds	_____	_____	_____	_____	... _____
Other cash receipts	_____	_____	_____	_____	... _____
Total Cash Receipts	_____	_____	_____	_____	... _____
Total Cash Available	_____	_____	_____	_____	... _____
Less: Purchases	_____	_____	_____	_____	... _____
Gross wages	_____	_____	_____	_____	... _____
Payroll expenses	_____	_____	_____	_____	... _____
Other services	_____	_____	_____	_____	... _____
Office supplies	_____	_____	_____	_____	... _____
Maintenance and repairs	_____	_____	_____	_____	... _____
Advertising	_____	_____	_____	_____	... _____
Automobile	_____	_____	_____	_____	... _____
Travel and entertainment	_____	_____	_____	_____	... _____
Consulting services	_____	_____	_____	_____	... _____
Rent	_____	_____	_____	_____	... _____
Telephone	_____	_____	_____	_____	... _____
Utilities	_____	_____	_____	_____	... _____
Insurance	_____	_____	_____	_____	... _____
Taxes	_____	_____	_____	_____	... _____
Interest	_____	_____	_____	_____	... _____
Other expenses	_____	_____	_____	_____	... _____
Subtotal	_____	_____	_____	_____	... _____
Less: Loan principal payment	_____	_____	_____	_____	... _____
Capital purchases	_____	_____	_____	_____	... _____
Startup costs	_____	_____	_____	_____	... _____
Reserve/escrow	_____	_____	_____	_____	... _____
Owner's withdrawal	_____	_____	_____	_____	... _____
Subtotal	_____	_____	_____	_____	... _____
Total Cash Disbursements	_____	_____	_____	_____	... _____
Cash Balance (closing)	_____	_____	_____	_____	... _____

64

APPENDIX L: CURRENT AND PROJECTED BALANCE SHEET

	Current	Projected
Assets:		
Current Assets:		
Cash and equivalents	_____	_____
Accounts receivable	_____	_____
Inventory (net)	_____	_____
Prepaid items	_____	_____
Other current assets	_____	_____
Total Current Assets	_____	_____
Fixed Assets (net):		
Furniture and fixtures	_____	_____
Leasehold improvements	_____	_____
Machinery and equipment	_____	_____
Land and building	_____	_____
Total Fixed Assets	_____	_____
Other Assets	_____	_____
Total Assets	_____	_____
Liabilities and Net Worth:		
Current Liabilities:		
Accounts payable	_____	_____
Taxes payable	_____	_____
Interest payable	_____	_____
Current portion of long-term debt	_____	_____
Short-term debt	_____	_____
Miscellaneous payables	_____	_____
Total Current Liabilities	_____	_____
Long-Term Liabilities:		
Long-term loan (net)	_____	_____
Convertible debentures	_____	_____
Total Long-Term Liabilities	_____	_____
Total Liabilities	_____	_____
Net Worth:		
Capital stock	_____	_____
Paid-in surplus	_____	_____
Retained earnings	_____	_____
Total Net Worth	_____	_____
Total Liabilities and Net Worth	_____	_____

65

APPENDIX M: FIXED-ASSET ACQUISITION SCHEDULE

Item   Date to Be Purchased   Cost

66

APPENDIX N: BREAK-EVEN POINTS

67

APPENDIX O: RÉSUMÉS OF KEY PERSONNEL

APPENDIX P: INDIVIDUAL AND ORGANIZATIONAL TAX RETURNS

APPENDIX Q: CHARACTER REFERENCES

APPENDIX R: _____

71

202

APPENDIX S: _____

72

203

APPENDIX T: _____

PART IV

SOURCES OF FUNDING

An Overview

The business plan provides us with an understanding of how much capital is necessary for the venture. Armed with that information, we can then explore the various sources of financing. There are four basic sources of funding:

- Your own savings and investments
- Debt financing (i.e., borrowing with the intent of paying back the loan)
- Equity financing [i.e., having individuals or companies (e.g., venture capitalists) invest in your business in exchange for partial ownership]
- Some combination of the above

A recent survey in *Inc.* magazine noted that in most cases the initial funding for new ventures came from multiple sources. Furthermore, venture capital was used in less than 10% of the cases. Be prepared to use more than one source of funding for your venture.

It is also recommended that you consult with other people familiar with the financing process (i.e., other entrepreneurs, consultants, members of the board of directors, other business associates, etc.) prior to seeking funding. They can provide you with valuable insight into the various options available and into the manner in which you should apply for financing.

We examine the first source of funding noted above—your own funds—in this section and examine debt and equity financing in Sections 2 and 3.

YOUR OWN FUNDS

You certainly should invest at least some of your own funds in your business. This will enable you to realize the greatest returns from the business if the venture succeeds. In addition, banks and venture capital companies generally balk at providing funds unless they see that you have made enough of a commitment to your business to invest your savings into it. Why should they take the risks if you haven't? Clearly, John DeLorean's small personal investment in his (now defunct) own car company—DeLorean Motor Corporation (DMC)—(estimated at less than $20,000 by some accounts), in exchange for a majority ownership position in the company, was most atypical of business financing.

Should Your Funds Be Treated as Equity or as Debt?

When you initially put your money into the business, it can be treated as your own piece of ownership of the business (in a similar way to equity financing but you, rather than outsiders, maintain ownership) or as a loan (as in the case with debt financing, however, the business owes you, rather than outsiders, the money).

There are several advantages of putting (at least a portion of) your personal funds into the business as debt rather than as equity. First, you, personally, will be able to collect interest on the loan, which the company writes off anyway. Second, if you put the funds in as a loan, you will be able to get the money out of the business easily—and tax free! This might not be the case if you put the money in as equity. If you loan the money to the business, and if the company succeeds, you will have the equity via retained earnings and can get the money out of the business if you so choose by having your company pay off the loan to yourself. If the company fails, equity investors are unlikely to get any money out of the business because lenders will have a prior claim to the assets.

One note of caution: The IRS does not take too kindly to closely held corporations whose debts provided by shareholders represent a large part of their working capital. If the IRS views such debts as equity, they will disallow the corporation from deducting interest on the debts. In general, if the loan "looks like a loan," it will be treated as debt; otherwise, it will be treated as equity. To protect yourself, it is advisable that you take the following steps:

1. Specify—in writing—a reasonable rate of interest and a schedule of repayment. The loan should not be payable on demand.
2. The debt should not be excessive. If the ratio of debt to equity exceeds 3:1, the IRS may treat it as equity.
3. Make payments for the loan on time.
4. Maintain a record of the debt on your books.
5. Demonstrate that outside creditors would make similar loans.

Putting Real Estate into the Business

If you are considering putting real estate into your business, rather than doing so directly, your family should maintain ownership of the property and should rent it to the business. Real estate tends to inflate in value over a period of years and it may be difficult for you to convert it into cash. If your family owns the real estate, however, the property can generate losses in the early years that can offset the income of your family members in high tax brackets (e.g., yourself). Later it can generate income that can increase the tax burden of low-income members of your family (e.g., your children).

Another advantage of renting real estate to your business is that if it is a corporation, you will have some justification for accumulating earnings. This is a way to avoid the double tax on dividends paid out. A corporation can justify an additional accumulation of earnings for the purpose of purchasing real estate at a *later date.*

DEBT AND EQUITY INSTRUMENTS

As noted earlier, in addition to financing your venture with your own funds, there are two other basic sources of funding: debt financing and equity financing. In addition, there are several "hybrid" forms of financing that have recently gained tremendous popularity among investors, having characteristics of both debt and equity.

As is true with any type of investment, risk and return go together. Debt assumes a guaranteed repayment schedule and provides the lender or creditor with a prior claim to the assets of the company over that of an equity investor. Thus the risk of providing a company with a loan is much less than it is in investing in shares of stock of that company; consequently, the potential returns for the lender are proportionately lower than they would be for an investor.

The most common debt and equity tools used to finance a business are as follows:

Common stock: purest form of equity in the company. Common stock holders receive no fixed or guaranteed return and have the lowest-priority claim against assets in the case of liquidation of the company. The risk (as well as the potential return) of common stock is the greatest of all debt and equity tools.

Preferred stock: a special category of stock which has certain advantages, such as guaranteed dividends and prior rights in the case of liquidation, over common stock.

Debt with warrants: a sweetened form of loan from the perspective of the investor. It allows the investor to purchase shares of common stock at a fixed price within a specified period while still collecting interest on the loan to the company. The most famous example of the use of debt with warrants is when the State Mutual Life Assurance Company, in the mid-1960s, loaned Ray Kroc's business $750,000 at an interest rate of $7\frac{1}{2}$ percent. As a sweetener, State Mutual received warrants to purchase 10 percent of the common stock of Kroc's company, McDonald's. About 10 years later State Mutual earned approximately $12 million on the sale of its stock in McDonald's.

Convertible debentures: allows the creditor to convert any remaining outstanding debt into stock at a specified price. It differs from debt with warrants in that the creditor need not receive all of the loan payments before purchasing the stock, whereas in the case of debt with warrants, the borrower must repay all of the loan and the lender has the choice of whether or not to exercise the warrants.

Subordinated convertible debt: similar to convertible debentures, except that the creditor has a lower claim to the assets in the case of liquidation or bankruptcy.

Straight debt: a simple loan or a debenture, where the borrower is obliged to repay the loan at an agreed-upon rate over an agreed-upon time. Generally, such loans are secured with some type of collateral—either owned by the business or by the entrepreneur personally.

As noted earlier, the entrepreneur's objective is to enhance the potential return for the investor while reducing the downside risk as much as possible. For that reason the hybrid forms of financing—debt with warrants and convertible debentures—have become very popular investment tools for investors because they strike a balance between risk and return.

In the next two sections we examine the various sources of debt and equity financing in greater detail.

Debt Financing

As noted earlier, there are several ways to finance new business ventures. One such way is through debt financing (i.e., the utilization of loans). An attractive feature of debt financing is that it provides the borrower with the necessary funds to begin a business without reducing his or her ownership of the company. In this section we examine the sources of debt financing for a business venture and discuss ways to enhance the likelihood of obtaining a loan for the business.

SOURCES OF DEBT FINANCING

Loans may be obtained from one or more of the following sources:

- Friends and relatives
- Life insurance policies
- Credit unions
- Commercial banks
- Savings and loan associations (S&Ls)
- Credit card companies
- Mortgage companies
- Personal loan companies
- The Small Business Administration (SBA)
- Other federal government sources
- State and local sources

Let's examine each of these sources in detail.

Friends and Relatives

You may be able to obtain some funds from friends or relatives. This is especially helpful when starting a venture. It is important, however, that you pay back such loans on time to avoid turning friends into enemies. In addition, to avoid problems with the IRS, such loans should be structured like any other loan; notes payable should be signed and a fair market interest rate should be stated. As an alternative to providing you with funds, friends, or relatives might be willing to cosign a note so that a bank would be more eager to lend money to you.

Life Insurance Policies

You can often borrow most of a life insurance policy's cash surrender value for your business. Make sure that you understand the terms of the policy before taking the loan to prevent the policy from being voided or the amount of money that is due to a beneficiary from being significantly reduced. This type of loan is attractive because the interest rate is generally low and the procedure to obtain the loan is relatively simple.

Credit Unions

If you belong to a credit union, you will be able to borrow funds from the union. The procedure is generally slightly more complex than it is for borrowing from a life insurance policy but more simple than borrowing from other lending sources.

Commercial Banks

Commercial banks can provide you with a loan at fair market interest rates if you can demonstrate that the business is sound. To most banks that will mean having an operating history of at least two or three years. Banks often require that the borrower maintain appropriate deposits with them. In addition, most banks will require personal guarantees for newer companies. You will soon come to realize that having a good relationship with a banker is a critical factor in the success of any business.

Loans may take on any one of the following forms:

- *Line of credit:* where the company may draw up to a specified sum as needed over a prescribed period. The period will run from 30 days to two years or more.
- *Inventory Loan:* similar to a line of credit, whereby repayment of the loan is made as the inventory is sold and receivables are satisfied.
- *Accounts Receivable Financing:* allows the company to receive in advance a maximum of approximately 65 to 80 percent of the face value of its receivables that are less than 60 days past due.
- *Factoring:* where the bank (or factoring company) purchases the receivables outright for a certain percentage of their face value.
- *Commercial Loan:* a "time" loan that is repaid over a specified time.

Savings and Loan Association (S&Ls)

S&Ls can provide you with a loan if you have the appropriate collateral. As with commercial banks, loans are often made against the funds that the borrower has in a savings account.

Credit Card Companies

Several entrepreneurs have financed businesses by obtaining lines of credit with their credit card companies. Although interest rates are high and the risks can be great as debts pile up, this method can be an effective way to obtain cash in a relatively short amount of time and may be the only financing alternative available for many businesses.

Mortgage Companies

In recent years, mortgage companies and other financial institutions have allowed people to establish a line of credit based on the equity that they have in their houses. Such "home equity loans," although somewhat risky, have enabled numerous entrepreneurs to raise the necessary capital for their businesses.

Personal Loan Companies

Personal loan companies often charge the highest rate of interest of any lending party. (Rates can be 20 to 40 percent.) However, many finance companies specialize in a particular industry and can therefore be less expensive and more reliable than some banks.

The SBA

The SBA provides financial assistance in the form of loans to qualifying businesses. The SBA can only lend you money if you are unable to obtain a loan on reasonable terms from a bank or to raise money without selling essential assets of your company. (More will be said about financial assistance available through the SBA later.)

Even former President Jimmy Carter and his mother, Miss Lillian, received assistance in the form of an SBA loan. The Carters used the $175,000 loan to construct a cotton gin building and other office facilities.

For further information on sources of funding from the SBA, contact

> U.S. Small Business Association
> 111 18th Street, NW
> Washington, DC 10417
> (202) 634-1818

Other Federal Government Sources

In addition to the SBA, several other government organizations can provide you with funding. Specifically, the Farmers Home Administration guarantees bank loans of up to 90 percent for businesses located in communities of less than 50,000 people. For further information, you can contact

> Farmers Home Administration
> Business and Industry Loan Program
> U.S. Department of Agriculture
> 14th Street and Independence Avenue, SW
> Washington, DC 20250
> (202) 447-7967

Also, the Department of Energy in collaboration with the National Bureau of Standards provides funding for companies that develop energy-related inventions. Funding is in the form of grants. For information, contact

> Office of Energy Related Inventions
> National Bureau of Standards
> Washington, DC 20234
> (301) 921-3695

State and Local Sources

In addition to requesting funds from federal sources, you might be able to obtain funding from state or local authorities. Because certain states (e.g., California, Connecticut, Massachusetts, Minnesota, New Jersey, Pennsylvania) have been more active than other states in promoting small business, the funding requirements and provisions will vary considerably from state to state. Where the business is located can make quite a difference in securing funds.

You can enhance the likelihood of obtaining state or local assistance by making the appropriate political contacts. However, the overriding factor in determining whether you will be funded is still sound financial planning.

State funding is generally available from either the Division of Commerce or the Department of Economic Development of the state. Local funding is often available from a local community development corporation (CDC), which is a group of nonprofit community organizations that encourage local development. Two excellent references for listings of organizations in your area that provide funding are:

- L. Smollen et al., *Sourceguide for Borrowing Capital* (Wellesley, MA: Capital Publishing Corp., 1977)
- *Directory of State Small Business Programs* (issued by the office of the Chief Counsel for Advocacy of the SBA)

FINANCIAL ASSISTANCE AVAILABLE THROUGH THE SBA

Types of Financial Assistance Available through the SBA

There are several types of financial assistance that you might obtain either through private lenders and then guaranteed by the SBA, or through the SBA itself. These programs, which vary somewhat from state to state, include:

- Regular loans
- Special loans
- Disaster assistance
- Pollution control financing
- Surety bonds
- The SBIR program

In addition, you might be able to obtain equity financing through small business investment companies (SBICs), which are discussed in detail in Section 3 of this part of the book.

Regular Business Loans.   Most of the regular SBA loans are made by private lenders (such as commercial banks, S&Ls, insurance companies, etc.) and then guaranteed by the SBA. The average size of a guaranteed loan is approximately $100,000 with a maturity of less than 10 years.

Special Loans.   The SBA also provides the following types of special loans:

- *Local development company loans:* to groups of local citizens who want to improve the economy in their area. The loan can be used to assist small businesses in the construction, expansion, and acquisition of plant or equipment.
- *Small general contractor loans:* to assist small construction firms with short-term financing. Funds can be used to finance residential or commercial construction or rehabilitation.
- *Seasonal line of credit guarantees:* to provide short-term financing for small firms with seasonal loan requirements.
- *Energy loans:* to companies engaged in the manufacturing, selling, installing, servicing, or developing of energy measures.
- *Handicapped assistance loans:* to owners of small businesses who are physically handicapped and to private nonprofit organizations which employ handicapped persons.

Disaster Assistance.   Disaster assistance is provided by the SBA in the form of:

- *Physical damage natural disaster recovery loans:* to repair or replace damaged or destroyed personal and business property
- *Economic injury natural disaster loans:* for working capital and to pay financial obligations which the small business owners would have met had the disaster not occurred

Pollution Control Financing.   The SBA assists small businesses in financing pollution control devices by guaranteeing their private financing. Terms are generally below prevailing interest rates and as long as 30 years.

Surety Bonds.   The SBA can guarantee up to 80 percent of losses incurred under bid, payment, or performance bonds issued to contractors on contracts valued up to $1.25 million.

The SBIR Program. The SBA also assists technology businesses by administering the Small Business Innovation Research (SBIR) program in conjunction with the following federal government agencies:

U.S. Department of Agriculture	(202) 475-5022
U.S. Department of Commerce	(202) 377-1472
U.S. Department of Defense	(202) 697-9383
U.S. Department of Education	(202) 357-6065
U.S. Department of Energy	(301) 353-5867
U.S. Department of Interior	(202) 634-1305
U.S. Department of Transportation	(617) 494-2051
U.S. Environmental Protection Agency (EPA)	(202) 382-5744
U.S. National Aeronautics and Space Administration (NASA)	(202) 453-2848
U.S. National Science Foundation (NSF)	(202) 357-7527
U.S. Nuclear Regulatory Commission (NRC)	(301) 443-7770

Funding, which is in the form of grants, is provided as follows:

- Phase I funding provides companies with $25,000 to $50,000 for six-month projects.
- Phase II funding of up to $500,000 is provided to up to half of the companies that receive Phase I funding to enable them to continue their work.
- Phase III funding for development and commercialization must be obtained through private financing.

Recently, several startup businesses in the biotechnology and information processing industries have received SBIR grants for new product ideas. For information on the SBIR program, contact:

U.S. Small Business Administration
Office of Innovation Research and Technology
1441 L Street, NW
Washington, DC 20416
(202) 653-6458

Eligibility for SBA Loans

The SBA can only make or guarantee a loan if a business cannot obtain funds on reasonable terms from a bank or other private source. In addition, there are standard eligibility requirements for loans based on the number of employees per firm, and in some cases, on the annual sales of the company. Contact your local SBA field office for details.

Credit Requirements for SBA Loans

To secure an SBA loan, you would have to demonstrate that you:

- Are of good character

- Have the ability to operate a business successfully
- Have enough capital in an existing business so that—with the SBA loan—your business will be able to operate soundly
- Will be reasonably able to repay the loan
- Have the ability to repay the loan and other fixed debts out of profits

The lending officer will make a decision based on the financial statements discussed earlier as well as on your general character and management capability.

Terms of the SBA Loan

The SBA can make direct loans of up to $150,000. Loans that are guaranteed by the SBA cannot exceed $500,000.

The SBA sets a maximum allowable interest rate for banks to charge on guaranteed loans based on the cost of money to the federal government.

Applying for an SBA Loan

If you are getting ready to start a business or are already in business, you should take these steps to apply for an SBA loan:

1. Prepare a business plan which includes:
   - A description of your business
   - A description of your experience and management capabilities
   - An estimate of how much you and others have to invest in the business and how much you will need to borrow
   - Detailed projected financial statements
   - Detailed accounts of all personal assets and liabilities
2. List collateral to be offered as security (i.e., mortgage on assets, assignment of warehouse receipts, personal guarantees, etc.).
3. Apply directly to the bank for a bank loan. If you are denied, ask the banker to make the loan under SBA's Loan Guarantee Plan. In such instances the bank will be working directly with the SBA.
4. If the guaranteed loan is not available, contact your local SBA field office.

HOW TO APPLY FOR A LOAN

Are You Credit Worthy?

Before a loan officer will lend money to a business, he or she must be satisfied with answers to the following questions:

- What sort of person is the prospective borrower? By all odds, the character of the borrower comes first. Next is his or her ability to manage the business.
- What is the borrower going to do with the money? The answer to this question will determine the type of loan, short or long term. Money to be

used for the purchase of seasonal inventory will require quicker repayment than money used to buy fixed assets.

- When and how does the borrower plan to pay it back? The loan officer's judgment of your business ability and the type of loan will be a deciding factor in the answer to this question.
- Is the cushion in the loan large enough? In other words, does the amount requested make suitable allowance for unexpected developments? The loan officer decides this question on the basis of your financial statements, which set forth the conditions of the loan and of the collateral pledged.

The answers to these questions should be found in your business plan, which must include the appropriate financial statements.

The loan officer will make a determination of your financial position based largely on your earnings statement and balance sheet, which measure growth potential and financial stability. The lender will be particularly interested in:

- General information:
  —Record of revenues and earnings
  —Projected earnings
  —Salaries of owners
  —Tax situation
- Receivables and payables:
  —Accounts receivable turnover
  —Percentage of total accounts owed by your largest account
  —Reserve for doubtful accounts
  —Condition of your client's payables
  —Ratio of debt to net worth
- Inventories:
  —Need for mark downs
  —Amount of raw material versus work in process versus finished goods
  —Obsolescence of inventory
- Fixed assets:
  —Condition of equipment
  —Depreciation policy
  —Future plans for additional purchases

Collateral

You will generally be required to have some type of collateral to back up the loan. The types of securities that are used for collateral include:

- Endorsers or comakers (cosigners)
- Accounts receivable
- Warehouse receipts
- Assigned leases
- Real estate

- Stocks and bonds
- Life insurance
- Personal savings

Lenders will certainly require a personal guarantee on any loans taken out by sole proprietorships or partnerships. They will, in addition, require a personal guarantee on many loans taken out by corporations, especially in the case of new corporations. Do not fall prey to the common misperception that people are not liable for loans taken out by a corporation.

Build a Relationship with a Banker

The worst time for you to ask for a loan is when you need it. By that time, it is often too late. Thus you should develop a relationship with a banker as early as possible. I would suggest that all "entrepreneurs-to-be" take out a $500 or $1000 loan while still in high school or college. Later, this will demonstrate to lenders that the entrepreneur has a record of borrowing and of paying back a loan on time.

In selecting a banker, you should avoid choosing one who is near retirement, as you will probably lose your rapport with the bank when the banker leaves. Also, it is often advisable not to choose a stand-out banker who is "on the move up," as your relationship with the bank may dwindle if the banker is either promoted or accepts a better position at another bank. To reduce the likelihood of these two problems occurring, get to know more than one banker at the bank where you are conducting business.

When you are confident in your selection of a banker, you should invite the banker to visit your business. You should treat this visit as an "army inspection." An unclean facility may be suggestive of loose controls or ineffective management.

Columns and Rows

When seeking debt financing, you must recognize that it is crucial to get to know the loan officer—above all, learn what is important to him or her. As Dick Levin, associate dean of the School of Business Administration at the University of North Carolina, notes, bankers tend to be "good-looking white Protestant males of average intelligence with a low need to take risks and a high need for structured support systems."[1] One thing about these bankers—they need and love financial statements. Be prepared with the appropriate quarterly pro forma statements; the more you have, the more difficult it will be for the banker to find out anything about the assumptions that have been used to produce the statements. In Dick Levin's words, "give 'em what they like best:

> columns and rows
> columns and rows
> columns and rows
> columns and rows."

[1]See D. Levin, *Buy Low, Sell High, Collect Early, and Pay Late* (Englewood Cliffs, NJ: Prentice-Hall, 1983).

Negotiate!

Loans are always negotiable; that is, you can negotiate the amount, the interest rate, the payment rate, and so on. However, if you don't ask, don't expect the loan officer to stray from the existing lending policy. One of the best times for you to negotiate with a banker is when you have run out of funds but the project has not yet been completed. (This is fairly common in land development projects.) In such a situation, bankers are more likely to "throw good money after bad money" than to foreclose the deal, because foreclosure will look bad for the lending officer and will hurt the bank's short-term earnings.

Although negotiation is advisable, it is unwise to haggle too much over interest rates, especially for a percentage point or less. This can hurt your relationship with the banker in the long run.

You can and should use more than one banker. This may enable you to get better terms on the loan—as I have indicated, the terms are generally negotiable—and will enable you to increase the leverage for the business.

Information on Loans

Some excellent references on borrowing funds for a new or existing venture are:

- L. Smollen et al., *Sourceguide for Borrowing Capital* (Wellesley, MA: Capital Publishing Corp., 1977)
- T. Martin, *Financing the Small Growth Business* (New York: Holt, Rinehart and Winston)
- D. Gumpert and J. Timmons, *The Insider's Guide to Small Business Resources* (New York: Doubleday)

In addition, the SBA has several good publications which may be obtained from your local SBA field office.

CONCLUDING REMARKS

Debt financing can provide you with the leverage needed to begin and sustain operations while enabling you to maintain ownership of the company. However, utilizing too much debt may result in severe cash flow problems. Thus it is often advisable that you utilize multiple types of financing for the business.

The small business owners who have had the most success with debt financing have been the ones who have planned effectively for their businesses. If you are in need of a loan either to start a business or to get a business going in the right direction, it is essential to:

- Set goals
- Develop cash flow projections and budgets
- Forecast revenues and earnings
- Evaluate the strengths and weaknesses of the business
- Assess environmental opportunities and threats

- Determine how the strengths can be used to capture the opportunities and to avoid the threats facing the business.

It is unlikely that a loan officer will assist a small business owner in obtaining funds unless he or she has demonstrated the ability to plan for his or her cash needs.

Let's now examine one other source of obtaining capital—equity financing.

Equity Financing

There has been a dramatic rise in the popularity of equity financing for new and existing businesses in recent years. This type of funding provides your corporation with the necessary cash to begin or expand operations without putting you severely into debt. However, it dilutes your ownership position in the company. In essence, the greater the amount of equity others have in your business, the more you are working for somebody else rather than for yourself. (Presumably, you began the business partly because you wanted to be your own boss!) Therefore, you should be cautious when giving up a portion of your (long-term) equity position to satisfy your immediate cash needs. Nonetheless, you should be familiar with the various sources of equity financing and of the expectations of equity investors.

As I have indicated earlier, you should utilize more than one form of financing to enable your business to grow.

INFORMAL SOURCES OF EQUITY FINANCING

In addition to your own funds, you might obtain equity financing from the following informal sources:

- Family and friends
- Private investors such as physicians, attorneys, or business owners
- Advisers and business contacts (e.g., accountants, attorneys, consultants, etc.)
- Employees (this is the idea of employee stock ownership, i.e., employees invest in the company in return for their long-term equity)
- Potential customers and suppliers
- Past employers

Pennies from Heaven

Recently, entrepreneurs have sought funding from "angels," wealthy individual investors who are most interested in providing capital to startup businesses. They generally invest under $100,000 (typically $25,000 to $50,000) in a venture, but will occasionally invest larger sums of money. An investor of this sort should certainly be considered as a prime candidate for membership on the board of directors.

Angels, which are also referred to as "adventure capitalists," can be found in private clubs throughout the nation. Joseph Mancuso, director of the Center for Entrepreneurial Management in New York, has organized "angel" chapters in several large cities. In addition, William Wetzel, professor of business administration at the University New Hampshire, has developed the Venture Capital Network, a computerized database to link entrepreneurs with investors. The cost is $100 for a six-month listing.

Informal sources will generally provide you with limited funds—perhaps up to $100,000—for your venture. If your business needs additional funding, you should consider formal sources of equity.

There are basically two formal methods of obtaining equity financing:

- Private placement of stock through investors or investment companies—such as venture capital firms—which does not require registration (but does require notification) with the Securities and Exchange Commission (SEC).

- Public stock offering, which requires that the company go through a lengthy and expensive registration process to register the securities with the SEC. (This will be discussed only briefly.)

PRIVATE PLACEMENT

There are several complex federal and state securities laws which must be taken into account when seeking equity financing for a business. Similar to tax laws, they become outdated with the passage of time. Thus the information provided here should only serve as a guide to the nature of securities laws that may affect you.

Although private placement laws may vary somewhat from state to state, there are three important rules under Regulation D of the (federal) Securities Act with which you should be familiar if considering a private placement. The purpose of the rules, as outlined below, is to eliminate unnecessary restrictions on the ability of small businesses to raise capital:

Rule 504 is useful for companies interested in raising small amounts of capital from numerous investors. It allows the issuer to sell up to $500,000 of its securities during a 12-month period regardless of the number or sophistication of the investors.

Rule 505 permits the sale of $5 million of a company's securities in any 12-month period to any 35 investors and to an unlimited number of "accredited investors," which includes institutional investors such as banks, insurance companies, investment companies, certain employee benefit plans, directors, executive officers, and general partners of the issuer, certain wealthy individuals (based on net worth, income requirements, and so on).

Rule 506 permits the issuer to sell an unlimited amount of its securities only to certain investors. The issuer may sell its securities to any 35 "sophisticated investors" (i.e., those that either individually or through a knowledgeable representative meet the requirements to be considered "sophisticated") and to an unlimited number of "accredited investors."

In addition, there are some general requirements common to all three of the rules above.

- The issuer has good reason to believe that each investor has the ability to evaluate the risks and merits of the investment, or are able to bear the economic risk of the investment.
- Each investor has access to the same information.
- The purchasers are not underwriters who will resell the stock.
- There is no general advertising of the offering.
- The securities are sold through direct communication between the issuer and purchaser.

I have only presented a preliminary overview of some of the regulations involving private placements. The SEC puts out a very useful guide which gives more detail on these regulations. It is entitled "Q&A: Small Business and the SEC" and may be obtained by contacting

> U.S. Securities and Exchange Commission
> 450 Fifth Street, NW
> Washington, DC 20549
> (202) 272-7460

In addition, you can contact the Office of Small Business Policy at the SEC— (202) 272-2644—for more information on securities regulations.

As noted earlier, the regulations vary from state to state. Thus I would also urge you to seek legal counsel from an attorney specializing in securities law to assist you with a private placement and to answer questions regarding specific securities regulations for your state.

A limited amount of capital—"seed capital"—is available to finance new ventures or merely new ideas, whereas other capital is available to finance growth businesses with some operating history.

Seed Capital

Many venture investors are willing to invest in pre-startups. However, because there are greater risks in providing seed capital to entrepreneurs than there are in providing capital to established businesses, the funding company will require a greater equity position in the new venture (i.e., higher risks/higher returns!). Generally, seed capitalists look for a 50 to 100 percent higher return on their investments than would the standard venture capital company. Funding is generally limited to $250,000.

Some of the major seed capital companies in this country are:

- Crosspoint Venture Partners (Palo Alto)
- Primus Capital Fund (Cleveland)

- Aegis Fund (Boston)
- Seed Ventures, Inc. (Malverne, PA)

See the Appendix at the end of this book for more complete information on these companies.

Other Equity Investors

There are several other sources of equity funding, most of which finance businesses with some operating history. Although, on occasion, these investors will finance startups, they will expect higher returns on such investments (to compensate for the higher risks) or a greater share of the ownership of the company in which they have invested. These sources of equity funding include:

- Venture capital firms
- Investment banking firms
- Insurance companies
- Large corporations
- Small business investment companies (SBICs) and minority enterprise small business investments companies (MESBICs)
- Accountants
- Banks
- Professional finders

Let's examine these sources of financing in greater detail.

Venture Capital Firms.[1]   These firms are either traditional partnerships that are established by wealthy families to manage a portion of their funds aggressively, or professionally managed pools that are funded by institutional investors. Some venture capital companies provide "seed capital" for startup businesses. Others invest in turnaround situations. However, the majority of venture capital companies invest in growth business. These sources will generally make investments of $1/2 million-$2 million.

Perhaps the most famous example of a venture capital firm's support of a growth company is when American Research and Development (ARD) invested $70,000 during the 1950s in a new company known as Digital Equipment Corporation. Today that investment is worth over $1 billion.

Recently, some entrepreneurs have made contact with venture capitalists at venture capital fairs. The fairs, which are conducted throughout the nation (but especially in areas where there is high growth in new ventures, such as San Francisco, Boston, Atlanta, Dallas, etc.), enable owners of fledgling companies to make proposals to investors.

The most notable fair is the one sponsored by the American Electronics Association in Monterey, California. There is a screening process for this fair whereby only the most qualified new ventures are invited to attend.

[1]An outstanding reference on the venture capital process is David Gladstone, *Venture Capital Handbook* (Englewood Cliffs, NJ: Prentice-Hall, 1988).

Some of the largest venture capital companies in the country include:

- TA Associates (Boston)
- Warburg Pincus Ventures (New York)
- Hambrecht & Quist Venture Partners (San Francisco)
- Hillman Ventures (Pittsburgh)
- Allied Capital (Washington, DC)
- Welsh, Carson, Anderson & Stowe (New York)
- Brentwood Associates (Los Angeles)
- U.S. Venture Partners (Menlo Park, CA)
- Mayfield Fund (Menlo Park, CA)
- Sprout Group (New York)
- Kleiner Perkins Caufield & Byers (San Francisco)
- Greylock Management (Boston)

A more complete listing, along with addresses and phone numbers is included in the Appendix. In addition, Stanley Pratt's directory of venture capital sources provides information on the size of investments, types of industries, and locations of venture capital companies. It is available from

Venture Economics, Inc.
16 Laurel Avenue
Box 348
Wellesley Hills, MA 02181
(617) 431-8780

The company's computerized data base of over 500 venture capital firms can be searched to identify prospective investors.

Finally, two associations can provide you with information on venture capital. These are:

Western Association of Venture Capitalists
3000 Sand Hill Road
Building 2, Suite 215
Menlo Park, CA 94025
(415) 854-1322
   (serves the western half of the nation)

National Venture Capital Association
Suite 700
1655 North Fort Myer Drive
Arlington, VA 22209
(703) 528-4370

Investment Banking Firms. These firms usually trade in more established securities, but occasionally form investor syndicates for venture proposals. Sometimes referred to as "dealmakers," these firms are in business to arrange financing and to structure deals for emerging growth businesses. Many sophisticated entrepreneurs consider the use of investment bankers as the rule, rather than the exception, for raising capital, as they can do so more quickly and efficiently than can the managers of the venture themselves.

Some of the larger investment banking firms are:

- ABS Ventures Limited Partnership (Baltimore)
- Drexel Burnham Lambert (New York)
- Salomon Brothers (New York)
- Morgan Stanley & Co. (New York)
- Montgomery Securities (New York)

Similar to the investment banking firms, but on a much smaller scale, are the "boutiques," which raise cash from banks, finance companies, insurance companies, and private individuals. Like investment banking firms, they will sometimes invest their own capital. Their clientele is generally local or regional, and they can usually arrange financing for companies in the $1 million to $10 million range.

Dealmakers will generally charge ½ to 3 percent of the capital raised to arrange for a debt placement and 4 to 8 percent to arrange for an equity placement. An extensive listing of private dealmakers is given in the September 1988 issue of *Venture* magazine.

Insurance Companies. Insurance companies often have required a portion of equity as a condition of their loans to smaller companies as protection against inflation. Some of the larger insurance companies that fund new ventures are:

- Allstate Insurance Co. (Northbrook, IL)
- Equitable Life Assurance Society (New York)
- Prudential Insurance Co. (Newark, NJ)

Large Corporations. Large corporations often invest in smaller companies in order to supplement their R&D programs and to keep abreast of technological innovations. Several corporations have started divisions or subsidiaries for just this purpose. These include:

- Amoco Venture Capital (Chicago)
- Xerox Venture Capital (Stamford, CT)
- Lubrizol Enterprises (Wickliffe, OH)
- Caterpillar Venture Capital (Peoria, IL)

Corporate venture groups are often an attractive source of capital because they can invest $10 million to $20 million in some ventures.

Recently, several large corporations have begun providing financial backup to their employees who wish to begin new ventures of their own. For example, Tektronix provided financial support to Jim Hurd, a former manager of solid-state engineering with the company, in order to begin Planar Systems in exchange for 49½ percent of the equity in the new business. In addition, Campbell Soup provided William Sharp, a research director of the company, with the necessary financial, marketing, R&D, and personnel assistance (including a $5 million research laboratory for the company) in return for a 30 percent equity position in the new venture. By providing employees with the necessary support to begin new ventures of their own, both the established companies and the new ventures have benefited tremendously.

Recently, several new ventures have developed collaborative agreements with large companies as a means of obtaining cash. For example, Immunex Corp., a genetic engineering startup in Seattle, signed a collaborative research contract whereby Hoffmann–LaRoche paid Immunex $500,000 up front (plus subsequent sales royalties) as well as monthly research payments so that it could manufacture and market Immunex drugs, pending regulatory approval.

Several other biotechnology companies have also entered into collaborative arrangements with larger corporations as a means of obtaining additional funding. For example, Collaborative Research Inc. entered into an arrangement with American Hospital Supply Corp. for the funds needed to test and market its immunological products, while Cetus Corp. received funding from Nabisco, Shell Oil, and Weyerhauser, and Genetic Systems Corp. had assistance from Cutter Laboratories.

Small Business Investment Companies (SBICs) and Minority Enterprise Small Business Investments Companies (MESBICs). These companies are licensed by the SBA and may provide management assistance as well as equity funding to emerging businesses. When dealing with an SBIC or an MESBIC, you should initially determine if it is primarily interested in an equity position—as venture capital—or merely in long-term lending on a fully secured basis. American Commercial Capital Corp. of New York, for example, lends money on a secured basis. (Thus there is less risk and, consequently, less potential return for the lender.) The company's clients therefore tend to be low-technology companies with fixed assets rather than high-technology companies with merely ideas. If the borrower does not succeed, American Commercial will take ownership of the secured assets.

There are several hundred SBICs in this country, most of which are found in such states as New York, California, Texas, Connecticut, and Massachusetts. Some SBICs specialize in specific industry groups (e.g., high technology, health care, etc.), whereas others provide funding for all types of ventures. SBICs generally fund businesses with a few years of operating experience.

The SBA sets a limit on the size of the venture to be funded by SBICs as follows:

- A maximum of $9 million in assets
- A maximum of $4 million in net worth
- A maximum average net income after taxes of $400,000 over recent years

SBICs have enabled several unprofitable or marginally profitable ventures to become profitable businesses. For example, American Frozen Foods, Inc. of Bridgeport, Connecticut, has grown from a 10-employee operation with sales of $600,000 and an operating loss in 1961 to a profitable $50 million company today. SBICs have also assisted NBI, a manufacturer of word processing systems in

Boulder, Colorado; Ault, Inc., a manufacturing firm in Minneapolis, Minnesota; Lifeline Systems of Waltham, Massachusetts, a manufacturer of community-based emergency response systems aid for the elderly and handicapped; and Pandick Press of New York in going from the "red" to the "black" within a few years. Some of the most notable SBICs in this country are:

- Citicorp Venture Capital Ltd. (New York)
- First Chicago Venture Capital (Chicago)
- Clinton Capital Corp. (New York)
- Chemical Venture Partners (New York)
- Churchill International (Waltham, MA)
- Rust Ventures (Austin, TX)

More complete information is included in the Appendix. In addition, you can obtain information of investment preferences and the capitalization of these SBICs from

National Association of Small Business Investment Companies
  (NASBIC)
1156 15th Street
Suite 1101
Washington, DC 20005
(202) 833-8230

In addition to SBICs, there are about 100 minority enterprise small business investment companies (MESBICs) that provide funding to businesses owned by racial minorities. They operate in a manner similar to other venture capital companies and therefore will evaluate proposals based on the owner's previous work experience and on the company's business plan.

Some of the larger MESBICs in the country are:

- Medallion Funding Corp. (New York)
- Transportation Capital Corp. (New York)
- Fulcrum Venture Capital Corp. (Washington)
- Opportunity Capital Corp. (San Francisco)
- MESBIC Financial Corp. (Dallas)
- Metro Detroit Investment Co. (Farmington Hills, MI)
- Chicago Community Ventures, Inc. (Chicago)

A more complete listing is included in the Appendix. In addition, you can obtain information on MESBICs from

American Association of Minority Enterprise Small
  Business Investment Companies (AAMESBIC)
915 15th Street, NW
Washington, DC 20005
(202) 347-8600

Accountants. Many entrepreneurs receive assistance from accounting firms, which perform many of the same services for their clients as investment bankers. These include establishing computerized networks of investors, providing important introductions to venture capitalists and other investors, assisting in the preparation of business plans and financial projections, evaluating capital needs, and screening and negotiating deals.

Each of the Big Eight accounting firms has an emerging business services or an entrepreneurial services group as noted below:

- Arthur Andersen & Co. (Small Business Practice)
- Arthur Young & Co. (Entrepreneurial Services Group)
- Coopers & Lybrand (Emerging Business Services)
- Deloitte Haskins & Sells (Emerging Business Services Group)
- Ernst & Whinney (Privately Owned and Emerging Business Services)
- Peat Marwick Main & Co. (Middle Market Practice)
- Price Waterhouse (Entrepreneurial Services Division)
- Touche Ross & Co. (Enterprise Group)

The Big Eight accounting firms are located in medium-sized and large cities throughout the nation.

Banks. Recently, several banks have begun funding new ventures through equity financing rather than merely through debt financing. Currently, there are over 100 banks that have venture capital subsidiaries. Although large banks such as BankAmerica have been funding new ventures through equity financing for years, smaller regional banks have recently turned to the venture capital business.

Despite the greater risks involved in providing equity financing as compared to debt financing, the potential rewards are commensurate with the risks. For example, BankAmerica's venture capital investment of $1 million in Quantum Corporation, a maker of disk drives, grew to about $20 million when Quantum went public. Continental Illinois Corp's $500,000 investment in Apple Computer grew over 80-fold in about five years. Because of the risks in financing new ventures, however, federal regulators allow banks to invest a maximum of 5 percent of their capital into venture capital subsidiaries.

Professional Finders. Professional Finders are firms or individuals familiar with sources of capital, which may be able to help a small company locate capital; they are generally not sources of capital themselves. You should exercise care by dealing only with reputable, professional finders whose fees are in line with industry practice. Furthermore, it should be noted that although finders may provide useful introductions, equity investors generally prefer to work directly with principals when making investments.

Although there are many reputable finders or brokers, there are thousands of finders who will provide little for you and who will demand up front fees for their "services." Thus be cautious in selecting a finder. If possible, select one who (1) has proven experience and can supply you with references, (2) possesses credentials in financial matters, (3) has operated a small business, and (4) has knowledge of and experience in your type of industry.

RESEARCH AND DEVELOPMENT LIMITED PARTNERSHIP

There is another source of funding that is often used by high-technology companies which has characteristics of both debt and equity financing. It involves a company sponsoring a Research and Development Limited Partnership (RDLP), which sells investment units to individual investors (most often, taxpayers in the highest tax brackets). The proceeds are used by the company to engage in R&D work. The investors or limited partners receive a sizable initial tax deduction (often 80 or 90 percent of their investment in the first year) and also expect to recover their investment in addition to a return on investment resulting from sales of the developed product.

One advantage of an RDLP to the entrepreneur is that unlike typical equity financing, it allows the company to raise capital without giving up ownership or control of the business. In addition, for new companies not yet generating income, they can pass along the tax benefits of writing off R&D expenditures to the investors; such tax benefits will be of little value to a firm not yet operating profitably. RDLPs are also advantageous in that they might represent the only means of financing R&D; lenders and investors are often reluctant to fund such risky ventures.

TAX LAWS FAVORING THE EQUITY INVESTOR

There are certain tax laws that can make your business a much more attractive investment than would otherwise be the case. One such law involves the manner in which you issue stock.

Prior to issuance of any shares of stock, the board of directors can issue 1244 stock under a section of the Internal Revenue Code (IRC 1244) that grants ordinary rather than capital treatment of losses on certain small business stock. If the losses were treated as capital losses, there would be a maximum annual deduction—presently $3000—for them if they cannot be offset against capital gains. By treating the losses as ordinary losses, however, the entire amount can generally be written off in one year.

1244 stock allows shareholders in most new ventures to deduct up to $50,000 (or $100,000 on a joint return) of bankruptcy losses against ordinary income. The requirements (which are rather lenient) for qualification for section 1244 stock include the following:

- The stock must be common stock, issued by a domestic corporation.
- The corporation must have over 50 percent of its gross receipts from other than "passive" sources (e.g., investments) for five years before the losses.
- The stock must be issued by the corporation for money or other property pursuant to a written plan containing several limitations.
- There can be no other kind of prior stock offering outstanding.
- The amount of contribution received for the stock and equity capital of the corporation must not exceed $1,000,000.
- Only individuals and partnerships qualify for 1244 benefits; corporations, trusts, and estates cannot claim 1244 treatment for stocks that they hold.

- The claimed losses cannot exceed the money or property given in exchange for the stock.
- The individuals receiving stock must be the original persons to whom the stock was issued. If you are thinking of incorporating an existing partnership, make sure that you take the following steps, in this order:
  1. Liquidate the partnership
  2. Distribute the assets to the partners
  3. Let the partners transfer the assets to the corporation in exchange for 1244 stock.

     (The order in which you do this is critical. If you, instead, transfer the assets directly to the new corporation, you will not qualify for 1244 stock.)

Thus, if you must issue stock, recognize that 1244 stock will "soften the blow" if the company does fail by allowing you and the other investors to deduct your losses in one year rather than over several years, which would be the case if they were treated as capital losses. Therefore, 1244 stock is a good way to raise capital for your business. It gives equity investors better tax treatment for their losses if your business goes broke.

PUBLIC STOCK OFFERINGS [2]

Your corporation might also be able to raise capital by a public stock offering. Recognize, however, that the costs of underwriting fees, legal fees, audits, prospectuses, and so on, can be as much as 20 percent of the amount raised. In addition, the terms of the public offering (as reflected by its valuation) are generally more attractive for mature companies than they are for start up companies.

During "bull" markets, small companies can raise large amounts of cash by an initial public offering (IPO). Numerous entrepreneurs (e.g., Bill Gates of Microsoft) have even realized "paper profits" in the hundreds of millions of dollars in their personal investment in their company at the time of an IPO.

Recently, many small companies have used some of the smaller stock exchanges (i.e., Denver, Vancouver, etc.) as vehicles for "going public." For example, Neti Technologies, Inc., a software company in Ann Arbor, Michigan, recently had an IPO on the Vancouver exchange. This exchange is advantageous over the larger national exchanges (i.e., New York Stock Exchange, American Stock Exchange) in that the entrepreneur can raise smaller amounts of capital—in many cases under $5 million—with looser filing requirements. Furthermore, the exchange is advantageous over smaller venture capital companies in that entrepreneurs generally maintain greater control of their business after securing the funding they require.

Two very useful publications on public stock offerings are:

- *Going Public: IPO Reporter*
- *New Issues*

[2]*Note:* Although the issues involved in public stock offerings are well beyond the scope of our discussion here, I have included a few points of interest, with the caution that entrepreneurs considering a public offering should contact an experienced securities attorney for information.

In addition, Ernst & Whinney's *Deciding to Go Public* and Deloitte Haskins & Sells' *Strategies for Going Public* are excellent booklets which address the key issues involved in public offerings. You can obtain copies from the local offices of these Big 8 accounting firms.

EMPLOYEE OWNERSHIP [3]

An effective use of "equity dilution" is the establishment of an employee ownership plan for the business. According to several studies (i.e., studies conducted by the University of Michigan, the Senate Finance Committee, and Cornell University), companies with substantial employee ownership plans were significantly more profitable than were comparable companies without such plans as well as more profitable than they had been prior to establishing the plans. Recently, Amtrol, Quad/Graphics, and Action Instruments have implemented employee ownership plans that have had very beneficial results for these companies.

Stock ownership has had tremendous benefits for employees as well. In particular, the early recruits of many high-technology startups have fared rather well in recent years. For example, when 3 Com Corp., a manufacturer of local-area-network equipment in Mountain View, California, began operating, managers received a 1% stake in the company, engineers a quarter to a third of that, and production people about 0.1 percent. As noted by 3 Com's president, William Krause, "ownership creates a special feeling it's hard to create otherwise."[4]

ESOPs: They Are Not Just Fables

There are several types of employee ownership programs, although employee stock ownership plans (ESOPs) are one very popular variety of them. ESOPs can be a particularly effective way of not only raising equity funding, but also of providing employee benefits, enhancing employee commitment and responsibility, and realizing substantial tax deductions for the business.

It is essential that you have a good lawyer—one that has had experience with such a plan—if you plan to establish an ESOP. To set up the plan, which can cost over $10,000 to install, your company would establish a trust for your employees which is designed to receive contributions (cash or securities), which are tax deductible, from your business. Employees are entitled to the stock in the trust (which will have appreciated tax-free) when they leave your company, at which time your company will usually purchase the stock back from them.

An attractive feature of ESOPs is that the employee trust creates a market for the stock, where there might not otherwise be a market if your company sought outside equity financing. Furthermore, the trust can borrow funds to buy the investor's stock, whereby both the interest and principal are tax deductible.

Of course, there is a major drawback: If your company does fail, the employees may lose their entire investment. However, it is not uncommon to hear reports of warehouse personnel, salespersons, truck drivers, and administrative personnel becoming millionaires after selling their stock to the trust at the time of their retirement.

[3]Much of the information in this section is based on a personal communication with Corey Rosen, Executive Director of National Association of Employee Ownership, in 1983.
[4]See *Business Week,* April 18, 1983, p. 81.

Pros and Cons of Employee Ownership

Although employee ownership dilutes the personal equity of an entrepreneur-founder, the positive impact for employees and for the organization as a whole may make it a very worthwhile investment. I have found that employee ownership is one of the best ways to get people to take on additional responsibilities (willingly) and to get them to "act like entrepreneurs." Effective small business owners are those who are prepared to share the responsibility, share the recognition, and share the wealth with those individuals who have been responsible for the growth of the company. It is for this reason that nearly 90 percent of Genentech's employees and 100 percent of Tandem Computer's employees own stock in their company.

Employee ownership can be extremely beneficial for a business. However, in the very early stages of a new venture, the ownership risks and rewards should be restricted to the primary participants who are making the major contribution to the business (i.e., the management team). After some initial level of stability has been reached, stock options or stock ownership can be used with other personnel, but only after long, careful thought.

Sources of Information on Employee Ownership

You can obtain more information on employee ownership by contacting

National Center for Employee Ownership
426 17th Street
Suite 650
Oakland, CA 94612

THERE IS NO "FREE LUNCH"

One important feature of equity financing is that it dilutes your ownership position of the business. There is an important rule to follow regarding equity financing: Do not "give away" your equity. This can be accomplished—to some extent—by utilizing your own funds as well as debt financing in addition to the equity funding that you are seeking.

Your equity in the business is one of your most valuable possessions. Although many entrepreneurs view equity financing as a way to obtain a "free loan," it actually comes with a heavy dilution, sometimes up to 70 percent or more, of your equity position. Naturally, equity financing (in combination with debt financing) should be used by many businesses, especially as the business grows. However, do not just surrender your equity in exchange for cash; you will also need to give up equity to attract marketing and managerial talent. If you have faith in your business—and if not, why start it in the first place?—the primary beneficiaries from the company's long-term growth should be those people involved in the managerial decisions that resulted in the growth. Thus you should exercise extreme care and good managerial judgment when seeking equity financing.

CONCLUDING REMARKS

As a final note, the following are some basic tips on obtaining funds for your business:

- Plan your capital requirements.
- Balance your debt and equity; do not overrely on one source of funding.
- Maintain a liquid position:
  —Avoid excessive fixed assets.
  —Avoid excessive inventories.
  —Maintain adequate working capital.
- Do not seek more funding than you need.

It is often extremely difficult for a business, especially a new venture, to obtain the desired funding. To improve the likelihood of obtaining funding, it is essential that you invest the time to plan your financial position and your financial needs. Demonstrate to investors that you are a competent manager and that you have a potential edge over your competitors. Clearly, this demonstrates the importance of preparing a business plan with the accompanying financial statements. Although preparing a business plan will not guarantee that you will receive the funding that you desire, not preparing one will guarantee that you will not receive the funding.

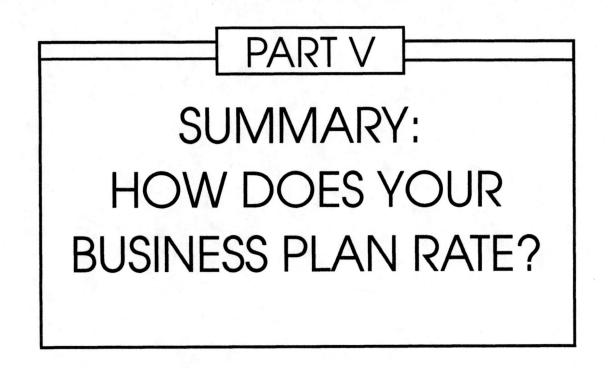

PART V

SUMMARY:
HOW DOES YOUR
BUSINESS PLAN RATE?

You can now use the information presented throughout this book to evaluate your own business plan. The information is presented in simple checklist form to enable you to evaluate your plan from the perspective of the investor and to concentrate on areas where the plan can be improved.

Place an "×" in the appropriate spaces below to indicate how your business plan compares to the "ideal" plan. Keep in mind that generally only *A* or *A*+ plans get funded. So, to enhance the likelihood of obtaining funding, you will have to demonstrate to investors that your plan is in the *A* or *A*+ range in as many categories as possible.

	F	D	C	B	A	"Ideal" Plan A+
I. DEFINITION OF BUSINESS:						
A. Product/Service:						
	___	___	___	___	___	Simple
	___	___	___	___	___	Describes competitive advantage(s)
	___	___	___	___	___	Proprietary position
B. Industry:						
	___	___	___	___	___	25+ percent growth
	___	___	___	___	___	Opens new markets
C. Target Market:						
	___	___	___	___	___	Clearly defined
II. MARKETING CAPABILITIES:						
A. Benefit to Users:						
	___	___	___	___	___	Significant user benefit
	___	___	___	___	___	Quantifiable user benefit
B. Marketability/Past success:						
	___	___	___	___	___	Past record of success

	F	D	C	B	A	"Ideal" Plan A+
C. Widespread Appeal:	___	___	___	___	___	___ Large number of potential customers
D. Ability to Sell:	___	___	___	___	___	___ Experienced in selling

III. MANAGEMENT CAPABILITIES:
A. Management:

	F	D	C	B	A	"Ideal" Plan A+
	___	___	___	___	___	___ Experienced management
	___	___	___	___	___	___ Management team
	___	___	___	___	___	___ Experienced external board of directors

IV. FINANCIAL ARRANGEMENT:
A. Acceptable Return:

	F	D	C	B	A	"Ideal" Plan A+
	___	___	___	___	___	___ 40+ percent compounded annual return
B. Exit:	___	___	___	___	___	___ Provision for "exit" delineated
C. Participation by Others:	___	___	___	___	___	___ Several other investors already involved

	F	D	C	B	A	"Ideal" Plan A+

C. Participation by Others: (continued)

—	—	—	—	—	—	Original owners/top management have invested substantially

D. Structured Deal:

—	—	—	—	—	—	Structured equitable financial arrangement delineated

V. AVOIDING THE TURNOFFS:
    A. Standardized vs. Customized Package:

—	—	—	—	—	—	Custom prepared for this venture

B. Product vs. Market Orientation:

—	—	—	—	—	—	Oriented to market

C. Financial Projections:

—	—	—	—	—	—	Realistic and justifiable

D. Examination of Risks:

—	—	—	—	—	—	Turned risks into opportunities

VI. PLAN PACKAGE:
     A. Cover:

—	—	—	—	—	—	Professional; spiral bound

	F	D	C	B	A	"Ideal" Plan A+
B. Format/Appearance:	___	___	___	___	___	Neat; carefully edited
C. Executive Summary:	___	___	___	___	___	Clear, concise executive summary
D. Body of Report:	___	___	___	___	___	Includes appropriate sections
E. Appendices:	___	___	___	___	___	Includes financials and other relevant information

APPENDIX

WHERE TO FIND FUNDING*

Following is one of the most comprehensive directories available of sources of equity funding in the United States. It includes venture capital companies as well as SBICs, corporate investors, and investment banking firms, arranged by state. Since venture capital companies and other sources of capital are often small businesses themselves, they are subject to the same changes affecting other small businesses (i.e., merger and acquisition, relocation, failure, etc.) Therefore, although we have made every effort to ensure accuracy in compiling this information, it will need to be updated periodically.

The directory can be an invaluable guide for entrepreneurs, if used properly. As noted earlier in this book, you can enhance your chances of getting funded by being introduced by another entrepreneur in which a venture capitalist has invested, or by some other third party contact of a venture capitalist. It is, therefore, advisable to use the directory to find out the names of the companies (and entrepreneurs) in which a venture capitalist has invested. Then, develop contacts with those entrepreneurs. You can even ask them to review your business plan. There's no substitute for being referred to an investor by another company in that investor's portfolio.

*This listing is presented merely for informational purposes. Neither the author or his associates, nor Prentice Hall and its representatives can attest to the character of the investors included in this directory, and are therefore not responsible for any investments made by them. The reader should exert extreme caution when seeking investors and should seek advice from experienced professionals when appropriate.

ALABAMA

FHL Capital Corporation
1550 Financial Center
505 20th Street North
Birmingham, Alabama 35203
(205) 328-3098

First Alabama Capital Corporation
16 Midtown Park East
Mobile, Alabama 36606
(205) 476-0700

First SBIC of Alabama
16 Midtown Park East
Mobile, Alabama 36606
(205) 476-0700

Hickory Venture Capital Corporation
699 Galatin Street, Suite A-2
Huntsville, Alabama 35801
(205) 539-1931

Porter, White & Yardley Capital, Inc.
15 N. 21st Street, Steiner Building
Birmingham, Alabama 35202
(205) 252-3681

Private Capital Corp.
2160 Highland Avenue
Birmingham, Alabama 35025
(205) 933-4618

Remington Fund, Inc. (The)
1927 First Avenue North
P. O. Box 10686
Birmingham, Alabama 35202
(205) 324-7709

Tuskegee Capital Corporation
4453 Richardson Road
Montgomery, Alabama 36108
(205) 281-8059

ALASKA

Alaska Business Investment
Corporation
301 W. Northern Lights Road
Anchorage, Alaska 99501
(907) 278-2071

Calista Business Investment
Corporation
516 Denali Street
Anchorage, Alaska 99501
(901) 279-5516

ARIZONA

Camelback Capital
645 S. Rockford Drive
Tempe, Arizona 85281
(602) 894-6994

Coronado Venture Fund
800 North Swan #130
Tucson, Arizona 85711
(602) 326-6778

El Dorado Ventures
2828 North Central Avenue
Station 1820
Phoenix, Arizona 85004
(602) 279-1101

F B S Venture Capital Company
14605 North Airport Drive, #325
Scottsdale, Arizona 85260
(602) 948-8017

Norwest Venture Capital
Management, Inc.
8777 East Via de Ventura, Suite 335
Scottsdale, Arizona 85258
(602) 483-8940

Pinnacle West Capital Corporation
P. O. Box 52133, Suite 800
Phoenix, Arizona 85072-2133
(602) 234-1142

Rocky Mountain Equity Corporation
4530 N. Central Avenue, Suite 3
Phoenix, Arizona 85012
(602) 274-7534

Valley National Investors
Valley Bank Center, 9th Floor
241 North Central Avenue
Phoenix, Arizona 85073
(602) 261-1577

Wescot Capital Corporation
2828 North Central Avenue, Suite
1275
Phoenix, Arizona 85004
(602) 279-0818

ARKANSAS

Capital Management Services Inc.
1910 N. Grant, Suite 200
Little Rock, Arkansas 72207
(501) 644-8613

Independence Financial Services
P.O. Box 3878
Batesville, Arkansas 72503
(501) 793-4533

Kar-Mal Venture Capital Inc.
2821 Kavanaugh Blvd.
Little Rock, Arkansas 72205
(501) 661-0010

Power Ventures Inc.
Hwy. 829
Malvern, Arkansas 72104
(501) 332-3695

Small Business Investment
Capital, Inc.
12103 Interstate 30
Little Rock, Arkansas 72203
(501) 455-6599

Stephens, Inc.
114 East Capitol Avenue
P.O. Box 3507
Little Rock, Arkansas 72203
(501) 374-4361

CALIFORNIA

Accel Partners
One Embarcadero Center, Suite
2102
San Francisco, California 94111
(415) 989-5656

Adler & Company
1245 Oakmead Parkway
Sunnyvale, California 94086
(408) 720-8700

Advanced Technology Ventures
1000 El Camino Real, Suite 210
Menlo Park, California 94025-4327
(415) 321-8601

Alafi Capital Company
P.O. Box 7338
Berkeley, California 94707
(415) 653-7425

Allergan Capital and Development
2525 Dupont Drive
Irvine, California 92715
(714) 752-4345

Allied Business Investors, Inc.
482 S. Atlantic Blvd., Suite 201
Monterey Park, California 91754
(818) 289-0186

Ally Finance Corporation
9100 Wilshire Blvd., Suite 408
Beverly Hills, California 90212
(213) 550-8100

Alpha Partners
2200 Sand Hill Road #250
Menlo Park, California 94025
(415) 854-7024

American Advance Ventures,
L.P.
2851 Fillmore Street
San Francisco, California 94123
(415) 921-1797

AMF Financial, Inc.
9910-D Mira Mesa Blvd.
San Diego, California 92126
(619) 695-0233

Apple Computer, Inc.
Strategic Investments & Corp
    Development
20525 Mariani Avenue
Cupertino, California 95014
(408) 973-3314

Arscott, Norton & Associates
375 Forest Avenue
Palo Alto, California 94301
(415) 853-0766

Asian American Capital
1251 W. Tennyson Road, Suite 4
Hayward, California 94544
(415) 877-6888

Asset Management Company
2275 East Bayshore Road
Palo Alto, California 94303
(415) 494-7400

Associated Venture Investors
    (AVI) Management, Inc.
3000 Sand Hill Road, #1 Suite
    105
Menlo Park, California 94025
(415) 854-4470

Atalanta Investment Company
8500 Melrose Avenue #212
Hollywood, California 90069-5106

Avalon Ventures
1020 Prospect Street, #405
La Jolla, California 92037
(619) 454-3803

Axton, Inc.
534 Drucilla Drive
Mountain View, California 94040
(415) 964-8139

Bancorp Venture Capital, Inc.
2082 Michelson Drive, Suite #302
Irvine, California 92715
(714) 752-7220

BankAmerica Capital Investments,
    Inc.
555 California Street, Department
    3908
San Francisco, California 94104
(415) 622-2230

Bartlett Schlumberger Capital
    Corp.
140 East Carillo Street
Santa Barbara, California 93101
(805) 963-6511

Bay Partners
10600 North DeAnza Blvd.,
    Ste. 100
Cupertino, California 95014-2031
(408) 725-2444

Bay Venture Group
One Embarcadero Center, Suite
    3303
San Francisco, California 94111
(415) 989-7680

Beckman Instruments, Inc.
2500 Harbor Blvd.
P.O. Box 3100
Fullerton, California 92634
(714) 871-4848

Benefit Capital, Inc.
721 Bonhill Road
Los Angeles, California 90049
(213) 820-8767

Berliner Associates
535 Middlefield Road #240
Menlo Park, California 94025
(415) 324-1231

Bessemer Venture Partners
3000 Sand Hill Road, #3 Suite
    225
Menlo Park, California 94025
(415) 854-2200

Biovest Partners
12520 High Bluff Drive #250
San Diego, California 92130
(619) 481-8100

Blalack Loop, Inc.
696 East Colorado Boulevard
    #220
Pasadena, California 91101
(818) 449-3411

BNP Venture Capital Corporation
3000 Sand Hill Road, #1
    Suite 125
Menlo Park, California 94025
(415) 854-1084

Boundary Fund
1900 West Garvey Avenue South,
    Suite 200
West Covina, California 91790
(818) 962-3562

Brentwood Associates
11661 San Vincente Blvd., Suite
    707
Los Angeles, California 90049
(213) 826-6581

Bridge Fund
237 Almendra Avenue
Los Gatos, California 95030
(408) 354-6611

Bridgemere Capital, Inc.
44 Montgomery Street #2900
San Francisco, California 94104
(415) 421-3311

Brownstein (Neil H.) Corporation
Neil H. Brownstein Corporation
3000 Sand Hill Road, #3 Suite 225
Menlo Park, California 94025
(415) 854-2200

Bryan & Edwards
3000 Sand Hill Road, #2 Suite 215
Menlo Park, California 94025
(415) 854-1555

Burr, Egan, Deleage & Company
Three Embarcadero Center, Suite
    2560
San Francisco, California 94111
(415) 362-4022

Business Equity & Dev. Corp.
1411 W. Olympic Blvd., Suite 200
Los Angeles, California 90015
(213) 385-0351

C F B Venture Capital Corporation
530 B Street, 2nd Floor
San Diego, California 92101
(619) 230-3304

Cable & Howse Ventures
435 Tasso Street, Suite 115
Palo Alto, California 94301
(415) 322-8400

California Capital Investors
11812 San Vicente Blvd.
Los Angeles, California 90049
(213) 820-7222

California Private Investment Corp.
388 Market Street, #900
San Francisco, California 94111
(415) 989-1915

Camden Investments, Inc.
9560 Wilshire Blvd., #310
Beverly Hills, California 90212
(213) 859-9738

Canaan Venture Partners
3000 Sand Hill Road, #1 Suite 205
Menlo Park, California 94025
(415) 854-8092

Capital Corporation of America
880 El Camino Del Mar
San Francisco, California 94121
(415) 221-8700

Capital Management Services
3000 Sand Hill Road, #280
Menlo Park, California 94025
(415) 854-3927

Carlyle Capital Corporation
444 South Flower Street #4650
Los Angeles, California 90017
(213) 689-9235

CALIFORNIA (cont.)

CBS Ventures
4350 Executive Drive
San Diego, California 92121
(619) 457-2773

CFB Venture Capital Corporation
530 B Street, 2nd Floor
P. O. Box 109
San Diego, California 92112
(619) 230-3304

Charterway Investment Corporation
222 S. Hill Street, Suite 800
Los Angeles, California 90012
(213) 687-8539

Churchill International
444 Market Street, 25th Floor
San Francisco, California 94111
(415) 398-7677

CIN Investment Company
444 Market Street, 25th Floor
San Francisco, California 94111
(415) 398-7677

Citicorp Venture Capital, Ltd.
Two Embarcadero Place
2200 Geng Road, Suite 203
Palo Alto, California 94303
(415) 424-8000

CommTech International
545 Middlefield Road #180
Menlo Park, California 94025
(415) 328-0190

Communications Ventures
3000 Sand Hill Road, #2 Suite
  175
Menlo Park, California 94025
(415) 854-3098

Concord Partners
435 Tasso Street, Suite 305
Palo Alto, California 94301
(415) 327-2600

Continental Investors, Inc.
8781 Seaspray Drive
Huntington Beach, California 90014
(714) 964-5207

Cornerstone Ventures/Rothschild,
  Unterberg, Toubin Ventures
3000 Sand Hill Road, #3
  Suite 260
Menlo Park, California 94025
(415) 854-2576

Crosspoint Investment Corp.
1951 Landings Drive
Mountain View, California 94043
(415) 964-0100

Cruttenden & Company
4600 Campus Drive
Newport Beach, California 92660
(714) 852-9000

Cypress Fund (The)
2740 Sand Hill Road
Menlo Park, California 94025
(415) 854-4193

Deucalion Venture Partners
655 Montgomery Street #1200
San Francisco, California 94111
(415) 989-1860

Developers Equity Capital
  Corporation
1880 Century Park East #311
Los Angeles, California 90067
(213) 277-2000

Devereaux Capital Corporation
98 Main Street #403
Tiburon, California 94920
(415) 781-8390

DFC Ventures Limited
100 Spear Street #1430
San Francisco, California 94105
(415) 777-2847

Diehl and Company
4695 MacArthur Court
Newport Beach, California 92660
(714) 955-2000

Dime Investment Corporation
3731 Wilshire Boulevard
Los Angeles, California 90010
(213) 739-1847

Dominion Ventures
300 Montgomery Street #600
San Francisco, California 94104
(415) 362-4890

Dougery, Jones & Wilder
2003 Landings Drive
Mountain View, California 94043
(415) 968-4820

Dowdell Corporation
555 Capital Mall, Suite 640
Sacramento, California 95814
(916) 444-0494

Draper Associates
3000 Sand Hill Road, #4, Suite 235
Menlo Park, California 94025
(415) 854-1712

Drexel Burnham Lambert
  Inc./The Lambda Funds
5 Palo Alto Square, 3000 El Camino Real
Palo Alto, California 94306
(415) 945-8500

DSV Partners
620 Newport Center Drive
Newport Beach, California 92660
(714) 752-7813

Early Stages Company (The)
244 California Street #300
San Francisco, California 94111
(415) 986-5700

Edgar, Dunn & Conover, Inc.
1717 Embarcadero Road
Palo Alto, California 94303
(415) 856-9800

EG & G Venture Partners
7000 East El Camino Real #270
Mountain View, California 94040
(415) 967-2822

El Dorado Ventures
2 North Lake Avenue, Suite 480
Pasadena, California 91101
(818) 793-1936

Enterprise Partners
5000 Birch Street #6200
Newport Beach, California 92660
(714) 833-3650

Entertainment-Media Venture
  Partners, LP
2121 Avenue of the Stars #460
Los Angeles, California 90067
(213) 284-8868

Environment Venture Fund
c/o Robertson, Coleman & Stephens
One Embarcadero Center
San Francisco, California 94111
(415) 781-9700

Fairfield Venture Partners
650 Town Center Drive #810
Costa Mesa, California 92626
(813) 754-5717

FAS/Bekhor International
701 B Street #1500
San Diego, California 92101
(619) 544-1600

Financial Technology Research Corp.
16633 Ventura Blvd. #1220
Encino, California 91436
(813) 784-8300

First American Capital Funding, Inc.
38 Corporate Park #B
Irvine, California 92714-5105
(714) 660-9288

First Century Partners
350 California Street, 20th Floor
San Francisco, California 94104
(415) 955-1671

First Dallas Group, Ltd.
1299 Fourth Street
San Rafael, California 94901
(415) 459-2385

First Interstate Venture Capital
5000 Birch Street #10100
Newport Beach, California 92660
(714) 253-4360

First SBIC of California
650 Town Center Drive, 17th Floor
Costa Mesa, California 92626
(714) 556-1964

First SBIC of California
5 Palo Alto Square, Suite 938
Palo Alto, California 94304
(415) 424-8011

First SBIC of California
155 N. Lake Avenue, Suite 1010
Pasadena, California 91109
(818) 304-3451

First Westinghouse Ventures
Corp.
620 Newport Center Drive,
#1575
Newport Beach, California 92660
(714) 721-0740

Genesis Capital, LP
20823 Stevens Creek Blvd., C2
Suite A
Cupertino, California 95014
(408) 446-9690

Geo Capital Ventures
3 Embarcadero Center #2560
San Francisco, California 94111
(415) 391-3399

Girard Capital, Inc.
4320 LaJolla Village Drive, Suite
#210
San Diego, California 92122
(619) 457-5114

Glaspell (Bruce) & Associates
Bruce Glaspell & Associates
P. O. Box 410686
San Francisco, California 94141
(415) 781-1313

Glenwood Management
3000 Sand Hill Road, #1 Suite
230
Menlo Park, California 94025
(415) 854-8070

Glynn Ventures
3000 Sand Hill Road, #2 Suite
210
Menlo Park, California 94025
(415) 854-2215

Goodman (David M.) & Associates
David M. Goodman & Associates
2705 Paseo Del Mar
Palos Verdes Estates, California
90274
(213) 377-6619

Grace Ventures Corporation
20300 Stevens Creek Blvd., Suite
330
Cupertino, California 95014
(408) 725-0774

Hallador, Inc.
1435 River Park Drive #505
P.O. Box 15299
Sacramento, California 95851
(916) 920-1115

Hambrecht & Quist Venture
Partners
235 Montgomery Street
San Francisco, California 94194
(415) 576-3300

Hamco Capital Corporation
One Post Street, 4th Floor
San Francisco, California 94104
(415) 393-9813

Happ Ventures
444 Astro Street #400
Mountain View, California 94041
(415) 961-1115

Harvest Ventures, Inc.
10080 N. Wolfe Road #365
Building SW 3
Cupertino, California 95014
(408) 996-3200

Health Capital Group
1520 West Cameron Avenue,
#300
West Covina, California 91790
(818) 962-8602

Henry & Company
9191 Towne Centre Drive #230
San Diego, California 92122
(619) 453-1655

Hewlett-Packard Company
3000 Hanover Street
Palo Alto, California 94304
(415) 857-7308

Hillman Ventures
2200 Sand Hill Road #240
Menlo Park, California 94025
(415) 854-4653

HMS Capital
170 Middlefield Road #150
Menlo Park, California 94023
(415) 324-4672

Hoebich Venture Management, Inc.
5770 Croy Road
Morgan Hill, California 95037
(408) 778-5271

Holding Capital Group
2851 Alton Avenue
Irvine, California 92714
(714) 340-1616

Hytec Partners, Ltd.
1406 Burlingame Avenue #32
Burlingame, California 94010
(415) 340-1616

IBK Capital Corporation
One First Street #2
Los Altos, California 94022
(415) 941-9221

Imperial Ventures, Inc.
9920 S. LaCienega Blvd., Suite 1010
Inglewood, California 90301
(213) 417-5888

Imperial Ventures, Inc.
P. O. Box 92991
Los Angeles, California 90009
(213) 417-5830

Indosuez Technology Group
3000 Sand Hill Road, #4 Suite 130
Menlo Park, California 94025
(415) 854-0587

Inman & Bowman
4 Orinda Way, Bldg. D, Suite 150
Orinda, California 94563
(415) 253-1611

Institutional Venture Partners
3000 Sand Hill Road, #2, Suite 290
Menlo Park, California 94025
(415) 854-0132

Inter West Partners
3000 Sand Hill Road, #3, Suite 255
Menlo Park, California 94025-7112
(415) 854-8585

Interscope Investments, Inc.
10900 Wilshire Blvd., #1400
Los Angeles, California 90024
(213) 208-8636

InterVen Partners
445 A Figueroa, Suite 2940
Los Angeles, California 90071
(213) 622-1922

Investors in Industry (3i) Capital
Corp.
450 Newport Center Drive, Suite
250
Newport Beach, California 92660
(714) 720-1421

CALIFORNIA (cont.)

Irvine Technology Fund
4600 Campus Drive
Newport Beach, California 92660
(714) 852-9000

Ivanhoe Venture Capital, Ltd.
737 Pearl Street, Suite #201
La Jolla, California 92037
(619) 454-8882

Jafco American Ventures, Inc.
2180 Sand Hill Road #320
Newport Beach, California 92660
(714) 852-9000

Julian, Cole & Stein
11777 San Vicente Blvd., Suite
522
Los Angeles, California 90049
(213) 826-8002

KB Ventures I
2180 Sand Hill Road #320
Menlo Park, California 94025
(213) 854-0746

Kleiner, Perkins, Caufield, &
Byers
Four Embarcadero Center, Suite
3520
San Francisco, California 94111
(415) 421-3110

Kyocera International, Inc.
Corporate Development
8611 Balboa Avenue
San Diego, California 92123
(619) 576-2500

Latigo Capital Partners
23410 Civic Center Way, Suite
E-2
Malibu, California 90265
(213) 456-5054

Lawrence WPG Partners, LP
555 California Street, 47th Floor
San Francisco, California 94104
(415) 622-6864

Leisy, Robert B.
14408 East Whitter Blvd. #B-5
Whittier, California 90605
(213) 689-4862

Lepercq Capital Partners
601 California Street
San Francisco, California 94108
(415) 981-1810

LF International
875 Mahler Road #225
Burlingame, California 94010
(415) 697-8936

Linc Venture Partners, Inc.
2119 West March Lane, Suite C
Stockton, California 95207
(209) 957-6666

Lucas, (Donald L.)
Donald L. Lucas
3000 Sand Hill Road, #3 Suite 210
Menlo Park, California 94025
(415) 854-4223

M B W Management Inc.
350 Second Street, Suite #7
Los Altos, California 94022
(415) 941-2392

Manning and Company
29438 Quailwood Drive
Rancho Palo Verdes, California 90274
(213) 377-4335

Marigold Capital Development, Inc.
25283 Cabot Road
Laguna Hills, California 92653
(714) 951-2525

Marwitt Capital Corporation
180 Newport Center Drive
Newport Beach, California 92660
(714) 640-6234

Matrix Partners
2500 Sand Hill Road
Menlo Park, California 94025
(415) 854-3131

Mautner (Leonard) Associates
Leonard Mautner Associates
1434 Sixth Street #10
Santa Monica, California 90401
(213) 393-9788

Mayfield Fund
2200 Sand Hill Road, #200
Menlo Park, California 94025
(415) 854-5560

McCown de Leeuw & Company
3000 Sand Hill Road, #3 Suite 290
Menlo Park, California 94025
(415) 854-6000

McKesson Corporation
One Post Street
San Francisco, California 94104
(415) 983-8666

McKewon & Timmons
701 B Street
San Diego, California 92101
(619) 544-1600

MedVenture Associates
Pier 33 South, 2nd Floor
San Francisco, California 94022
(415) 956-6818

Melchor Venture Management,
Inc.
170 State Street #220
Los Altos, California 94022
(415) 941-6565

Menlo Ventures
3000 Sand Hill Road, #4 Suite 100
Menlo Park, California 94025
(415) 854-8540

Merrill, Pickard, Anderson &
Eyre
Two Palo Alto Square, Suite 425
Palo Alto, California 94306
(415) 856-8880

Metropolitan Venture Company
5757 Wilshire Blvd. #670
Los Angeles, California 90036
(213) 938-3488

Microtechnology Investment, Ltd.
46 Red Birch Court
Danville, California 94526
(213) 838-9319

MIP Equity Fund
3000 Sand Hill Road, #4 Suite 280
Menlo Park, California 94025
(415) 854-2653

MK Global Ventures
2471 East Bayshore Road, Suite 520
Palo Alto, California 94303
(415) 424-0151

MK International Ventures N.V.
606 South Olive Street #1123
Los Angeles, California 90014
(213) 625-1611

Mohr Davidson Ventures
3000 Sand Hill Road, #1 Suite 240
Menlo Park, California 94025
(415) 854-7236

Montgomery Associates
600 Montgomery Street
San Francisco, California 94126
(415) 421-4200

Montgomery Bridge Funds
600 Montgomery Street
San Francisco, California 94111
(415) 627-2000

Montgomery Medical Venture L.P.
600 Montgomery Street
San Francisco, California 94111
(415) 627-2000

Montgomery Pathfinder Fund
600 Montgomery Street
San Francisco, California 94111
(415) 627-2000

Morgan, Olmstead, Kennedy &
  Gardner, Inc
606 S. Olive Street
Los Angeles, California 90014
(213) 625-1611

Mountain Pacific Equities
130 Newport Center, #110
Newport Beach, California 92660
(714) 760-8534

Murison, Heller & Partners
Belmont Shores
1301 Shoreway Road, Suite 301
Belmont, California 94002
(415) 593-2885

National Corporate Finance, Inc.
2082 SE Briston #203
Santa Ana, California 92707
(714) 756-2006

National Investment Management
23133 Hawthrone Blvd. #300
Torrance, California 90505
(213) 373-8944

Nelson Capital Corporation
3600 Wilshire Blvd.
Los Angeles, California 90010
(213) 386-3600

Nest Venture Partners
1086 East Meadow Circle
Palo Alto, California 94303
(415) 493-0921

New Enterprise Associates
235 Montgomery Street #1025
San Francisco, California 94104
(415) 956-1579

New Kukje Investment Company
958 S. Vermont Ave., #C
Los Angeles, California 90006
(213) 389-8679

New West Ventures
4350 Executive Drive #206
San Diego, California 92121
(619) 457-6722

Newtek Ventures
500 Washington Street #720
San Francisco, California 94111
(415) 986-5711

Norton Partners
375 Forest Avenue
Palo Alto, California 94301
(415) 853-0766

Oak Investment Partners
3000 Sand Hill Road, #3 Suite 240
Menlo Park, California 94025
(415) 854-8825

Oak Investment Partners
3000 Sand Hill Road, #3 Suite 240
Mountain View, California 94025
(415) 854-8825

Olympic Ventures Partners
101 California Street #4035
San Francisco, California 94111
(415) 362-4433

Onset
151 University Avenue
Palo Alto, California 94301
(415) 327-5470

Orange Nassau Capital Corporation
1500 Quail Street, Suite 540
Newport Beach, California 92660
(714) 752-7811

Oscco Ventures
3000 Sand Hill Road, #4 Suite 140
Menlo Park, California 94025
(415) 854-2222

Oxford Venture Corporation
233 Wilshire Blvd. #730
Santa Monica, California 90401
(213) 458-3135

Pacific Asset Partners
45 Belden Place
San Francisco, California 94104
(415) 362-6120

Pacific Capital Fund (PCF) Corp.
675 Mariner's Island Blvd., #103
San Mateo, California 94404
(415) 574-4747

Pacific Coast Capital
700 Larkspur Landing Circle,
  Suite 199
Larkspur, California 94939
(415) 924-8260

Pacific Inland Venture Partnership
  Ltd/Capital Fund Associates, LP
222 South Harlow #700
Anaheim, California 92805
(714) 535-5148

Pacific Venture Partners
3000 Sand Hill Road, #4 Suite 175
Menlo Park, California 94025
(415) 854-2266

Paragon Partners
3000 Sand Hill Road, #2, Suite 190
Menlo Park, California 94025
(415) 854-8000

Paribas Technology, Inc.
101 California Street #3150
San Francisco, California 94111
(415) 788-2929

Patricof (Alan) Associates, Inc.
Alan Patricof Associates, Inc.
2100 Geng Road
Palo Alto, California 94303
(415) 494-9944

PBC Venture Capital Inc.
P.O. Box 6008, 1810 Chester Avenue
Bakerfield, California 94111
(805) 395-3206

Peregrine Associates
1299 Ocean Avenue #306
Santa Monica, California 90401
(213) 458-1441

Princeton/Montrose Partners
2331 Honolulu Avenue #G
Montrose, California 91020
(818) 957-3623

Prototype Funding Corporation
1650 Borel Place #207
San Mateo, California 94402
(415) 571-6791

Pyramid Ventures, Inc.
600 Montgomery Street #3400
San Francisco, California 94111
(415) 986-0444

Quest Ventures
555 California Street
San Francisco, California 94104
(415) 986-1697

R&D Funding Corporation
3945 Freedom Circle #800
Santa Clara, California 95054
(408) 980-0990

R&D Partners
701 Welch Road #1119
Palo Alto, California 94304
(415) 328-2525

Riordan Venture Management
300 South Grand Avenue, 29th Floor
Los Angeles, California 90071
(213) 229-8453

Robertson, Colman & Stephens
One Embarcadero Center #3100
San Francisco, California 94111
(415) 781-9700

Rock (Arthur) & Company
Arthur Rock & Company
1635 Russ Building
San Francisco, California 94104
(415) 981-3921

Rogers & Whitney
3000 Sand Hill Road, #2 Suite 175
Menlo Park, California 94025
(415) 854-2767

CALIFORNIA (cont.)

Round Table Capital Corporation
655 Montgomery Street
San Francisco, California 94111
(415) 392-7500

San Joaquin Capital Corporation
1675 Chester Avenue #330
P.O. Box 2538
Bakerfield, California 93303
(805) 323-7581

San Jose Capital
100 Park Center #427
San Jose, California 95113
(408) 293-7708

Sand Hill Venture Group
3000 Sand Hill Road, #2 Suite 256
Menlo Park, California 94025
(415) 854-9600

Sanderling Partners
60 E. Sir Francis Drake Blvd.,
   Suite 300
Larkspur, California 94939
(415) 461-1520

SAS Associates
515 South Figueroa Street, Suite 600
Los Angeles, California 90071
(213) 624-4232

Seaport Ventures, Inc.
525 B Street, Suite 630
San Diego, California 92101
(619) 232-4069

Security Financial Management
   Corp.
100 Bush Street, Suite 1905
San Francisco, California 94104
(415) 981-8060

Security Pacific Capital
   Corp./First SBIC of California
650 Town Center Drive, 17th Floor
Costa Mesa, California 92626
(714) 556-1964

Seidler, Amdec Securities, Inc.
515 S. Figueroa Street
Los Angeles, California 90071-3396
(213) 624-4232

Sequoia Capital
3000 Sand Hill Road, #4 Suite
   280
Menlo Park, California 94025
(415) 854-3927

Shearson Lehman Brothers, Inc.
One Bush Street
San Francisco, California 94014
(415) 981-3680

Sierra Ventures Management Company
3000 Sand Hill Road, #1 Suite 280
Menlo Park, California 94025
(415) 854-1000

Sigma Partners
2099 Gateway #310
San Jose, California 95110
(408) 279-6300

Silicon Valley Management
15474 ViaVequero
Monte Sereno, California 95030
(408) 395-2200

Sofinnova, Inc.
Three Embarcadero #2560
San Francisco, California 94111
(415) 216-0544

Southern California Ventures
9920 LaCienega Blvd., Suite 510
Inglewood, California 90301
(213) 417-5830

Spectra Enterprise Associates
200 North Westlake Blvd., Suite 215
Westlake Village, California 91362
(805) 373-8537

Sprout Group
3000 Sand Hill Road, #1 Suite 285
Menlo Park, California 94025
(415) 854-1550

Stanford University Endowment
   Fund
c/o Treasurer's Office
209 Hamilton Avenue
Palo Alto, California 94301
(415) 723-1317

Stephens & Company
550 Montgomery Street
San Francisco, California 94111
(415) 781-8000

Summit Ventures
4000 MacArthur Blvd. #750
Newport Beach, California 92660
(714) 476-2700

Sutro & Company
55 South Flower Street, #3400
Los Angeles, California 90071
(213) 362-4008

Sutter Hill Ventures
Two Palo Alto Square, Suite 700
Palo Alto, California 94306-0910
(415) 493-5600

Symbolics, Inc.
21605 Plummer Street, #2154
Chatsworth, California 91313
(818) 998-3600

TA Associates
435 Tasso Street #200
Palo Alto, California 94301
(415) 328-1210

Taylor & Turner
220 Montgomery Street; Penthouse 10
San Francisco, California 94104
(415) 398-6821

Technology Funding, Inc.
2000 Alameda de las Pulges, Suite
   250
San Mateo, California 94403
(415) 345-2200

Technology Partners
1550 Tiburon Blvd. #A
Belvedere, California 94920
(415) 435-1935

Technology Venture Investors
3000 Sand Hill Road, #4 Suite 210
Menlo Park, California 94025
(415) 854-7472

Terranomics Ventures
50 California Street, 14th Floor
San Francisco, California 94111
(415) 981-3600

Thompson Clive, Inc.
3000 Sand Hill Road, #4 Suite 240
Menlo Park, California 94025
(415) 854-0314

Thorn-EMI Venture Fund Limited
131 Via Bonita
Alamo, California 94507
(415) 838-2045

Triangle Ventures
1611 The Alameda
San Jose, California 95126
(408) 977-1000

Trinity Ventures, Ltd.
20813 Stevens Creek Blvd., Suite 101
Cupertino, California 95014
(408) 446-9690

Twenty First Century Venture
   Partners
1850 Union Street #497
San Francisco, California 94123
(415) 931-9307

U. S. Venture Partners
2180 Sand Hill Road, Suite 300
Menlo Park, California 94025
(415) 854-9080

Union Venture Corporation
445 S. Figueroa Street, 12th Floor
Los Angeles, California 90071
(213) 236-4092

Unity Capital Corporation
10055 Barnes Carson Road
San Diego, California
(619) 452-3180

Vanguard Associates
300 Hamilton Avenue #500
Palo Alto, California 94301
(415) 324-8400

Venca Management
235 Montgomery Street #810
San Francisco, California 94104
(415) 781-4944

Venrock Associates
Two Pal Alto Square #528
Palo Alto, California 94306
(415) 493-5577

Ventana Growth Fund
1660 Hotel Circle North #730
San Diego, California 92108
(619) 291-2757

Venture Growth Associates
3000 Sand Hill Road, #3 Suite
  125
Menlo Park, California 94025
(415) 854-8001

Venture Tech Management, Inc.
30092 Ivy Glenn Drive #230
Lajuna Miguel, California 92677
(714) 495-7151

Vista Capital Corporation
701 B Street #760
San Diego, California 92101
(619) 236-1900

Vista Group (The)
610 Newport Center Drive #400
Newport Beach, California 92660
(714) 720-1416

VK Capital Company
50 California Street #2400
San Francisco, California 94115
(415) 391-5600

VMB, Inc.
315 Third Street #182
San Rafael, California 94901
(415) 456-2911

Volpe & Covington
One Maritime Plaza, 11th Floor
San Francisco, California 94111
(415) 956-8120

Walden Group of Venture Capital
  Funds (The)
750 Battery Street, 7th Floor
San Francisco, California 94111
(415) 391-7225

Wallner & Company
215 Coast Boulevard
La Jolla, California 92037
(619) 454-3805

Wedbush Capital Partners
615 South Flower Street #407
Los Angeles, California 90017
(213) 687-7000

Weiss, Peck & Greer Venture
  Partners, L.P.
555 California Street, Suite
  4760
San Francisco, California 94104
(415) 622-6864

Westamco Investment Company
8929 Wilshire Blvd., Suite
  #400
Beverly Hills, California 90211
(213) 652-8288

Weyhaeuser Venture Company
21515 Hawthorne Boulevard,
  Suite 310
Torrance, California 90503
(213) 543-2661

Williams (J.H.) & Company
J. H. Williams & Company
3000 Sand Hill Road, #1, Suite
  270
Menlo Park, California 94025
(415) 854-0500

Wilshire Capital Inc.
3932 Wilshire Blvd.
Los Angeles, California 90010
(213) 388-1111

Wolfensohn Associates, L.P.
3000 Sand Hill Road, #1 Suite
  220
Menlo Park, California 94025
(415) 854-4324

Wood River Capital Corporation
3000 Sand Hill Road, Suite 280
Menlo Park, California 94025
(415) 854-1005

Woodside Fund
850 Woodside Drive
Woodside, California 94062
(415) 368-5545

Xerox Venture Capital
2029 Century Park East #740
Los Angeles, California 90067
(213) 278-7940

Yosemite Capital Investment
448 Fresno Street
Fresno, California 93706
(209) 485-2431

COLORADO

American Health Care Fund
2084 South Milwaukee Street
Denver, Colorado 80120
(303) 692-8600

Boettcher Venture Capital
  Limited Partners, L.P.
828 17th Street
Post Office Box 54
Denver, Colorado 80303
(303) 628-8640

Centennial Business Development
  Fund
1999 Broadway #2100
Denver, Colorado 80202
(303) 298-9066

Colorado Growth Capital Inc.
1600 Broadway, Ste. 2125
Denver, Colorado 80202
(303) 831-0205

Colorado Venture Management
2995 Wilderness Place
Boulder, Colorado 80301
(303) 440-4055

Columbine Venture Fund, Ltd.
5613 DTC Parkway, Suite 510
Englewood, Colorado 80111
(303) 694-3222

Curtiss Simmons Capital
  Resources, Inc.
8101 East Prentice Avenue, Suite 308
Englewood, Colorado 80111
(303) 740-7600

Grayson and Associates
1700 Lincoln Street #4000
Denver, Colorado 80203
(303) 863-2312

Hill, Kirby & Washington
885 Arapahoe Avenue
Boulder, Colorado 80302
(303) 442-5151

InterMountain Ventures, Ltd.
1100 10th St., P.O. Box 1406
Greeley, Colorado 80632
(303) 356-5721

Investment Securities of Colorado,
  Inc.
4605 Denica Drive
Englewood, Colorado 80111
(303) 796-9192

Larimer & Company
P. O. Box 13977
Denver, Colorado 80201-3977
(303) 298-9066

COLORADO (cont.)

Masters Fund (The)
1426 Pearl Street SW #211
Boulder, Colorado 80302
(303) 443-2460

Pernovo, Inc.
1877 Broadway #405
Boulder, Colorado 80302
(303) 442-1171

Rockies Fund (The)
8301 E. Prentice Avenue #202
Englewood, Colorado 80111-2905
(303) 779-4208

Stephenson Merchant Banking
100 Garfield Street
Denver, Colorado 80206
(303) 355-6000

UBD Capital, Inc./United Equity Corp.
United Equity Corporation
1700 Broadway
Denver, Colorado 80274
(303) 863-6329

Venture Associates, Ltd.
1420 Eighteenth Street #150
Denver, Colorado 80202
(303) 295-1127

Weiss, Peck & Greer Venture
   Partners, L.P.
1113 Spruce #300
Boulder, Colorado 80302
(303) 443-1023

Woody Creek Capital, Inc.
1919 14th Street #330
Boulder, Colorado 80302
(303) 444-6000

CONNECTICUT

Abacus Ventures
411 West Putnam Avenue
Greenwich, Connecticut 06830
(203) 629-1100

Advanced Materials Partners
49 Locust Avenue, P. O. Box 1022
New Canaan, Connecticut 06840
(203) 966-6415

Advest, Inc.
280 Trumbull
Hartford, Connecticut 06111
(203) 525-1421

Babcock Group (The)
49 Locust Avenue, P. O. Box 1022
New Canaan, Connecticut 06840
(202) 972-3579

Beacon Partners Limited
71 Strawberry Hill #614
Stamford, Connecticut 06902
(203) 348-8858

Bridge Capital Advisors, Inc.
185 Asylum Street, 36th Street
City Place
Hartford, Connecticut 06103
(203) 275-6700

Cambridge Research &
   Development Group
21 Bridge Square
Westport, Connecticut 06880
(203) 226-7400

Canaan Venture Partners
105 Rowayton Avenue
Rowayton, Connecticut 02853
(203) 855-0400

Capital Impact Corporation
961 Main Street
Bridgeport, Connecticut 06601
(203) 384-5670

Capital Resource Co. of CT L.P.
699 Bloomfield Avenue
Bloomfield, Connecticut 06002
(203) 243-1114

CIGNA Venture Capital
   Inc./CIGNA Capital Advisers
S-307
Hartford, Connecticut 06152
(203) 726-7537

Connecticut Seed Ventures, L.P.
30 Tower Lane
Avon Park South
Avon, Connecticut 06001
(203) 677-0183

Conning and Company
101 Pearl Street
Hartford, Connecticut 06103
(203) 527-1131

Consumer Venture Partners
One East Putnam Avenue
Greenwich, Connecticut 06830
(203) 629-8800

DCS Growth Fund
P.O. Box 740
Old Greenwich, Connecticut 06870
(203) 637-1704

Driscoll X. (Francis) Associates,
   Inc.
Francis X. Driscoll Associates,
   Inc.
21 Silvermine Woods
Wilton, Connecticut 06897
(203) 762-0379

ELF Technologies, Inc.
P.O. Box 10037
High Ridge Park
Stamford, Connecticut 06904-2037
(203) 358-5120

Fairchester Associates
Soundview Plaza
1266 Main Street
Stamford, Connecticut 06902
(203) 357-0714

Fairfield Venture Partners
1275 Summer Street
Stamford, Connecticut 06905
(203) 358-0255

First Connecticut SBIC
177 State Street
Bridgeport, Connecticut 06604
(203) 366-4726

Grayrock Capital, Inc.
36 Grove Street
New Canaan, Connecticut 06840
(203) 966-8392

Greenwich Venture Partners,
   Inc.
239 Glenville Road #3-VE
Greenwich, Connecticut 06831
(203) 531-8707

HITK
777 Summer Street
Stamford, Connecticut 06901
(203) 323-7773

Jacobs (E. S.) & Co.
E. S. Jacobs & Co.
City Place
Hartford, Connecticut 06157
(203) 275-2743

Kobak (James B.) & Company
James B. Kobak & Company
774 Hollow Tree Ridge Road
Darien, Connecticut 06820
(203) 655-8764

Marcon Capital Corporation
49 Riverside Avenue
Westport, Connecticut 06880
(203) 226-6893

Marigold Capital Development,
   Inc.
32 Field Point
Greenwich, Connecticut 06830
(203) 869-4300

MarketCorp Venture Associates,
   L.P.
285 Riverside Avenue
Westport, Connecticut 06880
(203) 222-1000

Memhard Investment Bankers, Inc.
P. O. Box 617
Old Greenwich, Connecticut 06870
(203) 637-5494

Mordy and Company
2 Greenwich Plaza
Greenwich, Connecticut 06830
(203) 661-7132

Northeastern Capital Corporation
209 Church
New Haven, Connecticut
(203) 865-4500

Oak Investment Partners
One Gorham Island
Westport, Connecticut 06880
(203) 226-8346

Orien Ventures
36 Grove Street
New Canaan, Connecticut 06840
(203) 966-7274

Oxford Venture Corporation
Soundview Plaza
1266 Main Street
Stamford, Connecticut 06902
(203) 964-0592

Prime Capital Management Company
One Landmark Square, Suite 800
Stamford, Connecticut 06901
(203) 964-0642

Prince Ventures
31 Brookside Drive
Greenwich, Connecticut 06830
(203) 869-4114

Procordia Corporation
545 Steamboat Road
Greenwich, Connecticut 06830
(203) 661-2500

Regional Financial Enterprises
36 Grove Street
New Canaan, Connecticut 06840
(203) 966-2800

Saugatuck Capital Company
595 Summer Street
Stamford, Connecticut 06901
(203) 348-6669

SBIC of Connecticut
1115 Main Street, Suite 610
Bridgeport, Connecticut 06604
(203) 367-3282

Seibert, Donald C.
Donald C. Seibert
P. O. Box 740
Old Greenwich, Connecticut 06870
(203) 637-1704

Technology Transitions, Inc.
426 Colt Highway
Farmington, Connecticut 06032-2597
(203) 674-8474

Ventech Partners, L. P.
30 Tower Lane
Avon, Connecticut 06001
(203) 677-0183

Venture Partners
P. O. Box 31382, Central Station
Hartford, Connecticut 06103
(203) 828-1616

Vista Group (The)
36 Grove Street
New Canaan, Connecticut 06840
(203) 972-3400

Vista Technology Ventures
2410 Long Ridge Road
Stamford, Connecticut 06903
(203) 326-2751

Wehr (Neal) & Associates
Neal Wehr & Associates
One Campbell Avenue #73
West Haven, Connecticut 06516
(203) 934-6544

Whitehead Associates
15 Valley Drive
Greenwich, Connecticut 06830
(203) 629-4633

Xerox Venture Capital
800 Long Ridge Road
Stamford, Connecticut 06904
(203) 278-7940

DELAWARE

CIGNA Venture Capital, Inc.
Brandywine Office Building
One Beaver Valley Road
Wilmington, Delaware 19850
(302) 479-6000

Morgan Investment Corporation
902 Market Street
Wilmington, Delaware 19801
(302) 651-3808

DISTRICT OF COLUMBIA

Allied Capital Corporation
1666 K. Street, N.W., Suite 901
Washington, D.C. 20006
(202) 331-1112

Allied Financial Corporation
1666 K Street, N.W., Suite 901
Washington, D.C. 20006
(202) 331-1112

American Advance Ventures, L.P.
2000 L Street, NW #702
Washington, D.C. 20036
(202) 887-5379

American Security Capital Corporation
730 15th Street, N.W.
Washington, D.C. 20013
(202) 624-4843

Broadcast Capital, Inc.
1771 N. Street, N.W.
Washington, D.C. 20036
(202) 429-5393

Bund (Malcolm) & Associates, Inc.
Malcolm Bund & Associates, Inc.
2000 L Street, NW
Washington, D.C. 20036
(202) 293-2910

Corporate Finance of Washington,
  Inc.
1326 R Street, NW #2
Washington, D.C. 20009
(202) 328-9053

D.C. Bancorp Venture Capital
  Company
1801 K Street, N.W.
Washington, D.C. 20006
(202) 955-6970

Environmental Venture Fund
William D. Ruckelshaus Association
1100 Vermont Avenue #1200
Washington, D.C. 20005
(202) 887-9030

First Financial Management
  Services, Inc
5225 Wisconsin Avenue #602
Washington, D.C. 20015
(202) 384-8686

Fulcrum Venture Capital
  Corporation
2021 K Street, N.W., Suite 701
Washington, D.C. 20006
(202) 833-9590

Middle Atlantic Ventures
655 15th Street NW #300
Washington, D.C. 20005
(202) 393-8550

Minority Broadcast Investment
  Corp.
1820 Jefferson Place, NW
Washington, D.C. 20036
(202) 293-116

NBL Capital Corporation
4324 Georgia Avenue, N.W.
Washington, D.C. 20011
(202) 829-1154

DISTRICT OF COLUMBIA
(cont.)

Pierce Investment Banking
1910 K Street, NW #800
Washington, D.C. 20006
(202) 833-8031

Syncom Capital Corporation
1030 15th Street, N.W., Suite 203
Washington, D.C. 20006
(202) 293-9430

U.S. Venture Development Corp.
4801 Massachusetts Avenue, NW,
   Suite 400
Washington, D.C. 20016
(202) 364-8890

Wachtel & Company, Inc.
1101 Fourteenth Street, NW
Washington, D.C. 20005
(202) 898-1144

Washington Resources
   Corporation
1100 H Street NW
Washington, D.C. 20080
(202) 624-6483

Washington Ventures
1320 18th Street NW, Suite 100
Washington, D.C. 20036
(202) 895-2560

FLORIDA

Allied North-American Company
111 E. Las Olas Boulevard
P.O. Box 14758
Fort Lauderdale, Florida 33301
(305) 763-8484

Business Research Company
205 Worth Avenue
P. O. Box 2137
Palm Beach, Florida 33480
(305) 832-2155

Caribank Capital Corporation
255 E. Dania Beach Boulevard
Dania, Florida 33004
(305) 925-2211

CEA Investments, Inc.
101 East Kennedy Boulevard
   #3300
Tampa, Florida 33602
(813) 222-8844

Community Equity Investments,
   Inc.
302 North Barcelona Street
Pensacola, Florida 32501
(904) 433-5619

Gold Coast Capital Corporation
3550 Biscayne Boulevard, Suite 601
Miami, Florida 33137
(305) 576-2012

Himmel Equities, Inc.
3095 North Course Drive
Pompano Beach, Florida 33069
(305) 975-7276

Ideal Financial Corporation
780 N.W. 42nd Avenue, Suite 304
Miami, Florida 33126
(305) 442-4665

Interstate Capital Corporation
701 E. Camino Real
Boca Raton, Florida 33432
(305) 395-8535

J&D Capital Corporation
12747 Biscayne Boulevard
North Miami, Florida 33160
(305) 893-0300

Katho Capital Corporation
2000 W. Commercial Boulevard,
   Suite 108
Ft. Lauderdale, Florida 33309
(305) 776-5700

Market Capital Corporation
P. O. Box 31667
Tampa, Florida 33630-3667
(813) 247-1357

North American Company Ltd.
111 East Las Olas Boulevard
P.O. Box 14758
Fort Lauderdale, Florida 33302
(305) 462-0681

Printon, Kane & Company
2000 Glades Road #202
Boca Raton, Florida 33431
(800) 526-4952

Pro-Med Capital, Inc.
1380 Miami Gardens Drive, NE
North Miami Beach, Florida 33179
(305) 949-5900

Small Business Assistance Corp.
2612 W. 15th Street
Panama City, Florida 32401
(904) 785-9577

South Atlantic Venture Fund, L.P.
614 West Bay Street #200
Tampa, Florida 33606
(813) 253-2500

Southeast Venture Capital Funds
One Southeast Financial Center
Miami, Florida 33131
(305) 375-6470

Universal Financial Services
3550 Biscayne Blvd.,
   Suite 702
Miami, Florida 33137
(305) 573-1496

Venture Capital Management
   Corporation
P.O. Box 2626
Satellite Beach, Florida 32937
(305) 777-1969

Venture Group, Inc.
5433 Buffalo Avenue
Jacksonville, Florida 32208
(904) 353-7313

Venture Opportunities
   Corporation
c/o Robert E. Dady, Esq.
799 Brickell Plaza #900
Miami, Florida 33131
(305) 358-8181

Verde Capital Corporation
255 Alhambra Circle #720
Coral Gables, Florida 33134
(305) 444-8938

Western Financial Capital
   Corporation
1380 Miami Gardens Drive,
   N.E.
North Miami Beach, Florida 33179
(305) 949-5900

GEORGIA

Advanced Technology
   Development Fund
430 10th Street, NW #N114
Atlanta, Georgia 30318
(404) 875-4393

Anatar Investments, Inc.
Gas Light Tower, Suite 2218
235 Peachtree Street
Atlanta, Georgia 30303
(404) 588-0770

Arete Ventures, Inc.
990 Hammond Drive
Atlanta, Georgia 30328
(404) 396-2480

Aumma Capital Corporation
1200 Ashwood Parkway #350
Atlanta, Georgia 30338
(404) 668-0508

Bellsouth Ventures Corporation
1155 Peachtree Street NE
Suite 5501
Atlanta, Georgia 30367
(404) 249-4329

Corporate Finance Associates, Inc.
300 Embassy Row #670
Atlanta, Georgia 30328
(404) 399-5633

Crescent Management Company
5775 Peachtree-Dunwoody Road,
    Suite 330C
Atlanta, Georgia 30342
(404) 252-8660

Grubb & Williams, Ltd.
1500 Tower Place
3340 Peachtree Road
Atlanta, Georgia 30328
(404) 237-6222

Hook (Philipps J.) & Associates, Inc.
Philipps J. Hook & Associates, Inc.
5600 Roswell Road, Suite 300
Atlanta, Georgia 30342
(404) 252-1994

Investor's Equity, Inc.
2629 First Atlanta Tower
Atlanta, Georgia 30383
(404) 523-3999

Mighty Capital Corporation
50 Technology Park, Atlanta,
    Suite 100
Norcross, Georgia 30092
(404) 448-2232

Noro Moseley Partners
4200 Northside Parkway
Building 9
Atlanta, Georgia 30327
(404) 233-1966

North Riverside Capital Corporation
5775-D Peachtree Dunwoody
    Road, Suite 650
Atlanta, Georgia 30342
(404) 252-1076

Palms & Company
1800 Peachtree Rd NW #620
Atlanta, Georgia 30309
(404) 355-2221

Robinson-Humphrey Company,
    Inc. (The)
3333 Peachtree Road NE
Atlanta, Georgia 30326
(404) 266-6000

Summit Ventures
900 Circle 75 Parkway #1390
Atlanta, Georgia 30339
(404) 988-0355

UTech Venture Capital Corporation
990 Hammond Drive #620
Atlanta, Georgia 30328
(404) 396-2480

Wellman-Thomas, Inc.
5775 Peachtree Dunwoody Road
    #640-D
Atlanta, Georgia 30342
(404) 252-8660

HAWAII

Bancorp Hawaii SBIC, Inc.
111 South King Street, #1060
Honolulu, Hawaii 96813
(808) 521-6411

ILLINOIS

Abbot Capital Corporation
9933 Lawler Avenue, Suite 125
Skokie, Illinois 60077
(312) 982-0404

Allstate Insurance Company
Venture Capital Division
Allstate Plaza, E2
Northbrook, Illinois 60062
(312) 291-5681

Alpha Capital Venture Partners
3 First National Plaza, Suite
    1400
Chicago, Illinois 60602
(312) 372-1556

American Healthcare Fund
120 South LaSalle Street #630
Chicago, Illinois 60603
(312) 372-4900

Ameritech Development
    Corporation
10 South Wacker Drive
Chicago, Illinois 60606
(312) 609-6000

Amoco Venture Capital
    Company
200 E. Randolph Drive
Chicago, Illinois 60601
(312) 856-6523

Blair (William) Venture Partners
William Blair Venture Partners
135 South LaSalle Street
Chicago, Illinois 60603
(312) 853-8250

Boundary Fund
955 American Lane #301
Schaumberg, Illinois 60173
(312) 843-7020

Business Ventures, Inc.
20 N. Wacker Drive, Suite 550
Chicago, Illinois 60606
(312) 346-1581

Capital Strategy Group, Inc.
    (The)
20 North Wacker Drive
Chicago, Illinois 60606
(312) 444-1170

Caterpillar Venture Capital, Inc.
100 N.E. Adams Street
Peoria, Illinois 61629-4390
(309) 675-5503

Chicago Capital Fund
208 South LaSalle #200
Chicago, Illinois 60604
(312) 855-6050

Chicago Community Ventures
    Inc.
104 S. Michigan, #215
Chicago, Illinois 60603
(312) 726-6084

Cilcorp Ventures, Inc.
300 Liberty Street
Peoria, Illinois 61602
(309) 672-5158

Combined Fund, Inc. (The)
1525 E. 53rd Street, #908
Chicago, Illinois 60615
(312) 363-0300

Continental Illinois Venture
    Corporation
231 S. LaSalle Street
Chicago, Illinois 60697
(312) 828-8021

December Group, Ltd (The)
135 South LaSalle Street #1119
Chicago, Illinois 60603
(312) 372-7733

Earl Kinship Capital Corporation
400 Skokie Boulevard, #675
Northbrook, Illinois 60062
(312) 291-1466

First Capital Corp. of Chicago
3 First National Place, Suite
    1330
Chicago, Illinois 60670-0501
(312) 732-5400

First Chicago Investment
    Advisors
3 First National Plaza, Suite
    0140
Chicago, Illinois 60670
(312) 732-9711

First Chicago Venture Capital
3 First National Plaza, Suite
    1330
Chicago, Illinois 60670-0501
(312) 732-5400

ILLINOIS (cont.)

Frontenac Venture Company
208 S. LaSalle Street, #1900
Chicago, Illinois 60604
(312) 368-0044

Golder, Thoma & Cressey
120 S. LaSalle Street, Suite
630
Chicago, Illinois 60603
(312) 853-3322

Goldman & Co./Woodall
Publishing Co.
100 Corporate North #100
Bannockburn, Illinois 60015
(312) 295-8858

Hayes & Griffith Venture
Management L.P.
190 South La Salle Street
Chicago, Illinois 60603
(312) 444-6000

IEG Venture Management Inc.
401 North Michigan #2020
Chicago, Illinois 60611
(312) 644-0890

Longworth Ventures
135 South LaSalle Street
Chicago, Illinois 60603
(312) 372-3888

Luken Company (The)
135 South LaSalle Street
Chicago, Illinois 60603
(312) 263-4015

Marquette Venture Partners
1751 Lake Cook #550
Deerfield, Illinois 60015
(312) 346-8290

Mesirow Venture Capital
135 South LaSalle Street
Chicago, Illinois 60603
(312) 443-5752

Neighborhood Fund, Inc.
1950 E. 71st Street
Chicago, Illinois 60649
(312) 684-8074

North American Venture Group,
Limited (The)
55 West Monroe Street
Chicago, Illinois 60603
(312) 236-6800

Northern Capital Corp/Northern
Investment Corporation
50 South LaSalle Street
Chicago, Illinois 60675
(312) 444-3155

Patterson, Johnson & Wang
One East Wacker Drive #3000
Chicago, Illinois 60601
(312) 222-2660

Peterson Finance & Investment
Company
3300 Peterson Avenue, Suite A
Chicago, Illinois 60659
(312) 539-0502

Pivan Management Company
7840 Lincoln Avenue
Skokie, Illinois 60077
(312) 677-1142

Prince Venture Partners
10 South Wacker Drive, #2575
Chicago, Illinois 60606
(312) 454-1408

Productivity Fund (The)
First Analysis Management
20 North Wacker Drive #4220
Chicago, Illinois 60606
(312) 372-3111

Sears Investment Management Company
Xerox Center, 32nd Floor
55 West Monroe Street
Chicago, Illinois 60603
(312) 875-0416

Seidman Jackson Fisher & Company
233 N. Michigan Avenue, Suite 1812
Chicago, Illinois 60601
(312) 856-1812

Sucsy, Fisher & Company
135 South LaSalle Street #616
Chicago, Illinois 60603
(312) 346-4545

Tower Ventures Inc.
Sears Tower, BSC 43-50
Chicago, Illinois 60684
(312) 875-0571

Walnut Capital Corporation
208 South LaSalle Street #1043
Chicago, Illinois 60604
(312) 346-2033

Wind Point Partners, L.P.
Quaker Tower, 321 North Clark Street
Chicago, Illinois 60610
(312) 245-4949

INDIANA

Biddinger Investment Capital
Corporation
9102 North Meridian Street, Suite 500
Indianapolis, Indiana 46260
(317) 844-7390

Circle Ventures Inc.
20 North Meridian Street, 3rd Floor
Indianapolis, Indiana 46240
(317) 636-7242

Corporation for Innovation
Development
One North Capital Avenue #520
Indianapolis, Indiana 46204
(317) 635-7325

Equity Resource Company, Inc.
210 S. Michigan Street
South Bend, Indiana 46601
(219) 237-5255

First Source Capital Corporation
100 North Michigan
P.O. Box 1602
South Bend, Indiana 46601
(219) 236-2180

Heritage Venture Group, Inc.
2400 One Indiana Square
Indianapolis, Indiana 46204
(317) 635-5696

Middlewest Ventures, L.P.
20 North Meridian Street, Suite 500
Indianapolis, Indiana 46204
(317) 631-8822

Miller Venture Partners
235 Washington Street
P.O. Box 808
Columbus, Indiana 47202
(812) 376-3331

White River Capital Corporation
500 Washington Street
P.O. Box 929
Columbus, Indiana 47202
(812) 276-1759

IOWA

Allsop Venture Partners
2750 First Avenue, N.E.
Cedar Rapids, Iowa 52402
(315) 363-8971

Invest America Venture Group, Inc.
800 American Building
Cedar Rapids, Iowa 52401
(319) 363-8249

Iowa Venture Capital Fund, L.P.
800 American Building
Cedar Rapids, Iowa 52401
(319) 363-8249

Pappajohn Capital Resources
2116 Financial Center
Des Moines, Iowa 50309
(515) 244-5746

Retail Opportunities, Inc.
5205 Woodland Avenue
Des Moines, Iowa 50312
(515) 255-6521

KANSAS

Allsop Venture Partners
8700 Monrovia, Suite 212
Lenexa, Kansas 66215
(913) 492-9542

Kansas Venture Capital, Inc.
One Townsite Plaza #A1030
Topeka, Kansas 66603
(619) 233-1368

Ventures Medical
4330 Shawnee Mission Parkway,
  #335
Shawnee Mission, Kansas 66202
(913) 362-7044

KENTUCKY

Bluegrass Capital Corporation
1815 Plantside Drive
P.O. Box 35000
Louisville, Kentucky 40232
(502) 499-1004

Equal Opportunity Finance, Inc.
420 Hurstbourne Lane, Suite
  201
Louisville, Kentucky 40222
(502) 423-1943

Financial Opportunities Inc.
P. O. Box 35710
Louisville, Kentucky 40232-5710
(502) 451-3800

Hilliard-Lyons Patent
  Management, Inc.
10509 Timberwood Circle
Louisville, Kentucky 40223
(502) 429-0015

Humana, Inc.
500 West Main Street
Louisville, Kentucky 40202
(502) 580-1000

Kentucky Highlands Investment
  Corp.
911 North Main Street
London, Kentucky 40741
(606) 864-5175

Mountain Ventures Inc.
911 N. Main Street
P. O. Box 628
London, Kentucky 40741
(606) 864-5175

LOUISIANA

Commercial Capital, Inc.
P.O. Box 1776
Covington Lane, Louisiana 70434
(504) 893-7260

Dixie Business Investment Co.
P.O. Box 588
Lake Providence, Louisiana 71254
(318) 559-1558

First Southern Capital
  Corporation
6161 Perkins Road
Baton Rouge, Louisiana 70898
(504) 769-3004

Louisiana Equity Capital
  Corporation
451 Florida Street
P.O. Box 1511
Baton Rouge, Louisiana 70821
(504) 389-4421

Southern Cooperative
  Development Fund (SCDF)
1006 Surrey Street
Lafayette, Louisiana 70501
(318) 232-9206

Walnut Street Capital Company
2330 Canal Street
New Orleans, Louisiana 70119
(504) 821-4952

MAINE

Maine Capital Corporation
70 Center Street
Portland, Maine 04101
(207) 772-1001

North Atlantic Venture Fund
70 Center Street
Portland, Maine 04101
(207) 772-4470

MARYLAND

ABS Ventures Limited Partnerships
135 E. Baltimore Street
Baltimore, Maryland 21202
(301) 727-1700

Arete Ventures, Inc.
6110 Executive Boulevard #1040
Rockville, Maryland 20852
(301) 881-2555

Broventure Capital Management
16 West Madison Street
Baltimore, Maryland 21201
(301) 727-4520

Emerging Growth Partners
400 East Pratt Street #610
Baltimore, Maryland 21202
(301) 332-1021

First Maryland Capital, Inc.
107 W. Jefferson Street
Rockville, Maryland 20850
(301) 251-0033

Greater Washington Investors
5454 Wisconsin Ave., Suite 1315
Chevy Chase, Maryland 20815
(301) 656-0626

Grotech Partners, L.P.
2201 Old Court Road
Baltimore, Maryland 21208
(301) 828-4600

Meridian Ventures
21 West Road
Baltimore, Maryland 21204
(301) 296-1000

New Enterprise Associates
1119 St. Paul Street
Baltimore, Maryland 21202
(301) 244-0115

Security Financial & Investment
  Corp.
7720 Wisconsin Avenue, Suite 207
Bethesda, Maryland 20814
(301) 951-4288

Spectra Enterprise Associates
1119 St. Paul Street
Baltimore, Maryland 21202
(301) 244-0115

Suburban Capital Corporation
6610 Rockledge Drive
Bethesda, Maryland 20817
(301) 493-7025

T. Rowe Price Threshold
  Partnerships
100 East Pratt Street
Baltimore, Maryland 21202
(301) 547-2000

UTech Venture Capital
  Corporation
c/o Arete Ventures, Inc.
6110 Executive Boulevard #1040
Rockville, Maryland 20852
(301) 881-2555

MASSACHUSETTS

ABS Ventures Limited Partnership
200 Fifth Avenue
Waltham, Massachusetts 02154
(617) 890-9445

MASSACHUSETTS (cont.)

Acquivest Group, Inc.
5 Speen Street
Framingham, Massachusetts 01701
(617) 875-3242

Adams, Harkness & Hill, Inc.
One Liberty Square
Boston, Massachusetts 02109
(617) 423-6688

Advanced Technology Ventures
10 Post Office Square, Suite 1230
Boston, Massachusetts 02109
(617) 423-4050

Advent International
45 Milk Street
Boston, Massachusetts 02109
(617) 574-8400

Aegis Fund Limited Partnerships
One Cranberry Hill
Lexington, Massachusetts 02173
(617) 862-0200

American Research & Development (ARD)
45 Milk Street
Boston, Massachusetts 02109
(617) 423-7500

Amervest Corporation
10 Commercial Wharf W.
Boston, Massachusetts 02110
(617) 723-5230

Ampersand Ventures (formerly Paine Webber Venture Management Co.)
55 William Street, Suite 240
Wellesley, Massachusetts 02181
(617) 239-0700

Analog Devices Enterprises
Two Technology Way
Norwood, Massachusetts 02062
(617) 329-4700

Anthonyson & Sheehan, Inc.
180 Linden Street
Wellesley, Massachusetts 02181
(617) 431-1095

Applied Technology Investors, Inc.
55 Wheeler Street
Cambridge, Massachusetts 02138
(617) 354-4107

Atlantic Energy Capital Corporation
260 Franklin Street, Suite 1501
Boston, Massachusetts 02110
(617) 439-6160

Atlas Venture
One Cambridge Center
Cambridge, Massachusetts 02142
(617) 621-1600

Bain Venture Capital
Two Copley Place
Boston, Massachusetts 02116
(617) 572-3000

BancBoston Ventures, Inc.
100 Federal Street
Boston, Massachusetts 02110
(617) 434-3323

Battery Ventures, L.P.
200 Portland Street
Boston, Massachusetts 02114
(617) 367-1011

Berner (R.C.) & Company
R.C. Berner & Company
65 William Street
Wellesley, Massachusetts 62181
(617) 237-9472

Bessemer Venture Partners
83 Walnut Street
Wellesley Hills, Massachusetts 02181
(617) 237-6050

Beta Ventures, Inc.
One Post Office Square #3800
Boston, Massachusetts 02109
(617) 482-8020

BMW Technologies Inc.
800 South Street
Waltham, Massachusetts 02154
(617) 894-8222

Boston Capital Ventures
One Devonshire Place, Suite 2913
Boston, Massachusetts 02109
(617) 227-6550

Boston Ventures Management, Inc.
45 Milk Street, Fifth Floor
Boston, Massachusetts 02109
(617) 292-8125

Bristol Investment Trust
842A Beacon Street
Boston, Massachusetts 02215
(617) 566-5212

Burr, Egan, Deleage & Company
One Post Office Square, Suite 3800
Boston, Massachusetts 02109
(617) 482-8020

Charles River Ventures
67 Batterymarch Street
Boston, Massachusetts 02110
(617) 439-0477

Chatham Venture Corporation
450 Bedford Street
Lexington, Massachusetts 02173
(617) 863-0970

Churchill International
9 Riverside Road
Weston, Massachusetts 02193
(617) 893-6555

Claflin Capital Management, Inc.
185 Devonshire Street
Boston, Massachusetts 02110
(617) 426-6505

Coolidge Investment Corporation
One Boston Place #923
Boston, Massachusetts 02108
(617) 723-3098

Copley Venture Partners
600 Atlantic Avenue, 24th Floor
Boston, Massachusetts 02110
(617) 722-6030

Corning Venture Management
125 Pearl Street
Boston, Massachusetts 02110
(617) 451-6722

CP Ventures, Inc.
25 Mall Road, #300
Burlington, Massachusetts 01803
(617) 270-0685

Downer & Company
125 Pearl Street
Boston, Massachusetts 02110
(617) 482-8846

E G & G Venture Partners
45 William Street
Wellesley, Massachusetts 02181
(617) 237-5100

East Boston Community Development Corp.
72 Marginal Street
East Boston, Massachusetts 02128
(617) 569-5590

Eastech Management Company, Inc.
One Liberty Square, 9th Floor
Boston, Massachusetts 02109
(627) 338-0200

Fidelity Venture Associates, Inc.
82 Devonshire Street
Boston, Massachusetts 02109
(617) 570-6450

Fin-Tech
36 Washington Street
Wellesley Hills, Massachusetts 02181
(617) 237-7762

First Chicago Venture Capital
One Financial Center, 27th Floor
Boston, Massachusetts 02111
(617) 542-9185

Fleet Venture Partners
1740 Massachusetts Avenue
Boxborough, Massachusetts 01719
(617) 263-0177

Foster, Dykema, Cabot & Company
50 Milk Street
Boston, Massachusetts 02109
(617) 423-3900

Fowler, Anthony & Company
20 Walnut Street
Wellesley, Massachusetts 02181
(617) 237-4201

Genesis Venture Capital Group,
   Inc. (The)
100 Fifth Avenue
Waltham, Massachusetts 02154
(617) 890-7631

GFI Technology, Inc.
Watermill Center, 800 South Street
Waltham, Massachusetts 02154
(617) 891-4455

Global Investments Ltd. Partnership
600 Atlantic Avenue #2000
Boston, Massachusetts 02210
(617) 973-9680

Greylock Management Corporation
One Federal Street
Boston, Massachusetts 02110
(617) 423-5525

Gryphon Ventures
545 Boylston Street
Boston, Massachusetts 02116
(617) 542-9130

Hambrecht & Quist Venture
   Partners
One Hollis Street #102
Wellesley, Massachusetts 02181
(617) 237-2099

Hambro International Venture Fund
One Boston Place
Boston, Massachusetts 02106
(617) 722-7055

Hancock Venture Capital
One Financial Center
Boston, Massachusetts 02111
(617) 350-4002

Harbour Financial Company
357 Fox Hill Street
Westwood, Massachusetts 02090
(617) 461-0460

Highland Capital Partners
260 Franklin Street, Suite 1920
Boston, Massachusetts 02110
(617) 439-6630

HLM Management Company
10 Liberty Square
Boston, Massachusetts 02109
(617) 423-3530

Investors in Industry (3i) Capital
   Corp.
99 High Street, Suite 1530
Boston, Massachusetts 02110
(617) 542-8560

Little (Arthur D.) Enterprises, Inc.
Arthur D. Little Enterprises, Inc.
20 Acorn Park
Cambridge, Massachusetts 02140
(617) 864-5770

Massachusetts Capital Resource
   Company
545 Boylston Street
Boston, Massachusetts 02116
(617) 536-3900

Massachusetts Community
   Development Finance
   Corporation (CDFC)
131 State Street #600
Boston, Massachusetts 02109
(617) 242-0366

Massachusetts Technology -
   Development Corporation (MTDC)
84 State Street #500
Boston, Massachusetts 02109
(617) 723-4920

Matrix Partners
One Post Office Square
Boston, Massachusetts 02109
(617) 482-7735

McGowan Leckinger Berg
10 Forbes Road
Braintree, Massachusetts 02184
(617) 849-0020

MDT Advisers, Inc.
20 Acorn Park
Cambridge, Massachusetts 02140
(617) 864-5770

Media/Communications Partners
45 Milk Street
Boston, Massachusetts 02109
(617) 574-6719

Merrill, Pickard, Anderson &
   Eyre
281 Winter Street
Waltham, Massachusetts 02154
(617) 890-0670

Millicorp
c/o Millipore Corporation
80 Ashby Road
Bedford, Massachusetts 01730
(617) 275-9200

Morgan Holland Ventures
One Liberty Square
Boston, Massachusetts 02109
(617) 423-1765

Nautilus Fund, Inc.
c/o Eaton Vance Corp.
24 Federal Street
Boston, Massachusetts 02110
(617) 482-8260

New England Capital Corporation
One Washington Mall, 7th
   Floor
Boston, Massachusetts 02108
(617) 722-6400

Northeast SBIC Corporation
16 Cumberland Street
Boston, Massachusetts 02115
(617) 267-3983

Orange Nassau Capital
   Corporation
260 Franklin Street
15th Floor
Boston, Massachusetts 02110
(617) 439-6160

PaineWebber Venture
265 Franklin Street, Suite 1501
Boston, Massachusetts 02110
(617) 439-8300

Palmer Partners
300 Unicorn Park Drive
Woburn, Massachusetts 01801
(617) 933-5445

Pell, Rudman & Company, Inc.
40 Rowes Wharf
Boston, Massachusetts 02110
(617) 542-6633

Pioneer Capital Corporation
60 State Street, #3220
Boston, Massachusetts 02109
(617) 742-7825

Plant Resources Venture Funds
124 Mount Auburn Street, Suite
   310
Cambridge, Massachusetts 02138
(617) 492-3900

PON Capital Corporation
150 Braintree Executive Park
Grossman Drive
Braintree, Massachusetts 02184
(617) 849-1349

MASSACHUSETTS (cont.)

Raytheon Ventures
141 Spring Street
Lexington, Massachusetts 02173
(617) 860-2270

Regent Financial Corporation
10 Commercial Wharf W.
Boston, Massachusetts 02110
(617) 723-4820

Robertson, Colman & Stephens
155 Federal Street
Boston, Massachusetts 02110
(617) 542-9393

Schooner Capital Corporation
99 Bedford Street
Boston, Massachusetts 02111
(617) 357-9031

Security Pacific Capital
   Corp./First SBIC of
   California
50 Milk Street, 15th Floor
Boston, Massachusetts 02109
(617) 542-7601

Shawmut National Ventures
   Corporation
One Federal Street, 30th
   Floor
Boston, Massachusetts 02211
(617) 556-4700

Sigma Partners
342 Green Street
Northboro, Massachusetts 01532
(617) 393-7396

Sprout Group
Center Plaza, 6th Floor
Boston, Massachusetts 02108
(617) 570-8700

Subro Ventures Corporation
Watermill Center
800 South Street
Waltham, Massachusetts 02154
(617) 894-8750

Summit Ventures
One Boston Place #3420
Boston, Massachusetts 02109
(617) 742-5500

Symbolics, Inc.
11 Cambridge Center
Cambridge, Massachusetts 02142
(617) 621-7500

T A Associates
45 Milk Street
Boston, Massachusetts 02109
(617) 338-0800

Tanner Capital Corporation
Exchange Place, 32nd Floor
Boston, Massachusetts 02109
(617) 227-5225

Transatlantic Capital Corporation
24 Federal Street
Boston, Massachusetts 02110
(617) 482-0015

Transportation Capital Corporation
230 Newbury Street
Boston, Massachusetts 02116
(617) 536-0344

TVM TechnoVenture Management
45 Milk Street
Boston, Massachusetts 02109
(617) 574-6706

Ulin, Morton, Bradley, & Welling
75 Federal Street
Boston, Massachusetts 02110
(617) 423-0003

UNC Ventures
195 State Street #700
Boston, Massachusetts 02109
(617) 723-8300

UST Capital Corp.
40 Court Street
Boston, Massachusetts 02108
(617) 726-7171

Vadus Capital Corporation
260 Franklin Street, Suite 1501
Boston, Massachusetts 02110
(617) 439-6160

Venture Capital Fund of New
   England (The)
160 Federal Street, 23rd Floor
Boston, Massachusetts 02110
(617) 439-4646

Venture Founders Corporation
One Cranberry Hill
Lexington, Massachusetts 02173
(617) 863-0900

Venture Partners
164 Canal Street
Boston, Massachusetts 02114
(617) 523-3280

VIMAC Corporation
12 Arlington Street
Boston, Massachusetts 02116
(617) 267-2785

Zero Stage Capital Company,
   Inc.
One Broadway, 10th Floor
Cambridge, Massachusetts 02142
(617) 876-5355

MICHIGAN

Alan-Dean & Company, Inc.
20276 Mack Avenue
Grosse Pointe Woods, Michigan 48236
(313) 886-6116

Battery Ventures
308 West Huron
Ann Arbor, Michigan 48103
(313) 663-1666

Dearborn Capital Corporation
P.O. Box 1729
Dearborn, Michigan 48121
(313) 337-8577

Doan Resources, L.P.
4251 Plymouth Road
P.O. Box 986
Ann Arbor, Michigan 48105
(313) 757-9401

Enterprise Development Fund
308 West Huron
Ann Arbor, Michigan 48103
(313) 663-3213

Great Lakes Capital Management,
   Inc.
7001 Orchard Lake #330
West Bloomfield, Michigan 48322
(313) 737-4545

Growth Funding, Ltd.
321 Fisher Building
Detroit, Michigan 48202
(313) 871-3606

Houston & Associates Inc.
1471 South Woodward #210
Bloomfield Hills, Michigan 48013
(313) 332-1625

Lowe (Edward) Group, Inc. (The)
The Edward Lowe Group, Inc.
203 North Edward Street
Cassopolis, Michigan 49031
(616) 445-8685

MBW Management Inc.
4251 Plymouth Road
P.O. Box 986
Ann Arbor, Michigan 48106-0986
(313) 747-9401

Metro-Detroit Investment Company
30777 Northwestern Highway,
   Suite 300
Farmington Hills, Michigan 48018
(313) 851-6300

Michigan Product Development Fund
23935 Research Drive
Farmington Hills, Michigan 48027
(313) 474-3314

Michigan Tech Capital
  Corporation
Technology Park
601 W. Sharon Avenue
P.O. Box 364
Houghton, Michigan 49931
(909) 487-2970

Motor Enterprises, Inc.
3044 W. Grand Blvd.
Detroit, Michigan 48202
(313) 556-4273

Mutual Investment Company,
  Inc.
21415 Civic Center Drive
Southfield, Michigan 48076
(313) 357-2020

Newtek Ventures
4660 South Hagadorn Road
East Lansing, Michigan 48823
(517) 337-4411

Regional Financial Enterprises
325 East Eisenhower Parkway,
  Suite 103
Ann Arbor, Michigan 48104
(313) 769-0941

Ventures Group, Inc. (The)
601 Sharon Avenue
Houghton, Michigan 49931
(906) 487-2970

MINNESOTA

Altair Ventures, Inc.
1401 West 94th Street
Minneapolis, Minnesota 55431
(612) 884-7281

Capital Dimensions Venture Fund
Two Appletree Square,
Suite 244
Minneapolis, Minnesota 55425-1637
(612) 854-3007

Capital Dimensions Venture
  Fund (Formerly Control Data
  Community Ventures Fund)
Two Appletree Square, Suite 244
Minneapolis, Minnesota 55425-1637
(612) 854-3007

Cherry Tree Ventures
1400 Northland Plaza
3800 West 80th Street
Minneapolis, Minnesota 55431
(612) 893-9012

Consumer Growth Capital, Inc.
8200 Humboldt Avenue S.
Bloomington, Minnesota 55431
(612) 888-9561

Dain Bosworth, Inc.
100 Dain Tower
Minneapolis, Minnesota 55402
(612) 371-2711

DGC Capital Co.
525 Lake Avenue South, Suite 216
Duluth, Minnesota 55802
(218) 722-0058

FBS Venture Capital Company
8000 78th Street W, #300
Edina, Minnesota 55435-2890
(612) 829-1122

First Midwest Capital Corporation
914 Plymouth Building
12 S. Sixth Street
Minneapolis, Minnesota 55402
(612) 339-9391

IAI Venture Capital Group
1100 Dain Tower, P.O. Box 357
Minneapolis, Minnesota 55440
(612) 371-7935

Impact Seven, Inc.
P.O. Box 15555
Minneapolis, Minnesota 55415
(612) 338-8185

Medical Innovation Capital Inc.
1201 Margrette Avenue #400
Minneapolis, Minnesota 55403
(612) 332-5130

Microtechnology Investments, Ltd.
7900 International Drive
Minneapolis, Minnesota 55420
(612) 851-1500

Minnesota Seed Capital, Inc.
Parkdale Plaza #330
1660 South Highway 100
Minneapolis, Minnesota 55416
(612) 545-5684

North Star Ventures Inc.
100 S. Fifth Street, #2200
Minneapolis, Minnesota 55402
(612) 333-1133

Northland Capital Corp.
613 Missabe Bldg., 227 W. 1st Street
Duluth, Minnesota 55802
(218) 722-0545

Northwest Venture Partners
222 S. Ninth Street, #2800
Minneapolis, Minnesota 55402
(612) 372-8770

Norwest Growth Fund, Inc.
222 S. Ninth Street, #2800
Minneapolis, Minnesota 55402
(612) 372-8770

Norwest Venture Capital
  Management, Inc.
2800 Piper Jaffray Tower
Minneapolis, Minnesota 55402
(612) 372-8770

Oak Investment Partners
33 South Sixth Street
Multifoods Tower #3920
Minneapolis, Minnesota 55402
(612) 339-9322

Pathfinder Venture Capital
  Funds
7300 Metro Blvd., Suite 585
Minneapolis, Minnesota 55435
(612) 835-1121

Piper Jaffray Ventures Inc.
222 South 9th Street
P.O. Box 28
Minneapolis, Minnesota 55402
(612) 342-6000

Retailers Growth Fund Inc.
2318 Park Avenue
Minneapolis, Minnesota 55404
(612) 872-4929

Shared Ventures, Inc.
6550 York Avenue South, Suite
  419
Minneapolis, Minnesota 55435
(612) 925-3411

Threshold Ventures, Inc.
430 Oak Grove Street, Suite 303
Minneapolis, Minnesota 55403
(612) 874-7199

MISSISSIPPI

Columbia Ventures, Inc.
809 North State
Jackson, Mississippi 39215
(601) 354-1453

Sun Delta Capital Access Center
819 Main Street
Greenville, Mississippi 38701
(601) 335-5291

Vicksburg SBIC
302 First National Bank Building
Vicksburg, Mississippi 39180
(601) 636-4762

MISSOURI

Allsop (R.W.) Venture Partners
R.W. Allsop & Associates
55 West Port Plaza, Suite 575
St. Louis, Missouri 63146
(314) 434-1688

MISSOURI (cont.)

Bankers Capital Corp.
3100 Gillham Road
Kansas City, Missouri 64109
(816) 531-1600

Capital for Business, Inc.
11 S. Meramec, Suite 800
St. Louis, Missouri 63105
(314) 854-7427

De Vries (Robert J.) & Company
Robert J. De Vries & Company
800 West 47th Street
Kansas City, Missouri 64112
(816) 756-0055

Gateway Associates, L.P.
8000 Maryland Avenue #1190
St. Louis, Missouri 63105
(314) 721-5707

Harbour Group Investments
7701 Forsyth Boulevard #550
St. Louis, Missouri 63105
(314) 727-5550

Intech Group, Inc.
130 South Berniston #703
St. Louis, Missouri 63105
(314) 863-3888

InvestAmerica Venture
Commerce Tower Building, #2724
911 Main Street
Kansas City, Missouri 64105
(816) 842-0114

United Missouri Capital Corp.
1010 and Grand, P.O. Box 226
Kansas City, Missouri 64141
(816) 556-7333

MONTANA

Development Corporation of Montana
350 North Last Chance Gulch
P.O. Box 916
Helena, Montana 59601
(406) 442-3850

Montana Science and Technology
  Alliance
46 North Last Chance #213
Helena, Montana 59620
(406) 449-2778

NEBRASKA

Community Equity Corp. of Nebraska
6421 Ames Avenue
Omaha, Nebraska 68104
(402) 455-7722

Nebraska Research &
  Development Authority
646 NBC Center
Lincoln, Nebraska 68508
(402) 475-5109

NEVADA

HITK
3835 Greenleaf Drive
Las Vegas, Nevada 89120
(702) 453-3307

United Venture Capital, Inc.
2288 Main Street
Genoa, Nevada 89411
(702) 782-5114

NEW HAMPSHIRE

Granite State Capital, Inc.
599 Middle Street
P. O. Box 6564
Portsmouth, New Hampshire
  03801
(603) 436-5044

Harvard Venture Capital
27 Loop Road, P.O. Box 746
Merrimack, New Hampshire 03054
(603) 429-0858

Kearsarge Ventures LP
66 Hanover Street #202
Manchester, New Hampshire 03101
(603) 625-1466

North Atlantic Venture Fund
102 Bay Street
Manchester, New Hampshire 03103
(603) 644-8110

Signal Capital Corporation
Liberty Lane
Hampton, New Hampshire 03842
(603) 929-3000

Vencap, Inc.
1155 Elm Street
Manchester, New Hampshire 03101
(603) 644-6100

NEW JERSEY

Accel Partners
One Palmer Square
Princeton, New Jersey 08542
(609) 683-4500

Amerinex Corporation
Park 80 West, Plaza Two
Saddle Brook, New Jersey 07662
(201) 845-0500

Bradford Associates
22 Chambers Street
Princeton, New Jersey 08540
(609) 921-3880

Bridge Capital Advisors,
  Inc.
Glenpointe Centre West
Teaneck, New Jersey 07666
(201) 836-3900

Capital Circulation Corp.
208 Main Street
Fort Lee, New Jersey 07024
(201) 947-8637

Capital SBIC, Inc.
691 State Highway 33
Mercerville, New Jersey 08619
(609) 890-1500

Domain Associates
One Palmer Square
Princeton, New Jersey 08542
(609) 683-5656

DSV Partners
221 Nassau Street
Princeton, New Jersey 08542
(609) 924-6420

Edelson Technology Partners
Park 80 West, Plaza Two
Saddle Brook, New Jersey 07662
(201) 843-4474

Edison Venture Fund
90 Nassau Street
Princeton, New Jersey 08540
(609) 683-1900

ESLO Capital Corporation
212 Wright
Newark, New Jersey 07114
(201) 242-4488

Essex Vencap, Inc.
1401 Broad Street
Clifton, New Jersey 07015
(201) 773-6300

First Princeton Capital
  Corp.
227 Hamburg Turnpike
Pompton Lakes, New Jersey 07442
(201) 831-0330

Geocapital Ventures
2115 Linwood Avenue
Fort Lee, New Jersey 07024
(201) 461-9292

InnoVen Group
Park 80 West, Plaza One
Saddle Brook, New Jersey 07662
(201) 845-4900

Investment Partners of America
732 West 8th Street
Plainfield, New Jersey 07060
(201) 561-3622

Johnson & Johnson Development
  Corp.
One Johnson & Johnson Plaza
New Brunswick, New Jersey
  08933
(201) 524-6407

Johnston Associates, Inc.
181 Cherry Valley Road
Princeton, New Jersey 08540
(609) 924-3131

KBA Partners, L.P.
400 Kelby Street
Parker Plaza
Fort Lee, New Jersey 07024
(201) 461-8585

Main Capital Investment
  Corporation
426 Essex Street, Suite J
Hackensack, New Jersey 07601
(201) 489-2080

MBW Management, Inc.
365 South Street, 2nd Floor
Morristown, New Jersey 07960
(201) 285-5533

Med-Tech Ventures, Inc.
201 Tabor Road
Morris Plains, New Jersey 07950
(201) 540-3457

Monmouth Capital Corp.
P.O. Box 335
125 Wyckoff Road
Eatontown, New Jersey 07724
(201) 542-4927

Princeton/Montrose Partners
101 Poor Farm Road
Princeton, New Jersey 08540
(609) 921-1590

Printon, Kane & Company
830 Morris Turnpike
P.O. Box 910
Short Hills, New Jersey 07078
(201) 467-9300

Raybar Small Business
  Investment Corp.
255 West Spring Valley Avenue
Maywood, New Jersey 07607
(201) 368-2280

Richardson & McGrath Associates
104 Algonquin Trail
Oakland, New Jersey 07436
(212) 337-9608

Rutgers Minority Investment Co.
180 University Avenue
Newark, New Jersey 07102
(201) 648-5627

SL/Health Care Ventures
c/o Health Care Investment
  Corporation
Twin Towers at Metro Park
379 Thornall Street
Edison, New Jersey 08837
(201) 906-4600

Tucker Capital Corporation
19 Vandeventer
Princeton, New Jersey 08542
(609) 924-5710

U.S. Venture Development Corporation
30 Ethel Road
Edison, New Jersey 08817
(201) 287-9039

Unicorn Ventures, Ltd.
6 Commerce Drive
Cranford, New Jersey 07016
(201) 276-7880

Venturtech Management, Inc.
210 Main Street
P.O. Box 210
Gladstone, New Jersey 07934
(201) 234-2373

Waldorf Group, Inc.
201 Lower Notch Road
Little Falls, New Jersey 07424
(201) 256-8280

WSGP
310 South Street, Suite CN1913
Morristown, New Jersey 07960
(201) 898-0293

NEW MEXICO

ADS Financial Services, Inc.
524 Camino del Monte Sol
Santa Fe, New Mexico 87501
(505) 983-1769

Albuquerque SBIC
501 Tijeras Ave NW
Albuquerque, New Mexico 87103
(505) 247-4089

Associated Southwest Investors, Inc.
2400 Louisiana, N.E., #4
Albuquerque, New Mexico 87110
(505) 881-0066

Equity Capital Corporation
119 East Marcy, Suite 101
Santa Fe, New Mexico 87501
(505) 988-4273

Fluid Capital Corp.
3939 San Pedro Drive NE
Albuquerque, New Mexico 87110
(505) 884-3600

New Business Capital Fund Ltd.
134 Rio Rancho Drive
Rio Rancho, New Mexico 87124
(505) 891-0766

New Mexico Capital Corporation
3939 San Pedro Drive NE
Albuquerque, New Mexico 87110
(505) 884-3600

New Mexico Research &
  Development Inst.
Pinon Building #358
1220 South St. Francis Drive
Santa Fe, New Mexico 87501
(505) 827-5886

Sage Management Partners
1650 University Blvd., N.E., Suite
  500
Albuquerque, New Mexico 87102
(505) 768-6267

Southwest Capital Inc.
3500-E Commanche Rd., N.E.
Albuquerque, New Mexico 87107
(505) 884-7161

NEW YORK

Adler & Company
375 Park Avenue, Ste. 3303
New York, New York 10152
(212) 759-2800

Adler & Shaykin
375 Park Avenue, Suite 1401
New York, New York 10152
(212) 319-2800

Alimansky Venture Group, Inc.
605 Madison Avenue #300
New York, New York 10022
(212) 832-7300

Allen, Elliott & Alexander, Inc.
116 Deerhurst Park
P. O. Box F
Kenmore, New York 14217
(716) 875-4253

American Commercial Capital Corp.
310 Madison Ave., Suite 1304
New York, New York 10017
(212) 986-3305

American Corporate Services
515 Madison Avenue #1225
New York, New York 10022
(212) 688-9691

NEW YORK (cont.)

AMEV Capital Corporation
One World Trade Center, Suite
   5001
New York, New York 10048
(212) 323-9800

Applied Technology Investors
   Inc.
25 Central Park West #31
New York, New York 10023
(212) 245-6238

Atalanta Investment Company,
   Inc.
450 Park Avenue, Suite 2102
New York, New York 10022
(212) 832-1104

Athena Venture Partners
375 Park Avenue #3303
New York, New York 10152
(212) 759-2800

Axa Capital Corporation
445 West 45th
New York, New York 10036
(212) 421-7870

Baer & Company
277 Park Avenue, 47th Floor
New York, New York 10172
(212) 207-1651

BankAmerica Capital Corporation
335 Madison Avenue
New York, New York 10017
(212) 503-8456

Bartlett Schlumberger Capital
   Corp.
310 East 46th Street
New York, New York 10017
(212) 319-7500

Bernhard Associates
6 East 43rd Street
New York, New York 10017
(212) 986-7500

Bessemer Venture Partners
630 Fifth Avenue
New York, New York 10111
(212) 708-9300

Biotech Capital Corporation
600 Madison Avenue
New York, New York 10022
(212) 758-7722

Blair (D.H.) & Co.
D.H. Blair & Co.
44 Wall Street
New York, New York 10005
(212) 968-2269

Boston Capital Ventures
645 Madison Avenue
New York, New York 10022
(212) 750-6122

Braintree Management Limited
59 South Greely Avenue
Chappaqua, New York 10514
(914) 238-5221

Bridge Capital Advisors, Inc.
50 Broadway
New York, New York 10004
(212) 514-6700

BT Capital Corporation
280 Park Avenue
New York, New York 10017
(212) 850-1916

Butler Capital Corporation
767 Fifth Avenue, Sixth Floor
New York, New York 10153
(212) 980-0606

C W Group, Inc.
1041 Third Avenue
New York, New York 10021
(212) 308-5266

Cegmark International
15 Columbus Circle
New York, New York 10023
(212) 541-7010

Central New York SBIC Inc. (The)
351 S. Warren Street, Suite 600
Syracuse, New York 13202
(315) 478-5026

Charterhouse Group International,
   Inc.
535 Madison Avenue
New York, New York 10022
(212) 421-3125

Chase Manhattan Capital Corp.
One Chase Manhattan Plaza, 23rd
   Floor
New York, New York 10081
(212) 552-6275

Chemical Venture Capital Corp.
277 Park Avenue, 10th Floor
New York, New York 10172
(212) 310-4949

Chromos Capital Corporation
80 Broad Street, 29th Floor
New York, New York 10004
(212) 908-0380

Citicorp Venture Capital Ltd.
153 East 53rd Street, 28th Floor
New York, New York 10043
(212) 559-1127

Clinton Capital Corp.
79 Madison Avenue
New York, New York 10016
(212) 696-4334

CMNY Capital Company, Inc.
77 Water Street
New York, New York 10005
(212) 437-7078

Cofinam Incorporated
125 East 56th Street
New York, New York 10022
(212) 593-6100

Coleman Ventures, Inc.
5909 Northern Boulevard
East Norwich, New York 11732
(516) 626-3642

Computer Science Capital
300 East 40th Street
New York, New York 10016
(212) 599-3465

Concord Partners
535 Madison Avenue
New York, New York 10022
(212) 906-7100

Crown Advisors Limited
225 Broadway #612
New York, New York 10007
(212) 619-1840

Croyden Capital Corp.
45 Rockefeller Place, Suite 2165
New York, New York 10111
(212) 974-0184

CW Group Inc.
1041 Third Avenue
New York, New York 10021
(212) 308-5266

DeMuth, Folger & Terhune
One Exchange Plaza at 55 Broadway
New York, New York 10006
(212) 509-5580

De Than (Charles) Group
Charles De Than Group
51 East 67th Street
New York, New York 10021
(212) 988-5108

Deutsche Bank Capital Corp.
40 Wall Street
New York, New York 10005
(212) 612-0616

Drexel Burnham Lambert Inc/The
   Lambda Fund
60 Broad Street
New York, New York 10004
(212) 480-6000

EAB Venture Corporation
10 Hanover Square
New York, New York 10015
(212) 437-4182

Eberstadt Fleming Venture Capital
1270 Ave. of the Americas, 11th Floor
New York, New York 10020
(212) 713-7701

Edwards Capital Company
215 Lexington Avenue, #805
New York, New York 10016
(212) 686-2568

Elk Associates Funding Corp.
600 Third Avenue, #3810
New York, New York 10016
(212) 972-8550

Elron Technologies Inc.
1200 Avenue of the Americas
New York, New York 10036
(212) 819-1664

Environmental Venture Fund
F & G Associates
123 Grove Avenue #118
Cedarhurst, New York 11516
(516) 374-4040

Equico Capital Corp.
1290 Avenue of the Americas,
   Suite 3400
New York, New York 10019
(212) 397-8660

Euclid Partners Corporation
50 Rockefeller Plaza
New York, New York 10020
(212) 489-1770

Everlast Capital Corp.
350 Fifth Avenue, Suite 2805
New York, New York 10118
(212) 695-3910

Exeter Capital, L.P.
1185 Avenue of the Americas, #2700
New York, New York 10036
(212) 840-4040

Fahnestock and Company
110 Wall Street
New York, New York 10005
(212) 668-8000

Fairfield Equity Corporation
200 E. 42nd Street
New York, New York 10017-5893
(212) 867-0150

Ferranti High Technology, Inc.
515 Madison Avenue, #1225
New York, New York 10022
(212) 688-9828

Fidenas Corporation
900 Third Avenue
New York, New York 10022
(212) 308-2240

Fifty-Third Street Ventures, L.P.
420 Madison Ave., #1101
New York, New York 10017
(212) 319-5740

Financial Health Associates
160 East 72nd Street
New York, New York 10021
(212) 517-4406

First Boston Corporation
12 East 49th Street
New York, New York 10017
(212) 909-2000

First Century Partners
1345 Avenue of the Americas
New York, New York 10105
(212) 698-6383

Fleet Venture Partners
666 Third Avenue
New York, New York 10017
(212) 972-8126

Foster Management Company
437 Madison Avenue
New York, New York 10022
(212) 753-4810

Founders Equity, Inc.
200 Madison Avenue
New York, New York 10016
(212) 953-0100

Fredericks Michael & Company
1 World Trade Center
15th Floor, Suite 1509
New York, New York 10048
(212) 466-6620

Freshstart Venture Capital
   Corp.
313 West 53rd Street
New York, New York 10019
(212) 265-2249

Fundex Capital Corporation
525 Northern Boulevard
Great Neck, New York 11021
(516) 466-8550

Gabelli Value, Inc.
655 Third Avenue
New York, New York 10017
(212) 953-5722

General Instrument Corporation
767 Fifth Avenue
New York, New York 10153
(212) 207-6200

Genesee Capital Inc.
100 Corporate Woods
Rochester, New York 14623
(716) 272-2334

Geo Capital Ventures
655 Madison Avenue
New York, New York 10021
(212) 935-0111

GHW Capital Corp.
489 Fifth Avenue, 2nd Floor
New York, New York 10017
(212) 687-1708

Gibbons, Green, Van Amerongen
600 Madison Avenue
New York, New York 10022
(212) 832-2400

Globus Growth Group
44 West 24th Street
New York, New York 10010
(212) 243-1000

Goldmark Capital Associates, Ltd.
320 Park Avenue
New York, New York 10022
(212) 759-9080

Goldome Strategic Investments, Inc.
One Fountain Plaza
Buffalo, New York 14203
(716) 857-6486

Gould (Arthur P.) & Company
Arthur P. Gould & Company
One Wilshire Drive
Lake Success, New York 11020
(516) 773-3000

Grayson and Associates
16 East 53rd Street
New York, New York 10022
(212) 580-8817

Great Lakes Capital Corp.
100 Corporate Woods #300
Rochester, New York 14623
(716) 272-2308

Greenhouse Management
   Corporation (The)
10 Tinker Lane
East Setauket, New York 11733
(516) 751-7898

Grumman Venture, Inc.
111 Stewart Avenue
Bethpage, New York 11714
(516) 575-6815

Guinness Mahon, Inc.
126 East 56 Street, #15 FL Tower 56
New York, New York 10022-3513
(212) 355-5400

NEW YORK (cont.)

Hambro International Venture
  Fund
17 East 71st Street
New York, New York 10021
(212) 288-7778

Hanover Capital Corporation
505 Park Avenue
New York, New York 10022
(212) 838-5893

Harrison Capital, Inc.
2000 Westchester Avenue
White Plains, New York 10650
(914) 253-7845

Harvest Ventures
767 Third Avenue
New York, New York 10017
(212) 838-7776

Helfer Broughton, Inc.
90 West
New York, New York 10006
(212) 587-8200

Herbert Young Securities,
  Inc.
98 Cuttermill Road
Great Neck, New York 11021
(516) 487-8300

Himmel Equities, Inc.
450 Park Avenue #1905
New York, New York 10022
(212) 688-1301

HiTech Venture Consultants,
  Inc.
8 West 40th Street, 10th Floor
New York, New York 10018
(212) 819-9500

Holding Capital Group
685 Fifth Avenue, 14th Floor
New York, New York 10022
(212) 486-6670

Hutton Venture Investment
  Partners, Inc.
31 West 52nd Street
New York, New York 10019
(212) 969-9303

Hycliff Partners
6 East 43rd Street, 28th Floor
New York, New York 10017
(212) 986-7500

Ibero-American Investors
  Corp.
38 Scio Street
Rochester, New York 14604-2514
(716) 262-3440

Inco Venture Capital Management
One New York Plaza, 37th Floor
New York, New York 10004
(212) 612-5620

Instoria, Inc./Providentia, Ltd.
15 W. 54th Street, 2nd Floor
New York, New York 10019-5404
(212) 957-3232

Integrated Medical Venture Partners
733 Third Avenue, 8th Floor
New York, New York 10017
(212) 551-5215

Intercoastal Capital Corporation
385 Madison Avenue
New York, New York 10017
(212) 986-0482

Interfid, Ltd.
Dag Hammarskjold Plaza
New York, New York 10017
(212) 832-2324

Intergroup Venture Capital Corp.
230 Park Avenue
New York, New York 10017
(212) 661-5428

International Monetary Corporation
54 West 16th Street #5E
New York, New York 10011
(212) 929-7344

International Technology Ventures, Inc.
200 Park Avenue #5506
New York, New York 10166
(212) 972-5233

Investech, L.P.
515 Madison Avenue #2400
New York, New York 10022
(212) 308-5811

Irving Capital Corp./ITC Capital Corp
1290 Avenue of the Americas
New York, New York 10104
(212) 408-4800

Jacobs (E.S.) & Company, L.P.
E.S. Jacobs & Company, L.P.
375 Park Avenue
New York, New York 10152
(212) 688-7166

Japanese American Capital
  Corporation
19 Rector Street
New York, New York 10006
(212) 344-4588

Johnsen Securities, Inc.
767 Third Avenue
New York, New York 10017
(212) 838-7776

Jordan Company (The)
315 Park Avenue South
New York, New York 10010
(212) 460-1900

Josephberg Grosz & Co., Inc.
344 East 49th Street
New York, New York 10017
(212) 935-1050

Keegan (Warren) Associates,
  Inc.
Warren Keegan Associates,
  Inc.
210 Stuyvesant Avenue
Rye, New York 10580
(914) 967-9421

Key Venture Capital Corporation
60 State Street
Albany, New York 12207
(518) 447-3500

KG Capital Corporation
3100 Monroe Avenue
Rochester, New York 14618
(716) 586-6015

Kuhns Brothers & Laidlaw,
  Inc.
275 Madison Avenue
New York, New York 10016
(212) 949-5300

Kwiat Capital Corp.
576 Fifth Avenue
New York, New York 10036
(212) 391-2460

Laidlaw, Adams & Peck, Inc.
275 Madison Avenue
New York, New York 10016
(212) 949-5300

Lawrence, Tyrrell, Ortale &
  Smith
515 Madison Avenue
New York, New York 10022-5403
(212) 826-9080

Lepercq de Neuflize & Co., Inc.
345 Park Avenue
New York, New York 10154
(212) 702-6100

M&T Capital Corp.
One M&T Place, 5th Floor
Buffalo, New York 14240
(716) 842-5881

Manufacturers Hanover Venture
  Capital Corp./MH Capital
  Investors, Inc.
270 Park Avenue
New York, New York 10017
(212) 286-3220

Marks (Carl) & Company, Inc.
Carl Marks & Company, Inc.
77 Water Street
New York, New York   10005
(212) 437-7078

Martin Simpson & Company, Inc.
150 Broadway, Suite 1606
New York, New York   10038
(212) 406-5200

Mayfair Capital Partners, Inc.
757 Third Avenue
New York, New York   10017
(212) 750-5100

McCown de Leeuw & Company
900 Third Avenue, 28th Floor
New York, New York   10022
(212) 418-6539

Medallion Funding Corporation
205 E. 42nd Street, Suite 2020
New York, New York   10017
(212) 682-3300

Merrill Lynch Venture Capital, Inc.
717 Fifth Avenue, 22nd Floor
New York, New York   10022
(212) 980-0410

Minority Equity Capital Co., Inc.
275 Madison Avenue, Suite 1901
New York, New York   10016
(212) 686-9710

Morgan Capital Corporation
900 Third Avenue
New York, New York   10022
(212) 223-3303

Morgan Stanley Venture Partners
1251 Avenue of the Americas
New York, New York   10020
(212) 703-4000

Multi-Purpose Capital Corp.
31 S. Broadway
Yonkers, New York   10701
(914) 963-2733

NAB Nordic Investors Ltd.
c/o DNC Capital Corp.
600 Fifth Avenue
New York, New York   10020
(212) 315-6532

NatWest USA Capital Corp.
175 Water Street
New York, New York   10038-4924
(212) 602-1200

Nazem & Company
600 Madison Avenue
New York, New York   10022
(212) 644-6433

Nelson Capital Corp.
585 Stewart Avenue
Garden City, New York   11530
(516) 222-2555

New York State Science &
   Technology Foundation
CID Program
99 Washington Avenue #1730
Albany, New York   12210
(518) 473-9741

Norstar Venture Capital Corp.
One Norstar Plaza
Albany, New York   12207-2796
(518) 447-4050

North American Capital
   Corporation
510 Broad Hollow #205
Melville, New York   11747
(516) 752-9600

North American Funding Corp.
177 Canal Street
New York, New York   10013
(212) 226-0080

North American Ventures
   Funds
c/o Inco Venture Capital
   Management
One New York Plaza
New York, New York   10004
(212) 612-5620

North Street Capital Corp.
250 North Street, RA-6S
White Plains, New York   10625
(914) 335-7901

Northwood Ventures
485 Madison Avenue, 20th Floor
New York, New York   10022
(212) 935-4595

Novatech Resource Corporation
103 East 37th Street
New York, New York   10016
(212) 725-2555

NYBDC Capital Corp.
41 State Street
Albany, New York   12207
(518) 463-2268

Ocean Ventures Management
   Inc.
126 East 56th Street
New York, New York   10022
(212) 758-7760

Pan Pac Capital Corporation
121 East Industry Court
Deer Park, New York   11729
(516) 586-7653

Patricof (Alan) Associates, Inc.
Alan Patricof Associates, Inc.
545 Madison Avenue
New York, New York   10022
(212) 753-6300

Penntech Papers Inc.
Three Barker Avenue
White Plains, New York   10601
(914) 997-1600

Pennwood Capital Corporation
9 West 57th Street
New York, New York   10019
(212) 753-1600

Pierre Funding Corporation
270 Madison Avenue, Suite
   1608
New York, New York   10016
(212) 689-9361

Pioneer Ventures Company
113 East 55th Street
New York, New York   10022
(212) 980-9094

Pittsford Group (The)
8 Lodge Pole Road
Pittsford, New York   14534
(716) 223-3523

Poindexter (J.B.) & Company
J.B. Poindexter & Company
Three East 54th Street
New York, New York   10022
(212) 888-8900

Poly Ventures
Polytechnic University
Route 110
Farmingdale, New York   11735
(516) 249-4710

Preferential Capital Company
16 Court Street
Brooklyn, New York   11241
(718) 855-2728

Princeton/Montrose Partners
c/o Alan Patricof Associates,
   Inc.
545 Madison Avenue, 15th
   Floor
New York, New York   10022
(212) 753-6300

Printon, Kane & Company
590 Madison Avenue #312
New York, New York   10022
(800) 526-4952

Prospect Group, Inc. (The)
667 Madison Avenue
New York, New York   10021
(212) 758-8500

NEW YORK (cont.)

Prudential Venture Capital
717 Fifth Avenue #1600
New York, New York 10022
(212) 753-0901

Pyramid Ventures, Inc.
280 Park Avenue
New York, New York 10017

Questec Enterprises, Inc.
328 Main Street
Huntington, New York 11743
(516) 351-1222

Questech Capital Corp.
600 Madison Avenue
New York, New York 10022
(212) 758-8522

Quincy Partners
P.O. Box 154
Glen Head, New York 11545
(212) 355-7830

R & R Financial Corporation
1451 Broadway
New York, New York 10036
(212) 790-1400

R&D Funding
One Seaport Plaza, 33rd Floor
New York, New York 10038
(212) 214-1480

Rain Hill Group, Inc.
90 Broad Street
New York, New York 10004
(212) 483-9162

Rand Capital Corporation
1300 Rand Building
Buffalo, New York 14203
(716) 853-0802

Realty Growth Capital Corporation
271 Madison Avenue
New York, New York 10016
(212) 983-6880

Reprise Capital Corporation
585 Stewart Avenue #416
Garden City, New York 11530
(516) 222-2555

Research and Science Investors,
  Inc.
230 Park Avenue, Suite 1260
New York, New York 10169
(212) 867-9535

Retail Opportunities Inc.
605 Madison Avenue #300
New York, New York 10022
(212) 832-7333

Revere Fund Inc. (The)
575 Fifth Avenue, 17th Floor
New York, New York 10017
(212) 808-9090

Richardson & McGrath
  Associates
150 East 35th Street
New York, New York 10016
(212) 337-9608

Richter, Cohen & Co.
950 Third Avenue
New York, New York 10022
(212) 421-6300

Robertson, Colman & Stephens
535 Madison Avenue
New York, New York 10022
(212) 319-8900

Rothschild Ventures Inc.
One Rockefeller Plaza
New York, New York 10020
(212) 757-6000

Roundhill Capital
c/o D.H. Blair & Company
44 Wall Street
New York, New York 10005
(212) 969-2055

S/L Health Care Ventures
1250 Broadway 25th Floor
New York, New York 10001
(212) 714-1470

Salomon Brothers Venture
  Capital
Two New York Plaza
New York, New York 10004
(212) 747-7900

Samuel Montagu Holdings,
  Inc.
535 Madison Avenue
New York, New York 10022
(212) 702-5469

Schmitt (Peter J.) SBIC, Inc.
Peter J. Schmitt SBIC, Inc.
355 Harlem Road
West Seneca, New York 14240
(716) 825-1111

Schroder Ventures Managers
  Limited
One State Street
New York, New York 10004
(212) 269-6500

Sevin Rosen Management
  Company
200 Park Avenue #4503
New York, New York 10166
(212) 686-5115

Shearson Lehman Brothers, Inc.
American Express Tower
World Financial Center
New York, New York 10285
(212) 298-2000

Siemens Capital Corporation
767 Fifth Avenue
New York, New York 10153
(212) 832-6601

Sierra Ventures Management
  Company
645 Madison Avenue #2100
New York, New York 10022
(212) 750-9420

Situation Ventures Corporation
502 Flushing Avenue
Brooklyn, New York 11205
(718) 855-1811

Skora (Allan E.) Associates
Allan E. Skora Associates
49 West 12th Street
Executive Suite
New York, New York 10011
(212) 691-9895

Small Business Electronics Co.,
  Inc.
1220 Peninsula Boulevard
Hewlett, New York 11557
(516) 374-0743

Southern Tier Capital Corp.
55 S. Main Street
Liberty, New York 12754
(914) 292-3030

Spinnaker Funds
c/o Hamilton Robinson & Co., Inc.
30 Rockefeller Plaza, Suite
  #3320
New York, New York 10112
(212) 246-8600

Sprout Group
140 Broadway
New York, New York 10005
(212) 504-3600

Square Deal Venture Capital
805 Avenue L
Brooklyn, New York 11230
(718) 692-2924

SRK Management Company
126 East 56th Street
New York, New York 10022
(212) 371-0900

Stuart James Venture Partners
805 Third Avenue, 9th Floor
New York, New York 10022
(212) 758-4665

TA Associates
48 West 68th Street #5 E
New York, New York 10022
(212) 769-1858

Tappan Zee Capital Corp.
120 N. Main Street
New City, New York 10956
(914) 634-8890

Taroco Capital Corporation
19 Rector Street
New York, New York 10006
(212) 344-6690

Tessler & Cloherty, Inc.
155 Main Street
Cold Spring, New York 10516
(914) 265-4244

Thomar Publications, Inc.
383 South Broadway
Hicksville, New York 11801
(516) 681-2111

Tinicum, Inc.
885 Second Avenue
New York, New York 10017
(212) 832-3883

TLC Funding Corporation
660 White Plains Road
Tarrytown, New York
(914) 332-5200

Transportation Capital Corporation
60 E. 42nd Street
New York, New York 10165
(212) 697-4885

Triad Venture Capital
  Corporation
950 Southern Blvd.
Bronx, New York 10459
(212) 589-6541

Tucker, Anthony & RL Day, Inc.
120 Broadway
New York, New York 10271
(212) 618-7400

UTech Venture Capital
  Corporation
One Seaport Plaza
New York, New York 10292
(212) 214-5356

Vega Capital Corporation
720 White Plains Road
Scarsdale, New York 10583
(914) 472-8550

Vencon Management, Inc.
301 West 53rd Street #10F
New York, New York 10019
(212) 581-8787

Venrock Associates
30 Rockefeller Plaza, Room 5508
New York, New York 10112
(212) 247-3700

Venture Capital Fund of America,
  Inc.
509 Madison Avenue
New York, New York 10022
(212) 838-5577

Venture Funding Group
49 West 12th Street
Executive Suite
New York, New York 10011
(212) 691-9895

Venture Lending Associates
767 Fifth Avenue
New York, New York 10153
(212) 980-0606

Venture Opportunities Corporation
110 East 59th Street, 29th Floor
New York, New York 10022
(212) 832-3737

Venture SBIC, Inc.
249-12 Jericho Turnpike
Floral Park, New York 10101
(516) 352-4210

VS & A Communications
  Partners, LP
350 Park Avenue
New York, New York 10022
(212) 935-4990

Walnut Capital Corporation
20 Exchange Place
New York, New York 10005
(212) 425-6883

Warburg, Pincus Ventures, Inc.
466 Lexington Avenue
New York, New York 10017
(212) 878-0600

Weiss, Peck & Greer Venture
  Partners, L.P
One New York Plaza, 30th Floor
New York, New York 10004
(212) 908-9500

Welsh, Carson, Anderson &
  Stowe
One World Financial Center, Suite
  3601
New York, New York 10281
(212) 945-2000

Wertheim Schroder & Co.,
  Incorporated
200 Park Avenue
New York, New York 10166
(212) 492-6000

Whitney (J.H.) & Company
J.H. Whitney & Company
630 Fifth Avenue, Room 3200
New York, New York 10111
(212) 757-0500

Winfield Capital Corp.
237 Mamaroneck Avenue
White Plains, New York 10605
(914) 949-2600

Winthrop Ventures
74 Trinity Place
New York, New York 10006
(212) 422-0100

Wolfensohn Associates L.P.
599 Lexington Avenue
New York, New York 10022
(212) 909-8100

Wood River Capital Corp.
645 Madison Avenue #2100
New York, New York 10022
(212) 750-9420

Yang Capital Corporation
41-40 Kissena Boulevard
Flushing, New York 11355
(718) 445-4585

NORTH CAROLINA

Atlantic Venture Partners
Two Piedmont Plaza
2000 West First Street #101
Winston-Salem, North Carolina 27104
(919) 725-2961

Falcon Capital Corp.
400 W. 5th Street
Greenville, North Carolina 27834
(619) 752-5918

Heritage Capital Corporation
2290 First Union Plaza
Charlotte, North Carolina 28282
(704) 334-2867

Intersouth Partners
2222 East Chapel Hill
Nelson Highway
Research Triangle Park, North
  Carolina 27709
(919) 544-6473

Kitty Hawk Capital Ltd.
Independence Center #1640
Charlotte, North Carolina 28246
(704) 333-3777

Kobe Development Corp.
Charlotte Plaza #2400
Charlotte, North Carolina 28244
(704) 378-3342

NORTH CAROLINA (cont.)

NCNB SBIC Corporation
One NCNB Plaza, TO5-2
Charlotte, North Carolina 28255
(704) 374-5000

NCNB Venture Company, L.P.
One NCNB Plaza, P.O. Box 100
Charlotte, North Carolina 28255
(704) 374-5723

Ruddick Investment Company
2290 First Union Plaza
Charlotte, North Carolina 28282
(704) 333-7144

Southgate Venture Partners/Delta
Capital Corp.
227 N. Tryon Street, Suite 201
Charlotte, North Carolina 28202
(704) 372-1410

Trivest Venture Fund
1300 St. Mary's Street #210
Raleigh, North Carolina 27605
(919) 834-9984

Venture Capitalists, Inc.
813 Hawthorne Lane
Charlotte, North Carolina 28204
(704) 334-3314

Venture First Associates
2422 Reynolda Road
Winston-Salem, North Carolina
27106
(919) 722-9600

Wheat First Securities
First Center Building #101
2000 West First Street
Winston-Salem, North Carolina
27104
(919) 725-2961

NORTH DAKOTA

Dakota First Capital Corporation
51 Broadway, Suite 601
Fargo, North Dakota 58102
(701) 237-0450

OHIO

A.T. Venture Capital Group
900 Euclid Avenue, T-18, P.O. Box 5937
Cleveland, Ohio 44101-0937
(216) 687-4970

BancOne Capital Corporation
100 East Broad Street
Columbus, Ohio 43215
(614) 248-5832

Brantley Venture Partners, L.P.
20600 Chagrin Boulevard #520
Cleveland, Ohio 44122
(216) 283-4800

Capital Funds Corporation
800 Superior Avenue, 12th Floor
Cleveland, Ohio 44114
(216) 344-5776

Cardinal Development Capital
Fund
40 South 3rd Street, Suite 460
Columbus, Ohio 43215
(614) 464-5557

Center City MESBIC
40 South Main Street, Suite 762
Dayton, Ohio 45402
(513) 461-6164

Clarion Capital Corporation
35555 Curtis Boulevard
Eastlake, Ohio 44094
(216) 953-0555

First Ohio Capital Corp.
606 Madison Avenue
P.O. Box 2061
Toledo, Ohio 43604
(419) 259-7151

Glenco Enterprises
1464 East 105th Street, Suite 101
Cleveland, Ohio 44106
(216) 721-1200

Gries Investment Company
720 Statler Office Tower
Cleveland, Ohio 44115
(216) 861-1146

Heartland Group, Inc.
545 Hanna Building
Cleveland, Ohio 44115
(216) 696-6663

Hook Partners
815 National City Bank Building
Cleveland, Ohio 44114
(216) 621-3142

Lubrizol Enterprises, Inc.
29400 Lakeland Boulevard
Wickliffe, Ohio 44092
(216) 943-4200

Miami Valley Capital, Inc.
315 Talbott Tower
Dayton, Ohio 45402
(513) 222-7222

Morgenthaler Ventures
700 National City Bank Bldg.
Cleveland, Ohio 44114
(216) 621-3070

National City Capital
Corp./National City Venture Corp.
629 Euclid Avenue
Cleveland, Ohio 44114
(216) 575-2491

Primus Capital Fund
1375 E. 9th Street, Suite 2140
Cleveland, Ohio 44114
(216) 621-2185

River Capital Corporation
796 Huntington Building
Cleveland, Ohio 44115
(216) 781-3655

Scientific Advances, Inc.
601 West Fifth Avenue
Columbus, Ohio 43201
(614) 424-7005

SeaGate Venture Management Inc.
245 North Summit Street, #1403
Toledo, Ohio 43603
(419) 259-8605

Senmed Ventures Group
4445 Lake Forest Drive #600
Cincinnati, Ohio 45242
(513) 563-3264

SHV Investment Fund
300 Pike Street
Cincinnati, Ohio 45202
(513) 621-4014

Small Business Advocacy, Inc. (The)
526 Nilles Road #5
Fairfield, Ohio 45014
(513) 829-0880

Sokol (Si) & Associates
Si Sokol & Associates
50 West Broad Street
Columbus, Ohio 43215
(614) 228-2800

Tamco Investors, Inc.
P. O. Box 1588
375 Victoria Road
Youngstown, Ohio 44501
(216) 792-0805

Technology Ventures, Inc.
26949 Chagrin Boulevard
Beachwood, Ohio 44122
(216) 464-5968

OKLAHOMA

Alliance Business Investment
Company
One Williams Center, Suite 2000
Tulsa, Oklahoma 74172
(918) 584-3581

Davis Venture Partners, L.P.
One Williams Center, Suite 2000
Tulsa, Oklahoma 74172
(918) 584-7272

Holding Capital Group
7136 South Yale #208
Tulsa, Oklahoma 74136
(918) 492-8524

Signal Capital Corporation
One Leadership Square #400
Oklahoma City, Oklahoma 73102
(405) 235-4440

Southwest Venture Capital Inc.
2700 E. 51st Street, Suite 340
Tulsa, Oklahoma 74105
(918) 742-3177

TSF Capital Corporation
2415 East Skelly Drive #102
Tulsa, Oklahoma 74105
(918) 749-5588

Western Venture Capital Corp.
4880 S. Lewis
P. O. Box 702680
Tulsa, Oklahoma 74105
(918) 744-6275

Woody Creek Capital, Inc.
320 South Boston #831
Tulsa, Oklahoma 74103
(918) 582-5811

OREGON

Cable & Howse Ventures
1800 One Main Place, 101 SW
  Main
Portland, Oregon 97204
(503) 248-9646

Earl Kinship Capital Corporation
10300 Southwest Greenburg Road,
  Suite 240
Portland, Oregon 97223
(503) 244-7307

InterVen Partners
227 SW Pine Street
Portland, Oregon 97204
(503) 223-4334

Northern Pacific Capital Corp.
1201 SW 12th Avenue
Portland, Oregon 97205
(503) 241-1255

Norwest Venture Capital
  Management, Inc.
1300 SW Fifth Ave., Suite 3018
Portland, Oregon 97201
(503) 223-6622

Olympic Venture Partners/Rainier
  Venture Partners
10300 Southwest Greenburg Road
Portland, Oregon 97223
(503) 245-5900

Oregon Resource & Technology
  Corporation
One Lincoln Center #430
Portland, Oregon 97233
(503) 246-4844

Orians Investment Company
529 SW Third Avenue, Suite 600
Portland, Oregon 97204
(503) 224-7885

Rosenfeld & Company
1211 Southwest Sixth Avenue
Portland, Oregon 97204
(503) 228-3255

Shaw Venture Partners
851 S.W. Sixth Avenue #800
Portland, Oregon 97204
(503) 228-4884

Tektronix Development Co.
P.O. Box 4500
M S 94-383
Forest Grove, Oregon 97076
(503) 629-1121

Trendwest Capital Corporation
803 Main Street #404
P.O. Box 5106
Klamath Falls, Oregon 97601
(503) 882-8059

PENNSYLVANIA

Adler & Shaykin
1631 Locust Street
Philadelphia, Pennsylvania 19103
(215) 985-9999

Alliance Enterprise Corporation
1801 Market Street
Philadelphia, Pennsylvania 19103
(215) 977-3925

Aluminum Company of America
1501 Alcoa Building
Pittsburgh, Pennsylvania 15219
(412) 553-2677

Capital Corporation of America
225 South 15th Street #920
Philadelphia, Pennsylvania 19102
(215) 732-1666

Century IV Partners
1760 Market Street
Philadelphia, Pennsylvania 19103
(215) 751-9444

CEO Venture Fund
4516 Henry Street #402
Pittsburgh, Pennsylvania 15213
(412) 687-3451

Core States Enterprise Fund
One Penn Center #1360
Philadelphia, Pennsylvania 19103
(215) 568-4673

Enterprise Venture Capital Corp.
  of Pennsylvania
227 Franklin Street, #215
Johnstown, Pennsylvania 15901
(814) 535-7597

Entrepreneurial Seed Fund
125 North 8th Street
Philadelphia, Pennsylvania 19106
(215) 931-0100

Erie Small Business Investment
  Company
32 West Eighth Street #615
Erie, Pennsylvania 16501
(814) 453-7964

First Valley Capital
  Corporation
640 Hamilton Mall, 8th
  Floor
Allentown, Pennsylvania 18101
(215) 776-6760

Fostin Capital Corp.
681 Andersen Drive
Pittsburgh, Pennsylvania 15220
(412) 928-8900

Genesis Seed Management
  Company
3 Great Valley Parkway, Suite
  105
Malvern, Pennsylvania 19355
(215) 640-1447

Greater Philadelphia Venture
  Capital Corporation, Inc.
225 S. 15th Street, Suite 920
Philadelphia, Pennsylvania 19102
(215) 732-1666

Hillman Ventures, Inc.
2000 Grant Building
Pittsburgh, Pennsylvania 15219
(412) 281-2620

Howard, Lawson & Company
2 Penn Center Plaza
Philadelphia, Pennsylvania 19102
(215) 988-0010

Innovest Group, Inc.
1700 Market #1228
Philadelphia, Pennsylvania 19103
(215) 564-3960

PENNSYLVANIA (cont.)

Keystone Venture Capital
  Management Co.
211 South Broad Street
Philadelphia, Pennsylvania 19107
(215) 985-5519

Kopvenco
3100 Koppers Building
Pittsburgh, Pennsylvania 15219
(412) 227-2222

Meridian Venture Partners (MVP)
The Fidelity Court Building
259 Radnor-Chester Road
Radnor, Pennsylvania 19087
(215) 293-0210

Nepa Venture Fund, L.P.
125 Goodman Drive
Bethelehem, Pennsylvania 18015
(215) 865-6550

New Hope Capital Corporation
1936 Street Road
New Hope, Pennsylvania 18938
(215) 794-3273

Pennsylvania Growth Investment
  Corp.
1000 RIDC Plaza #311
Pittsburgh, Pennsylvania 15238
(412) 963-9339

Philadelphia Capital Advisors
Philadelphia National Bank Building
Broad & Chestnut Streets
Philadelphia, Pennsylvania 19107
(215) 629-2727

Philadelphia Commercial
  Development Corp
714 Market Street #433
Philadelphia, Pennsylvania 19106
(215) 238-7676

Philadelphia Industries, Inc.
1401 Walnut Street, 2nd Floor
Philadelphia, Pennsylvania 19102
(215) 569-9900

Philadelphia Ventures, Inc.
1760 Market Street
Philadelphia, Pennsylvania 19103
(215) 751-9444

PIDC Penn Venture Fund
123 South Broad Street, 22nd Floor
Philadelphia, Pennsylvania 19109
(215) 875-3520

Pittsburgh Seed Fund Partners
4516 Henry Street #102
Pittsburgh, Pennsylvania 15213
(412) 687-5200

PNC Venture Capital Group
5th Avenue & Wood Street, 19th
  Floor
Pittsburgh, Pennsylvania 15222
(412) 355-2245

Robinson Venture Partners
6507 Wilkins Avenue
Pittsburgh, Pennsylvania 15217
(412) 661-1200

S.R. One, Ltd.
One Franklin Plaza
Philadelphia, Pennsylvania 19101
(215) 751-4257

Safeguard Scientifics, Inc.
630 Park Avenue
King of Prussia, Pennsylvania 19406
(215) 265-4000

Security Pacific Capital
  Corp./First S B I C of California
P.O. Box 512
Washington, Pennsylvania 15301
(412) 223-0707

T D H II Limited
c/o K.S. Sweet Associates
259 Radnor-Chester Road
Radnor, Pennsylvania 19087
(215) 964-0112

Trivest Venture Fund
P.O. Box 36
Lignoier, Pennsylvania 15658
(412) 471-0151

Venture Associates
Two Penn Center Plaza #410
Philadelphia, Pennsylvania 19102
(215) 988-0010

Venwest Partners
Westinghouse Electric Building
Gateway Center
Pittsburgh, Pennsylvania 15222
(412) 647-5859

Wyndmoor Associates Ltd.
8600 Elliston Drive
Wyndmoor, Pennsylvania 19118
(215) 233-3023

Zero Stage Capital Company, Inc.
1346 South Atherton Street
State College, Pennsylvania 16801
(814) 231-1330

PUERTO RICO

North America Investment Corp.
Banco Popular Center, Suite 1710
Hato Rey, Puerto Rico 00919
(809) 751-6178

Venture Capital PR, Inc.
Calle 58, (Altos) Condado
58 Caribe Street
Santurce, Puerto Rico 00907
(809) 721-3550

RHODE ISLAND

Domestic Capital Corporation
815 Reservoir Avenue
Cranston, Rhode Island 02910
(401) 946-3310

Earl Kinship Capital
  Corporation
2401 Hospital Trust Tower
Providence, Rhode Island 02903
(401) 831-4800

Fleet Venture Partners
111 Westminster Street
Providence, Rhode Island 02903
(401) 278-6770

Moneta Capital Corporation
Governor Financial Center
285 Governor Street
Providence, Rhode Island 02906
(401) 861-4600

Narragansett Capital Corp.
40 Westminster Street
Providence, Rhode Island 02903
(401) 751-1000

Old Stone Capital Corp.
150 South Main
Providence, Rhode Island 02901
(401) 278-2559

River Capital Corporation
555 South Main Street #321
Providence, Rhode Island 02903
(401) 861-7470

SOUTH CAROLINA

Carolina Venture Capital Corporation
14 Archer Road
Hilton Head Island, South
  Carolina 29928
(803) 842-3101

Charleston Capital Corporation
111 Church Street
P.O. Box 328
Charleston, South Carolina 29402
(803) 723-6464

Low Country Investment
  Corporation
P. O. Box 10447
Charleston, South Carolina 29411
(803) 554-9880

Reedy River Ventures
P.O. Box 17526
400 Haywood Road
Greenville, South Carolina 29606
(803) 297-9196

TENNESSEE

American Health Capital
  Ventures, Inc.
278 Franklin Road #240
Brentwood, Tennessee 37027
(615) 377-0416

Bradford (J.C.) & Company
J.C. Bradford & Company
330 Commerce Street
Nashville, Tennessee 37201
(615) 748-9000

Capital Services & Resources,
  Inc.
5159 Wheelis Drive #106
Memphis, Tennessee 38117
(901) 761-2156

Chickasaw Capital Corporation
67 Madison Avenue
Memphis, Tennessee 38103
(901) 523-6470

Davis Group
1431 Cherokee Trail, Box 59
Knoxville, Tennessee 37920
(615) 579-5180

Financial Resources, Inc.
2800 Sterick Building
Memphis, Tennessee 38103
(901) 527-9411

Hickory Venture Capital
  Corporation
165 Madison Street, 5th Floor
P.O. Box 84
Memphis, Tennessee 38101
(901) 523-4255

Lawrence, Tyrell, Ortale & Smith
3100 West End Avenue #500
Nashville, Tennessee 37203
(615) 383-0982

Leader Capital Corporation
158 Madison Avenue, P.O. Box
  708
Memphis, Tennessee 38101-0708
(901) 578-2405

Massey Burch Investment Group,
  Inc.
First Nashville Center #103
310 25th Avenue South
Nashville, Tennessee 37203
(615) 329-9448

Tennessee Equity Capital Corp.
1102 Stonewall Jackson
Nashville, Tennessee 37220
(615) 373-4502

Tennessee Valley Center, Inc.
152 Beale Street
P.O. Box 300
Memphis, Tennessee 38103
(901) 523-1884

Tennessee Venture Capital Corp.
P.O. Box 2567
Nashville, Tennessee 37219
(615) 244-6935

Valley Capital Corporation
100 W. Martin Luther King Blvd.,
  #806
Chattanooga, Tennessee 37402
(615) 265-1557

TEXAS

Acorn Ventures, Inc.
2401 Fountainview, Suite 950
Houston, Texas 77057
(713) 977-7421

Alliance Business Investment
  Company
910 Louisiana
Houston, Texas 77002
(713) 224-1873

Allied Bancshares Capital Corp.
P.O. Box 3326
Houston, Texas 77063
(713) 226-1625

American Equities, Inc.
One Republic Plaza
333 Guadalupe #600
Austin, Texas 78701
(512) 499-1582

Americap Corporation
7575 San Felipe #160
Houston, Texas 77083
(713) 780-8084

BancTexas Capital, Inc.
1601 Elm Street, Suite 200
Dallas, Texas 75201
(214) 969-6100

BCM Technologies, Inc.
1709 Dryden, Suite 901
Houston, Texas 77030
(713) 795-0105

Bentsen Investment Company
4600 Post Oak Place #100
Houston, Texas 77027
(713) 627-9111

Brittany Capital Company
2424 LTV Tower, 1525 Elm Street
Dallas, Texas 75201
(214) 954-1515

Business Capital Corp.
4809 Cole Avenue, Suite 250
Dallas, Texas 75205
(214) 522-2739

Capital Marketing Corporation
P. O. Box 1000
Keller, Texas 76248
(817) 656-7380

Capital Southwest Corp.
12900 Preston Road, Suite 700
Dallas, Texas 75230
(214) 233-8242

Cash (Berry) Southwest
  Partnership
Berry Cash Southwest
  Partnership
13355 Noel Road #1375 LB 65
Dallas, Texas 75240
(214) 392-7279

Central Texas SBIC
514 Austin Avenue
P.O. Box 2600
Waco, Texas 76702-2600
(817) 753-6461

Charter Venture Group, Inc.
2600 Citadel Plaza Drive, 6th
  Floor
Houston, Texas 77008
(713) 863-0704

Citicorp Venture Capital Ltd.
717 North Harwood #2920-LB87
Diamond Shamrock Tower
Dallas, Texas 75201
(214) 880-9670

Criterion Venture Partners
1000 Louisiana Suite 620
Houston, Texas 77002
(713) 751-2400

Curtin & Company, Inc.
2050 Houston Natural Gas Building
Houston, Texas 77002
(713) 658-9806

Davis Venture Partners, L.P.
2121 San Jacinto Street
Dallas, Texas 75206
(214) 954-1822

Dougery, Jones & Wilder
Two Lincoln Center, Suite 1100
5420 LBJ Freeway
Dallas, Texas 75240
(214) 960-0077

TEXAS (cont.)

Energy Capital Corporation
953 Esperson Bldg.
Houston, Texas 77002
(713) 236-0006

Enterprise Capital Corporation
4543 Post Oak Place #130
Houston, Texas 77027
(713) 621-9444

FCA Investment Company
30900 Post Oak Boulevard, #1790
Houston, Texas 77056
(713) 965-0061

Financial Services-Austin, Inc.
301 West Sixth Street
P.O. Box 1987
Austin, Texas 78767
(512) 472-7171

First Dallas Financial Company
3302 Southland Center
Dallas, Texas 75201
(214) 922-0070

First Dallas Group, Ltd (The)
5420 LBJ Freeway #1100
Dallas, Texas 75240
(214) 385-4500

First Houston International
  Corporation
1900 West Loop South #1370
Houston, Texas 77027
(713) 850-1100

First Texas Capital Corporation
Occidental Tower
5005 LBJ Freeway #1550
Dallas, Texas 75244
(214) 450-1475

Gatti Tomerlin & Martin
  Corporation
1250 NE Loop 410 #500
San Antonio, Texas 78209
(512) 821-6909

Grocers SBI Corporation (The)
3131 E. Holcombe Boulevard,
  Suite 101
Houston, Texas 77021
(713) 747-7913

GTM Corporation
909 Fannin Street #700
Houston, Texas 77010
(713) 853-2047

Hicks & Haas
300 Crescent Court, #1700
Dallas, Texas 75201-1841
(214) 871-8300

Hinsley Venture Capital, Inc.
9494 Southwest Freeway #100
Houston, Texas 77074
(713) 981-9494

Holding Capital Group
2440 Parkside
Irving, Texas 75061
(214) 252-2799

Houston Venture Partners
Capital Center Penthouse
401 Louisiana
Houston, Texas 77002
(713) 222-8600

Idanta Partners
201 Main Street, Suite 3200
Ft. Worth, Texas 76102
(817) 338-2020

Jaffe, (Richard) & Co., Inc.
Richard Jaffe & Co., Inc.
7318 Royal Circle
Dallas, Texas 75230
(214) 739-1845

Livingston Capital Ltd.
P.O. Box 2507
Houston, Texas 77252
(713) 872-3213

Lone Star Capital Ltd.
2401 Fountainview, Suite 950
Houston, Texas 77057
(713) 266-6616

Lummins, Hamilton & Co.
712 Main Street #3000
Houston, Texas 77002
(713) 236-4719

Mapleleaf Capital Corporation
55 Waugh Drive, #170
Houston, Texas 77007
(713) 880-4494

May Financial Corporation
3302 Southland Center
Dallas, Texas 75201
(214) 922-0070

MESBIC Financial Corp. of Dallas
12655 N. Central Expressway, #814
Dallas, Texas 75243
(214) 991-1597

MESBIC Financial Corp. of Houston
811 Rusk #201
Houston, Texas 77002
(713) 228-8321

MESBIC of San Antonio, Inc.
2300 Commerce Street
San Antonio, Texas 78207
(512) 224-0909

Mid-State Capital Corp.
510 North Valley Mills Drive
Waco, Texas 76710
(817) 776-9500

MSI Capital Corporation
6510 Abrams Road, Suite 650
Dallas, Texas 75231
(214) 341-1553

MVenture Corporation
1717 Main Street
Momentum Place, 6th Floor
Dallas, Texas 75201
(214) 939-3131

N Vest Capital Corporation
5025 Arapaho #400
Dallas, Texas 75248
(214) 661-9393

North Riverside Capital
  Corporation
400 North St. Paul
Dallas, Texas 75201
(214) 220-2717

Omega Capital Corporation
755 S. 11th Street, #250
Beaumont, Texas 77701
(409) 835-5928

Orange Nassau Capital
  Corporation
13355 Noel Road, Suite 635
Dallas, Texas 75240
(214) 385-9685

Phillips-Smith Specialty Retail
  Group
15110 Dallas Parkway #310
Dallas, Texas 75248
(214) 387-0725

Porcari, Fearnow & Associates,
  Inc.
1333 West Loop South
Houston, Texas 77207
(713) 840-7500

Preferred Capital
  Corporation
1900 West Loop South #1150
Houston, Texas 77027
(713) 840-7500

Red River Ventures Inc.
777 E. 15th Street
Plano, Texas 75074
(214) 422-4999

Republic Venture Group, Inc.
2820 Republic Bank Tower
P.O. Box 655961
Dallas, Texas 75265-5961
(214) 922-3500

Retzloff Capital Corporation
15000 Northwest Freeway
Houston, Texas 77040
(713) 466-4690

Rotan Mosle Technology Partners,
  Ltd.
3800 Republic Bank Center
700 Louisiana
Houston, Texas 77002
(713) 236-3180

Rowles (R. Patrick) & Company,
  Inc.
R. Patrick Rowles & Company,
  Inc.
4299 San Felipe #100
Houston, Texas 77027
(713) 521-0388

Rust Ventures LP/Austin Ventures
1300 Norwood Tower
114 West 7th Street
Austin, Texas 78701
(512) 479-0055

San Antonio Venture Group.,
  Inc.
2300 W. Commerce
San Antonio, Texas 78207
(512) 223-3633

SBI Capital Corporation
6305 Beverly Hill
Houston, Texas 77057
(713) 975-1188

Schnitzuis & Vaughan
3410 Republic Bank Center
700 Louisiana Street
Houston, Texas 77002
(713) 222-2170

Sevin Rosen Management
  Company
13455 Noel Road #1670
Dallas, Texas 75240
(214) 960-1744

South Texas Small Business
  Investment Co
120 South Main Street
P. O. Box 1698
Victoria, Texas 77902
(512) 573-5151

Southern Orient Capital
  Corporation
2419 Fannin, Suite 200
Houston, Texas 77002
(713) 225-3369

Southwest Venture Partnerships
300 Convent Street, Suite 1400
San Antonio, Texas 78205
(512) 227-1010

Southwestern Venture Capital of
  Texas
N. Frost Center, Suite 700
1250 NE Loop 410
San Antonio, Texas 78209
(512) 822-9949

Southwestern Venture Capital of
  Texas
1336 E. Court Street
Sequin, Texas 78155
(512) 379-0380

Sterling Group, Inc. (The)
Eight Greenway Plaza #702
Houston, Texas 77046
(713) 877-8257

Strategic Development Marketing Corp.
Four Forest Plaza #660
12222 Merit Drive
Dallas, Texas 75251
(214) 991-1990

Stuart & Company
901 Main Street, Suite 2903
Dallas, Texas 75202
(214) 744-0750

Sunwestern Investment Group
12221 Merit Drive
Three Forest Plaza, Suite 1300
Dallas, Texas 75251
(214) 239-5650

T.V.P. Associates
2777 Stemmons Freeway #925
Dallas, Texas 75207
(214) 689-4265

Telpar, Inc.
4137 Billy Mitchell
Addison, Texas 75001
(214) 233-6631

Tenneco Ventures, Inc.
1010 Milam, Suite T2919
P. O. Box 2511
Houston, Texas 77001
(713) 757-8776

Texas Capital Corp.
1341 W. Mockingbird, #1250E
Dallas, Texas 75347
(214) 638-0652

Texas Commerce Investment Co.
Texas Commerce Bank Building
712 Main Street; Suite 3100
Houston, Texas 77002
(713) 236-4719

The Woodlands Venture Fund, Ltd.
2170 Buckthorne Place, Suite 350
The Woodlands, Texas 77380
(713) 363-7115

Triad Ventures, Limited
301 West Sixth Street
P.O. Box 1987
Austin, Texas 78767
(512) 472-7171

Underwood Neuhaus & Company, Inc.
909 Fannin Street
Houston, Texas 77210-4522
(713) 853-2200

Ventures Medical
16945 North Chase Drive #2150
Houston, Texas 77060
(713) 873-5748

Wesbanc Ventures, Ltd.
2401 Fountainview, #950
Houston, Texas 77057
(713) 977-7421

West Central Capital Corp.
440 Northlake Center #206
Dallas, Texas 75238
(214) 348-3969

Western Corporation
1300 Post Oak Boulevard #1717
Houston, Texas 77056
(713) 622-3222

Woodland Capital Company
3007 Skyway Circle North
Irving, Texas 75038
(214) 659-9500

UTAH

Utah Ventures
419 Wakara Way
Salt Lake City, Utah 84108
(801) 584-2555

VERMONT

North Atlantic Venture Fund
Seven Burlington Square #600
Burlington, Vermont 05401
(802) 658-7820

Northern Community Investment
  Corp.
20 Main Street
P. O. Box 904
St. Johnsbury, Vermont 05819
(802) 748-5101

VIRGINIA

Atlantic Venture Partners
801 North Fairfax Street
Alexandria, Virginia 22314
(703) 548-6026

VIRGINIA (cont.)

Atlantic Venture Partners
P. O. Box 1493
Richmond, Virginia 23212
(804) 644-5496

Basic Investment Corporation
6723 Whittier Avenue #201
McLean, Virginia 22101
(703) 356-4300

Capital Associates Inc.
13873 Park Center Road #340
Herndon, Virginia 22071
(703) 481-1130

East West United Investment
  Company
815 W. Broad Street
Falls Church, Virginia 22046
(703) 237-7200

Hillcrest Group/James River
  Capital Associates
9 S 12th Street
Richmond, Virginia 23219
(804) 643-7358

Metropolitan Capital Corp.
2550 Huntington Avenue
Alexandria, Virginia 22303
(703) 960-4698

Norfolk Investment Company
100 West Plume Street, Suite
  208
Norfolk, Virginia 23510
(804) 622-0013

Research Industries, Inc.
123 N. Pitt Street
Alexandria, Virginia 22314
(703) 548-3667

River Capital Corporation
1033 N. Fairfax Street
Alexandria, Virginia 22314
(703) 739-2100

Sovran Funding Corporation
One Commercial Place
Norfolk, Virginia 23510
(804) 441-4041

Tidewater Small Business
  Investment Corp
1300 First Virginia Bank
  Tower
Norfolk, Virginia 23510
(804) 627-2315

Venture America
8081 Wolftrap Road #200
Vienna, Virginia 22180
(703) 641-9300

Washington Finance
100 East Broad Street
Falls Church, Virginia 22046
(703) 534-7200

Wheat First Securities
707 East Main Street, P.O. Box 1357
Richmond, Virginia 23211
(804) 649-2311

WASHINGTON

Broadmark Capital Corporation
777 108th Street NE #1750
Bellevue, Washington 98004
(206) 462-1600

Cable & Howse Ventures
777 108th Avenue, N.E., #2300
Bellevue, Washington 98004
(206) 646-3030

Capital Resource Corporation
1001 Logan Building
Seattle, Washington 98101
(206) 623-6550

Environmental Venture Fund
William D. Ruckelshaus Assoc.
1900 Washington Building
Seattle, Washington 98101
(206) 583-8899

F B S Venture Capital Company
405 114th Avenue S E #335
Bellevue, Washington 98004
(206) 453-5251

Fluke Capital Management
11400 S E 6th #230
Bellevue, Washington 98004
(206) 453-4590

Genesis Capital Limited Partnership
P.O. Box 5065
Bellevue, Washington 98009
(206) 454-7211

Northwest Business Investment
  Corp.
West 929 Sprague Avenue
Spokane, Washington 99204
(509) 838-3111

Olympic Venture Partners/Rainier
  Venture Partners
One Bellevue Center #1710
411 108th Avenue N E
Bellevue, Washington 98004
(206) 455-1470

Pacific Rim Ventures
P.O. Box 332
Burlington, Washington 98233
(206) 755-9057

Palmer Group (The)
903 NE 50th
Seattle, Washington 98101
(206) 547-4264

Palms & Company
6702 139th Avenue N E
Redmond, Washington 98502
(206) 885-4401

Peoples Capital Corporation
1415 Fifth Avenue
Seattle, Washington 98171
(206) 344-5463

Phoenix Partners (The)
1000 2nd Avenue, #3600
Seattle, Washington 98104
(206) 624-8968

Pierce Nordquist Associates
4020 Lake Washington Blvd N E,
  Suite 203
Kirkland, Washington 98033
(206) 624-9540

Seafirst Capital Corporation
701 Fifth Avenue
P.O. Box 34103
Seattle, Washington 98124-1103
(206) 358-7441

Walden Group of Venture Capital
  Funds (The)
F T 101901 147th Place N E
Bellevue, Washington 98007
(206) 643-7572

WISCONSIN

Allsop (R W) & Associates
R W Allsop & Associates
815 East Mason Street
  #1501
P.O. Box 1368
Milwaukee, Wisconsin 53201
(414) 271-6510

Baird (Robert W.), Inc.
Robert W. Baird, Inc.
P. O. Box 672
Milwaukee, Wisconsin 53201
(414) 765-3889

Bando-McGlocklin Capital
  Corp.
13555 Bishops Court, Suite
  205
Brookfield, Wisconsin 53005
(414) 784-9010

Capital Investments, Inc.
744 N. 4th Street
Milwaukee, Wisconsin 53203
(414) 273-6560

Diana Corporation (The)
111 East Wisconsin Avenue, Suite
  1900
Milwaukee, Wisconsin 53202
(414) 289-9797

Future Value Ventures, Inc.
622 N. Water Street, Suite
  #500
Milwaukee, Wisconsin 53202
(414) 278-0377

Impact Seven, Inc.
Industrial Road
Turtle Lake, Wisconsin 54889
(715) 986-4171

Invest America Venture Group,
  Inc.
600 East Mason Street
Milwaukee, Wisconsin 53202
(414) 276-3839

Lubar & Company, Incorporated
3380 First Wisconsin Center
Milwaukee, Wisconsin 53202
(414) 291-9000

M & I Ventures Corporation
770 N. Water Street
Milwaukee, Wisconsin 53203
(414) 765-7910

Madison Capital Corporation
100 State Street
Madison, Wisconsin 53703
(608) 256-8185

Marine Venture Capital, Inc.
111 E. Wisconsin Avenue
Milwaukee, Wisconsin 53202
(414) 765-2274

Matrix Venture Funds, Inc.
808 North Third Street
  #400
Milwaukee, Wisconsin 53203
(414) 289-9593

Palm & Company, Inc.
233 South Street
Waukesha, Wisconsin 53186
(414) 544-4971

Super Market Investors,
  Inc.
P.O. Box 473
23000 Roundy Drive
Pewaukee, Wisconsin 53072
(414) 547-7999

Twin Ports Capital Company
1228 Poplar Avenue
Superior, Wisconsin 54880
(715) 392-5525

Venture Investors of Wisconsin, Inc.
100 State Street
Madison, Wisconsin 53703
(608) 256-8185

Wind Point Partners, L.P.
1525 Howe Street
Racine, Wisconsin 53403
(414) 631-4027

Wisconsin Community Capital Inc.
14 W. Mifflin Street, #314
Madison, Wisconsin 53703
(608) 256-3441

Witech Corporation
231 West Michigan Street, P. O. Box 2949
Milwaukee, Wisconsin 53201
(414) 347-1550

WYOMING

Capital Corporation of Wyoming, Inc.
P.O. Box 3599
Casper, Wyoming 82602
(307) 234-5438

Wyoming Industrial Development Corp.
145 South Durbin
Casper, Wyoming 82602
(307) 234-5351

INDEX